RUSSIA AS IT IS.

BY

COUNT A. DE GUROWSKI.

NEW-YORK:
D. APPLETON AND COMPANY,
346 & 348 BROADWAY.
LONDON: 16 LITTLE BRITAIN.
1854.

PREFACE.

For some time Russia has more and more attracted general attention. This mighty colossus, over-topping Europe and Asia, is for many but a dark cavern filled with demoniac forces, which, let loose, are to extinguish light, engulf civilization, and stop the onward progress of the European world, spreading over it all the plagues and curses of darkness. How far these apprehensions are well founded and justified, I shall attempt to elucidate in the following pages. I shall try to give an insight into the heart, the life and the muscles of this political giant.

Conscience and truth have directed my pen in explaining the internal conditions of the Russian people, and the construction of their political society. Their institutions are presented here, as they exist in reality, as they are determined by existing and obligatory laws. Customs, manners, sentiments, opinions and aspirations, as they are drawn from the daily life of the people.

Overarched by despotism and caste, this people has still its sunny aspects. Good and evil intermix there, as in every other human society. The features, the character, and the actual state of the Russian nation are here laid before the reader, perhaps for the first time, in an unprejudiced and not superficial manner. It is however not a history, albeit the subjects unfolded and treated here are among the prominent elements of history. Every manifestation, every kind of utterance in social life, belongs to the boundless historical domain.

Russia and its people, generally unknown, are judged by their external form or government, and thus mostly from an external manifestation. But it is not this side alone, not the lives or deeds of sovereigns, not the battles and extensions of geographical boundaries, not the concluded treaties and diplomatic tricks which exclusively form the objects of history. All this summed up together, often gives no true idea of the life indwelling in a nation, a life running below and mostly in a direction opposite to the governmental external form. This under-current reveals the real character of a people, its signification in the future destinies of the whole or of a part of the human family. From this stand-point Russia is spoken of in these pages.

Going rather rapidly over the past, I had in view to explain the formation of the present ruling power, which in itself is a social element and agency, like any other. I attempt to do it justice as far as, in given conditions and crises undergone by the nation, this power resulted from unavoidable necessities, and in such moments has been beneficial to the national existence.

In the life, in the history of a nation, of a people, as well as when surveying the history even of our whole race; all the elements, forces, agencies, together with the transient social forms and modes of government, ought to be equitably pondered and treated; and the good and evil evolving therefrom impartially explained. Therefore neither general nor special history, nor its various compounds, ought to be dogmatically comprehended. Its aggregate is the result of human individual or common activity. It is the reflection of passions, convictions, sentiments, schemes, aims, aspirations, impulses lofty, generous or mean, egotistical or expansive, wide-embracing. All these moving forces have often been represented by individualities, as by heroes, founders of empires, leaders, legislators; or by special bodies, corporations or castes, or by masses of people enjoying the right of a political and social life. Thus history is as many-faced as is man, its maker, with the unwonted versatility of his powers of mind, with the still more unfathomed accords and discordances of passions, sentiments and impressions throbbing in his heart. Many historical phenomena, many prevailing moral convictions, through several generations, many social structures lasting for centuries, would remain unexplained enigmas if considered as results of an accident or of blind fatality, and if the reason of their protracted existence were not sought as having deep roots in human nature, and depending from certain almost absolute laws regulating the general historical movement. Some from among these laws will be subsequently pointed out.

The variety of historical phenomena springing uninterruptedly from the versatility of human nature, explains why every, even the most extreme idea or conception relating to the social organization, can be logically developed and supported in opposite ways, with seemingly powerful and conclusive historical evidences and illustrations. In this manner absolutists, papists, liberals, democrats, socialists, can with equal force and profusion draw maxims and examples from history, that inexhaustible and everliving source. Therefore, history would seem to be a chaotic abyss filled with testimonies alike for good and evil, testimonies by which both can be justified, and their right to social existence established. However, it is not so. In consequence of the above-mentioned versatility of man, on account of the countless passions stirring and urging his actions, we find in history continual ups and downs, vicissitudes resulting from the victory of a certain principle, tendency, or even of an individual will, over that of few or many. But as the final aim of the life and activity of every single individual is the real or fancied amelioration of his condition, even if to reach it he often commits violent deeds, or is directed by a gloomy misconception of duties towards himself and the human brotherhood, in the same way history embraced in its whole gravitates towards a final aim, that of securing every man's higher development. This development consists in the victory of human, mental and social liberty—his absolute selfhood—over transient expediencies, destroying or limiting the rights of all for the sake of the few, whatever may be the strength and momentary supremacy of the like expediencies.

Reason and conscience prevail finally in history. From all this apparently discordant clashing of forces struggling for duration and space, there arises an overruling accord, marking a slow but uninterrupted progress, leading and directing the ascension of the individual into the higher and purer regions of humanity.

History is the record of the doings of aggregate humanity, and not only of her so-called types, name them conquerors or philosophers, founders of religions or of empires. History embraces the life of all these numberless individuals where from are formed the races, the nations, the people. Uncounted drippings, small springs, muddy as well as clear brooks and rivulets form the mighty stream running for thousands of miles. So various actions and incentives, external or from within, agencies explained or hidden to the common eye, grandeur and weakness, shape out the history of each nation. And as the streams and rivers fill the abysses of the ocean, so these single histories united form the world-history or that of our race.

Judging the actions of an individual, it is fair to

account for his position, his character, his past, his individual feelings, his moral or even physical powers ; it is fair to have in view the incentives acting from without, the circumstances and elements among which he moves ; the same rule ought to be applied in judging a nation, a people. The Slavic race in general, or Russia in particular, ought to be appreciated according to that principle of common justice. By it the social elements existing in Russia are to be ascertained and their validity examined. Then only things will appear in their true light ; then it will be found, that beyond the Autocracy there exists in Russia a people with a destiny reaching beyond the temporary darkness enveloping it, which is caused by successive exigencies rather than by everlasting historical laws. Not the ruling power or the existing government, not the superior strata of society, contain the promise of the future. The people alone is its bearer ; the people, the present lower classes, however behind-hand and uncivilized they may now appear. From the people will pour out a current changing the actual state, breaking its encompassing form. To such a future this book points.

It may perhaps fall into hands of some acquainted with my previous writings, and to those I am in duty bound to give an explanation. They are aware that not for the first time the destinies of the Slavic race and of Russia, form the subject of my publications. I was among the first who gave to the conception of Panslavism a scientific and historical explanation, searching therein for a clew to the apparently savage and aggressive expansion of Russia. If I have changed my point of view concerning the mode by which Panslavism is to fulfil its destinies, my convictions are not at all changed as to the essential signification of the Slavi and of Russia in the great family of nations. Once I thought that autocracy would be the great and luminous beacon in this movement ; this I no longer believe. In this consists the change of my convictions, and this I am about to explain.

For nearly thirty years my existence was agitated by the political tempests overwhelming my fatherland as well as other parts of Europe. Thus I had occasion to do as much as any for ideas and individual convictions, at the risk of my neck, not to mention worldly losses actually sustained. I dearly acquired the right to act independently for myself. In my youth with other patriots, I took an active part in the affairs of Poland, the country of my birth. After I had been for several years the object of violent individual persecutions, by our joint efforts was effected the insurrection of 1830–'31, during which I tried to establish the republican government, and whose disastrous end threw me upon the world a condemned exile. Years of wandering were spent in Europe and principally in Paris. I had thus an opportunity to mingle on a large scale with ideas of every shade, and men of all opinions ; to observe and judge various events, and to devote my time to social and historical studies. A revolution in my mind was effected. Analyzing with conscientious scrutiny the causes of the political death of Poland, I lost the faith in any possibility of her resurrection. The destiny of the Slavic race, dawning now on the horizon, could not depend on one of its feeblest, withered and destroyed branches. Russia alone represented the Slavic vitality in the moving complications of Europe and of the Western world. Among the various reasons of the destruction of Poland, the most deleterious was, the utter want for centuries of any centralizing idea, of any organized and directing power. Russia's growth was the result of the existence of such an influence. At that time not only political theoreticians, but new systems aiming to reform society in its foundations, as for example that of the St. Simonians, whose conceptions I studied and shared ; all of them established as an axiom that society ought to be directed by a supreme will embodied in one individual, ruling or inspiring the rest. Thus sprang up in my mind the fallacious belief shared with many others, that an energetic concentration of power was an absolute necessity for the existence, the development and progress of society at large as well as for single nations. According to such a notion, civilization was to be spread from above, and the more a nation was behind-hand, the greater the need of such a supreme leader. All the political as well as social schools resounded with expositions about the necessity of organization, to be obtained by the unity of direction. The more my mind was overpowered by such ideas, the deeper I felt the curse of the existence of an exile, rootless on a foreign soil; a dejection so admirably described by Ballanche, who says that "man has not the choice of his fatherland; but if he exiles himself to avoid living under institutions disliked by him, then he remains without a tie, he is a stranger on earth." The devotion and interest felt for my ancient country, became wholly superseded by my interest for the whole race, of which Poland was, after all, rather an insignificant offshoot.

For the last thirty years all general historical studies, as well as the philosophical comprehension of history, were directed to elucidate the character of various races, and their bearing on the affairs of the world. To the distinct characteristics of whole races which of old took possession of Europe, rather than to single nations, were traced all great historical events and the progressive evolutions of civilization. Thus originated those generalizations introduced in the philosophy of history, as that for example of German civilization, which framed out the whole political and intellectual state of Europe after the downfall of the Roman world. By birth a Slavi, I looked around to see where was alive the powerful trunk of my race, and found that Russia alone represented it. Thus originated with me the idea of Panslavism. Its signification is the union of disseminated Slavic families—some of whom vegetate miserably under the foreign dominion of the Magyars, Turks and Germans, into a homogeneous whole, around one mighty stock. Panslavism does not aim to give laws to Western Europe, but only not to receive any from her, or from Ouralian invaders.

The study of, and devotion to the great truths revealed by Fourier, nay, his personal advice, influenced powerfully my decision. Whoever has read his works, knows how repeatedly Fourier points to Russia and even to a Czar, as to the means of the speediest realization of the theory of association. And thus I went to Russia and to the Czar.

At that moment the Emperor Nicholas shone with the light of an autocrat, kindling the beacon of civilization. He proclaimed his wish to evolve it from the national Slavic genius. To such a focus converged all the aspirations of the Slavi, from the Elba, the Danube, the Carpathian and the Balkan Mountains. With many others, I was dazzled by the apparent brilliancy of the aim, and became conscientiously a believer in the lofty and providential calling of Czarism. For several years I was in a position to observe its nature, its action, and how far it could fulfil the mission which in my ardent imagination and wishes I assigned to this supreme, this almost superhuman power. Penetrating, however, more deeply, not only into the nature of the man, but into that of the institution itself, my enthusiasm began to cool. Still I strained my reason to hold out, hoping for the best. One by one the scales fell from my eyes, and finally I violently broke the voluntary chain, retook the staff of the exile, and with it my liberty.

It is scarcely worth while to mention the showers

of abuse poured on me from various quarters. These never have impressed me and never can. Acting under the dictates of conviction, I never hesitated to secede from an idea, or change a route, when by following them the inward harmony of conscience could have become endangered. Often in this thorny journey have I had the sad satisfaction to be right, to be justified by events—notwithstanding accusations and recriminations. Thus years previous to the events of 1848, in one of my writings I doubted the possibility of Germany becoming easily an unit ; and until the present time events have confirmed my premonitions. Seceding openly eighteen years ago from my former countrymen and co-exiles, I gave as reason the utter impossibility of the reconstruction of Poland, especially by foreign help and interference. There is not yet the slightest sign on the horizon to overthrow my assertions. Neither my writings nor my acts could have contributed to bring forth this result.

A homeless wanderer over the world, I reached America. Here my once youthful aspirations were reinvigorated. I found a partial realization of that for which as yet Europe vainly craves. From these shores I cast a glance on the past, on the rockings of the European world, and on the destinies of the race from which I descended, on those of the country abandoned forever.

The social organization, the institutions of America, raise her into the higher regions of humanity. How long will it be before Europe follows in the wake of her younger sister? Europe must still traverse many crises ere she shall free herself from the mental and political fetters forged by centuries as long as the past of the whole race. In this struggle the special group of the Slavic family must necessarily act its part. The present book aims to show how in the future, the Slavi may harmonize with the eternal laws of nature and the general destinies of mankind. All the European races and nations, which for centuries stood prominent in history, in bloody struggles, have tried their hands to establish social freedom and harmony. Hitherto their efforts have been unsuccessful. It may be, that the Slavi, who come the last, who have suffered and suffer the most, will give a more propitious lift to this great work,—which heretofore, as regards Europe, has been like the task of Tantalus.

THE AUTHOR.

NEW-YORK, *March*, 1854.

CONTENTS.

RUSSIA AS IT IS.

INTRODUCTION.

THE destinies of Europe, and of the ancient world, oscillate between liberty and absolutism: and Russia *at present* turns the scale in favor of the partisans of the past, and against the apostles and worshippers of a political and social disenthralment. In this struggle Russia, on the one side, presses with all the might, possessed by an autocracy, leading the cardinal stem of a mighty and numerous race of the human family. Thus, in the general course of events, that are moving and shaking the world, Russia represents two historical elements: that of the arbitrary power and that of a race. As a race, the Russian people has its distinct characteristics, prevailing as well in its history as in its internal organism; characteristics unknown, misunderstood, or misrepresented. The following pages, it may be, will contribute to throw some light on questions filling out the foreground on the world-scene.

The country, the people, are both old and new. Old, because belonging, as a race, to the first historical peoplings of Europe; and new, because in its outward manifestation

1*

as a state, Russia's appearance is recent, nay, even the last, on the records of Europe.

The Russian people probably occupied a great part of the region where it is settled now, before history dawned upon them. It is the region belonging to the Slavic race, of which the Russian is now the only independent representative among the other states and nations. The historical origin of the Russian people is merged in the darkness extending over the origin of the whole race. The same mystery surrounds the cradle of all aboriginal races and primitive nations of the ancient world.

Numerous and various are the hypotheses built up and successively destroyed, concerning the original and primitive distribution of inhabitants, over the European continent. It is beyond the limits of the present work, however, to array the ethnographical, ethnological, legendary, traditional and historical researches, discoveries, testimonies or assumptions, concerning the first races or families, who, in common or successively, wandered and spread themselves in all directions throughout Europe.

Among these, number the Slavi. Their historical current, as generally that of other old nations, does not spring from a positive epoch or spot, at once, as from a tabula rasa. Every historical period has always a kind of eponymus. It always presupposes a long and dark lapse of time, that is to say, some pre-existing world, still closely connected to the succeeding one.

The Slavic race stretches back to the common cradle of all historical races. If the Pentateuch is to be accepted as recording the distribution of the human family over the earth, the Slavi claim to descend from Riphaat, through Gomer, grandson of Japhet, as the Celts issue from Ascanaz, the Germans from Throgorma, two others of the Gomeriden. The sound *Rh*, vibrating through the remotest antiquity in regions occupied by the Slavi, seems to support this biblical hypothesis. Thus Rha is the name of the river Wolga, and the same sound is to be met with in the ancient names of mountains north of the Danube, of the meotic estuary, and of the Don, as *Kamennoï poïas*, even to the range near *Malaia Zemblia.* If Armenia was the point wherefrom, in the Phalegic epoch, the races emigrated, those who turned towards the north or west, entered probably originally the passes of the Caucasus, whence they continued their further migrations. To these regions, ethnology retraces their roots : some of their most ancient legends and myths, as, for example, those of the Asi, the protoplasts of the Germans, point to the east; and myths and legends are seldom without some basis of truth. The Slavi on their way to Europe seem to have wandered north and south of the Euxine, leaving, under various denominations, traces of their passage. North the Meotic Cymbri, south the Eniochi, Eneti, called by ancient writers *gens antiquissima*, the Paphlagonians, those subduers of the horse, and, according to Strabo, breeders of the mule, are claimed by some historical investigators, as the ancestors of the Slavi. At any rate, antiquity mentions on the Lych and the Termodontos names of tribes, which are to be found again among tribes north of the Danube, very probably towards the Don, as mentioned by Herodotus. Thus, for example, the Myriandini, who, according to his account, refused to join the Scythians, when invaded by Darius—reminding them that they, the Myriandini, did not participate in the Scythian invasion of Media and Asia Minor. According to the thread of the Genesis, the Slavi, following the Celts and Germans, would thus form the third among the primitive families of Northern Europe.

The modern researches of ethnology establish a different filiation. The close connection of the Slavic language with the Zend and Sanscrit, places the Slavic among the prominent members of the Indo-European family. Ethnologically, it became the sixth immigrant to Europe, succeeding the Greek, the Latin, the Celtic, the German, and the Samogitian or Lithuanian language. Thus the Slavi would have formed the rear-guard of tribes leaving Hindoo-Kosh and Parapomisus for their distant western home, where the Slavi finally spread themselves more extensively than any of those races immigrating before them.

The learned Denina and Adelung in some measure suggest, that perhaps the Slavi formed the aborigines of Europe, from the Atlantic to the Wolga. In the most remote and darkest times, these regions were called generally, Scythian;—but Scythians, even of a less obscure epoch, those of Herodotus and of the classical times, seem, after all, not to have represented a perfectly distinct race, or even tribe, but rather a confederation of various inhabitants in the north of Europe; possibly of Slavic, German or Gethic, Gothic, or even Celtic origin, and of various Finnic or pure Asiatic interlopers. In a more limited sense the same is very likely the case with the generalization called by the writers of the last classical epoch—as, for example, by Ptolemy and others—the Sarmathian one, which inherited the preceding generalization, the Scythian, in the Ptolemean geography. If there be any plausibility in Denina's opinion, the Slavi would in consequence have claims to a previous occupancy, being afterwards conquered and encroached upon by the Celts and Germans, to whom they taught the use of the plough, peculiar to the Slavic race. To the Eniochi, the Eneti, the constellation of the *Ursa Major* represented the plough in the heavens. It is still a positive and as yet unexplained historical fact, that when for the first time history reveals the Slavi under this their special and generic name, both along and beyond the Danube, as is testified by Jornandes, then by Procopius and other successive Byzantine writers—together with the name of Slavi is mentioned that of the Antes and Veneti, as forming one and the same family. But Venetes and Anti are mentioned by Cæsar more than five centuries before in Armorica or French Bretagne; and even in the Breton dialect there are words and names of Slavic meaning; and Slavic influence, at any rate, is to be traced very distinctly to the Weser and to the ancient Vindelicia.

Whatever hypothesis may be admitted concerning the Slavic race and its settlement, either according to the biblical or the Indo-European theory, this is certain, that the Slavi count among the autochtone families of Europe. Another point can likewise scarcely be contested, that from the time of the first occupation—which epoch escapes, and probably will for ever escape chronological research, to the moment of historical daybreak upon the Slavi—they occupied more or less the same regions where they were found then, and which they occupy now. Between the Sava, the Drawa, the Wistula, the Danube, the Euxine, to the northern slopes of the Waldai hills, and to the Wolga, is their primitive and incontestable home. History never will elucidate how far they extended to the furthermost limits of Western Europe,—where, at any rate, they were overlaid and wholly absorbed by other races. Not so, however, in their incontestable patrimony. There, although overrun for long centuries by Scythians or Asiats, then by Geths, by Goths as at the epoch and during the reign of Hermanric, by the Huns of Attila, by Bojan, the Awars, the Allans, then by Magyars and their kindred the Turks: there they remained, still indestructible, and outliving all these submersions. Their innate natural toughness has carried them victoriously through, even up to the present time, as in Croatia, Pannonia, Servia, etc.

When the North and the East precipitated themselves upon the ancient world; when tribes and peoples rolled onwards in waves, dislocating and displacing the old landmarks—and, it may be, even some centuries previous to that precise epoch—there on the water-sheds between the Weser, the Elba, the Vistula, as well as between the Danube and the Sava, was carried on an uninterrupted struggle between the various German and Slavic populations, for the possession of these lands. Whatever may be the evidences brought forward by German writers, the question which of the two, as regards priority of time, was the rightful possessor of the contested lands, will ever remain a point at issue. If, however, the Slavi formed the third biblic or the sixth Indo-European immigration, then advancing towards the west, they must have run against the rear-guard of the Germans in the above-named region—in the same way as the Germans pressed upon the Celts from the Schelde to the Swiss Alps—and so the conflict began. At one time the Germans, at another the Slavi, remained the masters of the field, strengthening themselves in their occupation of the country, to be again overrun or expelled. Thus, about the epoch of the final downfall of the Roman Empire, the contested regions were in various parts occupied by Gothic and German tribes, as Vandals, Bourgignons, Longobards, Lygians, etc., as well as by some remains of the Celts, as, for instance, the Boii. During their stay—protracted through centuries—on the Slavic soil, some of the German tribes received their name, which survives to the present time. Thus the Suevi, who, previously to the time of Tacitus, dwelt probably on both sides of the Elba—and, it may be, reached to the Vistula—received theirs. The name of Sueve has no root, nor any origin in any German dialect. It seems to be derived from the Slavic *Swoi*, that is, a man in his own right, *sui juris*. Other tribes, as, for example, the Lygians (Germ. Lygier), were wholly destroyed in the conflict, and disappeared at a very early period from history. Others finally, who, like the Bourgignons, dwelt for a long time on the Vistula, where at present is Lechia or Poland—in their progress to Gallia or France—brought and introduced there the nasal sound *on en*, unknown to Germans, but peculiar to the Polish branch of the Slavi.

When the Germans advanced to Italy and Gallia, and further, when the dominion of Attila was broken, the Slavi filled the then nearly abandoned lands, particularly along the banks of the Elba, as well as south towards the Adriatic. During the time of Charlemagne began the new conflict between the adjoining races. For centuries it was carried on along the whole line, with a fury of extermination scarcely known in history, and especially under the Imperial houses of Saxony and Frankony. In the south, notwithstanding that about the same time the Magyars, an Ouralian tribe, invaded the Slavic country, ravaging them, as well as southern Germany and even France, their hereditary toughness enabled them better to resist this conquest. The chroniclers of that time have preserved records of the unbridled fierceness and ferocity of these Asiatic invaders, who finally settled in Pannonia, on the top of several conquered Slavic tribes. Even to the present time, from Bohemia to the Cattaro there extends an uninterrupted chain of Slavic populations. In the north the protracted struggle ended partly in the extermination of the Slavi, partly in their Germanization throughout the shores of the Baltic, beyond the Elba and the Oder, to the banks of the river Warta. Nay, it may be said, that the struggle was never interrupted. Protestantism contributed mightily to denationalize the Slavi in these regions, and the contest exists still, for example, on the foot of the Sudette mountains in Silesia, in the Dukedom of Posen, on the Vistula in the land of the Caschouben. But now it has acquired a more humane manifestation; the remnants indeed of the Slavic race recede and disappear before the superiority of culture introduced by the Germans, together with their ruling and prevailing political nationality. The inhabitants of the actual kingdom of Saxony, as far and even beyond Lunebourg, have been once Slavi. Nearly all the names of the villages have a Slavic root or termination; the names of the manors (burg, castle) where the conquerors dwelt, are German.

All the writers and chroniclers of the mediæval epoch, beginning with the Gothic bishop Jornandes, speak of the Slavic race as occupying, in an uninterrupted continuity, immense regions of Europe. It would be an easy task to array quotations in numbers numberless. Roger Bacon, that giant of intellect and learning of this epoch, speaks of the Slavi, Russians, Muscovites, as extending through "immensa spatia," down south and towards the east; and further, that the Slavic language was then spoken by the greater part of the inhabitants of Europe.

At an early period likewise in the mediæval epoch, the Slavi, probably those lying south of the Danube, submerged Greece and the peninsula of the Morea, giving to it its name, from *More*, sea. The termination of many places, mountains and rivers in ancient Peloponnese, are still Slavic. The recent researches of the learned Fallmerayer prove this to be the case beyond any possible doubt.

As mentioned before, the Slavic race is from the beginning recorded in history, as forming three cardinal branches, viz: the Veneti or Vendi, the Antes, and the Slavi. The branch of the Veneti penetrated the furthest towards the west of Europe, and it is her fate that was principally sketched out in the above lines. Some of the Slavic historians or investigators maintain that these Veneti descend from the branch who wandered primarily from Caucasus to Europe south of the Euxine. Thus Eniochi, Eneti, Paphlagonians of Asia, ancient Veneti of Italy, Vendi, Veneti, Vinuli, Lini, Henyds, Gwinyads, around the Sudetten and the western part of the Crapack mountains, on the Elba, along the shores of the Baltic down to the Vistula, are one and the same family.

Certain it is that the Eniochi, Eneti of Asia disappeared therefrom even before the dawn of history, and are mentioned only "pro memoriâ" in its earliest records. The Veneti of Italy mentioned by Cato, Livy, etc., as "gens antiquissima" are the descendants of the Eniochi, and in their turn protoplasts or brothers of the northern Vendi. Whatever, however, may be the origin of the Slavic Vendi, it is a great and unpardonable confusion, committed principally by some recent English ethnographs and ethnologists, to mistake them for the Vandals, Vandalians—so terribly famous in the destruction of the Roman Empire. These Vandals have been of German or Gothic origin, and the confusion arises from the fact that they first appeared dwelling for a certain time on the Vistula, and advanced continually through Slavic regions towards the south of Europe. But the Vandals, before they reached Italy were already Christians and Arians. Thus their difference of creed with the Trinitarians or Catholics, was the principal reason of the atrocities put to their account; as their ferocity was principally shown in the destruction of Catholic churches, above all in Africa. At that time the Venden, like all the Slavi, were still pagans, nature worshippers, having consecrated groves and forests, fountains and streams. Their mythology was an embodiment of the elements of nature, and there are no traces among the Slavi of human or animal sacrifices.

The Antes, who at the time of Jornandes, Procopius, etc., were living along the Danube, covered the same country which they occupy now. Probably they extended north to the Dniester and Dnieper, mixing there with the branches of the third principal stock or the Slavi proper.

Wherever any of the Slavic families are met with in, or discovered through, history, they invariably appear as fixedly settled, as agriculturists. Living in villages and forming thus communities. Very likely the "Scythes Agricolæ" along the Dnieper, quoted by Herodotus in opposition to the nomadic Scythes, were Slavic tribes of the Scythian confederacy. If there be a positive Scythic family in history, it must be of Ouralian stock. Neither does this stock, nor any of its branches, ever appear to have been originally devoted to agriculture. Neither as Huns, Alans, Tartars, Turkomans, Kalmucks or Magyars.

The Emperor Mauritius towards the end of the sixth century, describes the Slavi as being eminently agriculturists. German writers acknowledge that the Slavi taught to the Germans both agriculture and horticulture. At any rate, the name of the plough, *Pflug* in German (*Plug* being the real Slavic name) is of pure Slavic origin. The respective characteristics of the two races as mentioned by various historians, support the above inference in favor of the Slavi. The primitive Germans were seldom tillers of the soil, but more generally roving and predatory tribes. Cæsar, and above all Tacitus, describes them as such.

"Nor are they so easily induced to till the earth or to await the harvest, as to plunge into the midst of enemies and wounds. They esteem it base indeed to seek through labor what they can obtain by bloodshed, etc." Quite the opposite, however, are the characteristics of the Slavi, who often were overrun and subjugated, but never, or at least very seldom, became invaders. When they overran Greece, the Byzantine Emperors directed them there. The Slavi seem to have been likewise the great traders and carriers of goods in very remote times, from the Baltic and the north, to the Adriatic and Black Sea. Settled rather than nomadic populations devote themselves to trade. The trader wandering to distant, sometimes unknown countries, does not take with him wife and family, neither could he leave them behind in a state of insecurity. Thus fixed settlements and an organised state of society are to be presupposed with a trading population, and even as giving birth to it. Such, therefore, were the Slavi. The commerce in amber and other productions of the north was carried to Italy by the Veneti, Venden. Rich and populous cities are mentioned in their regions at a time when nothing of the kind of autochtone foundation existed among the Germans. Thus, for example, the city of Wineta, on the west of the Island of Usedom, in Pommern, a country totally germanized, but whose name still shows its Slavic origin, being derived from *Po-more*, along the sea.

This city Wineta is described as having paved streets, temples with brazen doors and gates, and as being the emporium of the Baltic trade. At that very distant epoch, and in a region so remote from the centre of civilization, then gathered around the Mediterranean, cities could not spring up as though evoked by some magic spell, but long years, if not centuries, went to work slowly to raise and fill them with industry and wealth. Among the whole Slavic family, the Russian people alone preserved most eminently until even to the present day, this characteristic feature; being still among the best traders of Europe.

What the Veneti were westwards, the Slavic tribes (called the Slavi), were northeastwards in Europe; quiet agriculturists at the earliest period. The necessity of providing for subsistence in that rough climate, pointed to this even more absolutely. In general, the preëminent toughness of the Slavi, their resistance and the final overcoming of various conquests and submissions to other tribes and populations, during, it may be, thirty centuries: can principally be explained by the fact—that the invaders, mostly of Asiatic descent, and of roving nomadic mode of life, found a rather sedentary people, which could neither be expelled, destroyed or absorbed, on account of its intimate communion with the soil, and the consequent virtuality. In the West, germanization operates principally through expropriation.

The north or northeast of Europe, where Russia proper now is, was occupied at a distant period by that branch of the race which in all probability gave the name of the Slavi to the whole stock. Philologists derive this name from *Slowo*, verb, or *Slawa*, glory. Putting aside these dissertations about the origin of the name, we need only observe that its origin and existence in these regions is incontestible. According to all probability, the branch of the family carrying the verb, the *Slowo*, immigrating from the Caucasus north of the Terek, of the Black sea, took possession of the land: from the meotic estuary, between the Dnieper and the Wolga up to the common source of both these rivers in the heights of Woldaï, called also the Wolkonski forest, or that of the wolf and the horse (*Wolk*, wolf, *Kon*, horse). On those heights, around the lakes of Ilmen, Staraï-Russa (old Russia,) Peypus, and others, near the banks of the river Wolchowa, this tribe seems to have established itself, as its principal seat. A quiet hospitable people, probably the hyperboreans of the classical world, the Arymaspi, Arymphœi of Pliny, Pausanias, Ammian Marcellin, etc. There the dawn of the mediæval epoch found wealthy, populous and powerful republics and commercial cities, such as Novgorod and Pskoff. There too are places called *Slawïanskïa Klïutschy*, Slavic sources. The name of Novgorod, ancient as it is, presupposes the existence of another city, more ancient still, Novgorod signifying new town. The legend attributing the foundation of Novgorod to dissatisfied amazons,* confirms the supposition. Novgorod was the most flourishing city in Northern Europe when darkness covered the rest of it. To Novgorod, Danish princes were sent by their parents, to be educated and find wives. Trade flourished there from the remotest times. It was the great thoroughfare between the North and Asia. From the bays of the Baltic, through Lake Ladoga, the river Wolchow to Novgorod, Lake Ilmen or Staraïe-Russy, Petschory, through the lakes of Peypus, Gdoff, the river Welikaïa to Pskoff, then through the Volga and her tributaries, the land of the Permïans, the Kama, through the Don and Dnieper to the Black sea, to Colchis, Trebizonde, and through the Caspian, reaching the Armenians, the Persians, and the Hindoos.

All these regions formed the cradle of the present Russian Empire. With these republics Russian history begins. The chief fact of this historical epoch is the Northman establishment, and the extension of their dominion in the course of about half a century, from Nov-

* See appendix A.

gorod along the Dwina, and the Dnieper down to Kiïeff, where the capital was established, and shortly afterwards to the mouth of the Borysthenes into the Black sea. The establishment of the Northmen in Novgorod and Pskoff was no conquest. Ruryk and his followers were called in peacefully by the Novgorodians, who were quarrelling among themselves, rather to administer than to rule them. Nothing was changed in the old republican organization. The followers of Ruryk were not numerous, and could not—as some historians maintain—have exerted a powerful influence, or modified or changed the character and the physiological features of the autochtones. This Scandinavian influx was on the surface, but neither the blood, the customs, the manners, nor the language were affected by it. The Northmen did not mix with the people at large, and their descendants are the *Kniazïa*, the princes, and some few other noble families of Russia. With the grandson of Ruryk, the Northmen feature wholly disappears, being absorbed by the Slavic virtuality. The names of the *Wïeliki Knïaz's*, Grand Dukes, became Slavic, and the grandson of Ruryk had to be presented by his uncle to the Boyars and the people of Kiïeff in the forum or market-place of the city, *ploschtschad*, to be accepted by their common consent as their sovereign ruler. The oldest Slavic and Russian epic, called the "Song of the Band of Igor," (*piesn o polkie Igorowym*,) describing the feats of this follower and successor of Ruryk, is purely Slavic, as well in language as in form.

Kiïeff became the centre of the new growing Empire, Novgorod and Pskoff remaining Republics for several centuries, up to, indeed, the end of the fifteenth. In the tenth and eleventh centuries, Kiïeff was the most splendid and luxurious city north of the Alps. It was a Capua for Poles who came there as conquerors. The monks, and architects of that epoch, constructed churches in imitation of St. Sophia, and other edifices. Henry the First, of France, married Helena, a Russian princess, and thus, at this distant epoch, the Capets became connected with the Grand Dukes. Their conquests were extended from Kiïeff; near and distant tribes were overcome and subdued, as, for example, the Polowtse, the Pïetschyngi, the Ongry (a branch of the Magyars,) etc. From Dwina to Kiïeff, as well as far eastwards in the interior, reaching to Moscow itself in the course of time, small principalities were now founded for the progeny of the reigning Grand Dukes, and thus arose that division which proved afterwards so fatal, in facilitating the conquest by the Tartars. The dominion and the parceling extended westwards to the Carpathians, and the present Galicia formed one of the divisions. From Kiïeff, at that distant period even, the Greek Empire and Byzantium, were invaded, attacked, and stormed.

As the Republics of Novgorod and Pskoff gave birth to the Empire, it is clear that liberty and the commune were anterior to monarchical power, that is, to autocracy, to political or social enslavement. Freedom and a kind of self-government, in Russia as well as in other Slavic regions, were the source of social order. The remotest traditions of the Bohemians, Poles and Russians, as well as the political habits of the southern Slavi preserved to more recent times, never point to hereditary power, to absolute rulers, or to castes and nobility. Every where, the chiefs were elected from and by the people, without regard to their birth, their mode of life or occupation. Thus legend and tradition show a ploughman raised to the supreme dignity among the Tschechs; in Poland Piast, a wheelwright was chosen, and from him issued a long line of kings, a line, however, which became extinct in the male descent in the fourteenth, and in the female in the sixteenth century. In Bohemia, as well as in Poland, tradition names a Leshko, a Samo, a merchant, and a jeweller, elected as chiefs. Through the whole Slavic race, kings, princes and nobility, are creations of the secondary epoch, and can be traced out chronologically. From the elders in a commune sprang the nobles; they and the princes appear for the first time in the internal or external troubles and wars. But still the ancient liberties and free election, were preserved in some way or other. Thus the Cossacks, a genuine Slavic shoot, continued to elect their military commanders and chiefs up to the present century. The Hussites of Bohemia extended the idea of partial religious liberty—imported to Prague from England or Savoy—in a struggle for social and political emancipation, and thus they were the predecessors of the Puritans, the Independents, and, politically at least, as radical as the others. Ziska's hatred of princes and nobles is recorded in history. Jean of Rokitsany, one of the Hussitian leaders, promulgated from the castle of Prague a political magna charta, whose principal purport was, the abolition of royalty and family privileges. The nobility of Poland, even after having absorbed, at a very early period, all the political life and power belonging to the people and the nation—having in the course of time enslaved the peasantry and destroyed the franchises of the burghers;—still, herself, as a political body, remained faithful to the traditions of liberty and equality. The state was always called a republic, and all the nobles were absolutely equal. Titles and all similar distinctions, are of a more recent and foreign introduction. Royalty was, in principle, an elective dignity, even during the hereditary lineages of the Piasts and the Jagellons; and every nobleman, the richest or the poorest, could pretend to it. The thus celebrated "liberum veto" (*the veto of the free*), which gave to every nobleman, or at least to any member of the diet, the right to suspend and to annihilate all the acts of a session, by the single word *niepozwalam*, "I don't allow it," was looked upon by the nobility or body politic, as a *unicum et specialissimum jus cardinale* (or unique and special cardinal right). Whatever may be the merits of such usage, and without denying its mischievious and fatal influence on the destiny of Poland, it remains as an historical evidence of a notion of political equality reaching the utmost limits of an organized body.

In Russia, that is in the hereditary possessions founded by the Grand Dukes of Kiieff, political liberty very soon expired. However, it never disappeared from among the people as a normal communal organisation, even when they became wholly enslaved. In the course of ages, on the ruins of ancient freedom, a vast monarchy was created and consolidated—hewn out by means and courses common to the like historical formations. Russian history is a terrible tale of blood, and of almost superhuman labors and toils. In all struggles, in the most fearful national cataclysms Russia has gone through, she was always supported by her own resources; and assisted herself out of several abysses without any state or nation having extended to her a helping hand. Isolated and surrounded on all sides by enemies, she relied absolutely upon herself. Thus after more than 250 years, she overcame the Tartar dominion; and when towards the end of the 15th century, Iwan Wasilewitch the Great, finally liberated his country, then first only did England and other European states congratulate him and ask for his alliance. In the same way nobody assisted the Russian nation to reconquer its independence in the beginning of the 17th century.

There is one feature in which the growth and extension of Russia differs from that of almost every other European state. She extended herself principally over aboriginal regions, conquering and establishing her dominion over kindred populations, and branches issuing from the same stock with herself. Never did she imitate the Goths in subjugating the Iberians, or the Longobards establishing themselves on the necks of the Italians, or the Franks in subduing Gauls, Goths, Bretons, etc.; or the Saxons, Danes, Normans in imposing themselves on the primitive Britons as well as successively on each other; nor the result of this conglomorate, the English, in conquering the Gael-Scot, and the Celto-Irish. Russian conquests over foreign races are comparatively few compared with the whole; insignificant in themselves, they are limited to the outskirts of the grand Slavic domain. The Baltic provinces being a mixture of native remains of the Finns, together with a small sprinkling of German conquerors, never really enjoyed, and never could claim, an independent existence. The two real foreign conquests are Finland, the Caucasian and Transcaucasian regions. The protracted struggle with the mountaineers of the Caucasus, called generally Circassians, cannot be considered as just or unjust in itself.

It is a cruel necessity, deplored throughout the whole empire, in St. Petersburgh as well as by all ardent Circassophiles. Its origin can be traced as far back as the Xth century, when Swatoslaw, one of the Grand Dukes of Kiïeff seized upon the ancient kingdom of the Bosphorus. In the 16th century Iwan Wasilewitch, Grand Duke of Moscow, after having put an end to the Tartar dominion over Russia, invaded the Oriental region of the Caucasus, establishing military posts all along the Caspian sea. In 1594 Alexander, King of Georgia, recognised the supremacy of the Sovereigns of Moscow in order to find protection with them against the invasions of the Tartars and Mongols. Towards the end of the 18th century, Heraclius, King of Georgia, menaced by the Turks and Persians, signed a treaty, by which every sovereign of this country was to be a vassal of the Russian Czars, and finally, in the year 1800, the widow of Heraclius ceded to them all her rights and lands, and by a ukase, published by Paul, Georgia became incorporated into the Russian Empire. The Caucasian mountains lie between the two, and consequently the mountaineers are able to continually interrupt the communication between Russia and Georgia. It is the same as if the Indians should concentrate along the Rocky Mountains and thence invade and extend their depredations over California, Oregon and the Western States. It looks now like a war of extermination, whose final end is not easy to be foreseen.

Thus, if ever a nation was nursed and cradled in wars, it was Russia, some of them even menacing the destruction of her national independent existence. Slow and difficult were her first steps, at an epoch when the whole of Europe, as well as her surrounding neighbors, were powerful, organized states, which, during the days of her weakness and prostration, cut off and secured to themselves large slices of her patrimony. But the more Russia approached the hour of her political manhood, the more her progress became accelerated. She is now, indeed, more strongly cemented and more cohesive than is supposed or admitted by many politicians and writers.

At the first census made by Peter the Great, in the first half of his reign, the population of Russia amounted to above nine millions. That of Poland, at that time, was about fourteen millions. Sweden, with the possessions on the southern Baltic shores, as Pomerania, part of Livonia and Esthonia, about six millions; in the South the Tartars kept Kazan, Azoff, Crimea, and being then the tributaries of the Sultan, formed with the whole Ottoman Empire a mass outnumbering the Russians at least three times. And now Sweden is crippled, Poland is no more, and the death-knell is booming over Turkey. By a turn of events, unparalleled in history, Russia not only reconquered from her neighbors her ancient possessions lost for centuries; but broke them down successively one by one. The struggle with Poland lasted for nearly as many centuries as they can count for their political existence. In the tenth and eleventh centuries the Poles conquered Kiïeff, then the seat of the Empire. During the Tartar dominion, the Lithuanians conquered several principalities west and south of the Russians and Tartars; and when Lithuania became united with Poland in the 14th and 15th centuries, Kiïeff and south Russia, became Polish dependencies. In the beginning of the 17th century the Poles entered Moscow, twice establishing a short domination over the whole Empire. The Russian Czars, the Schuyskis, died in a Polish fortress, and the founder of the present Imperial dynasty, Feodor Romanoff was for several years a prisoner in Warsaw. But then in that same century the wheel of fortune turned very strangely. Sobieski signed the first treaty by which Poland began to yield to Russia and give up whole territories. Kiïeff was lost. Then Russia availed herself of the internal dissensions, tearing the old Polish Republic. The unbounded pride of some of the eminent Polish families called forth and introduced into Poland, Russian influence and Russian armies. Religious intolerance, the persecution of the Protestants (called dissidents,) as well as of the Schismatics or members of the Eastern church, totally weakened Poland, and so Russia became the mistress of large and warlike regions.

The Polish nobility, as an exclusively ruling body, never acted under the impulse of elevated statesmanlike foresight and conceptions. In this they differed totally from the Venetian or English aristocracy. Few of the Polish kings were real statesmen, and their efforts and aims were mostly paralyzed by the unruliness of the nobility. Thus in the 14th century, Casimir the Great, called "*rex rusticorum*, (the King of the peasants,) vainly tried to prevent the final enslavement of the peasantry by the rapacious nobles. In the 15th century, Casimir Jagellon, called by the German and Italian writers of that epoch the greatest sovereign and statesman of his age, was continually wrangling with his subjects for action and power. The same was the case with Stephen Batory, and with Wladislas IVth of the house of Vasa, the last statesman on the Polish throne. The reckless, ungovernable, and politically egoistical spirit of the nobility destroyed Poland beyond recovery, and caused her death. In all other respects she was brave and chivalrous beyond limit, generous and pure as any other nation whatever, in her manners, customs and domestic life. The Polish nobility, from the first moment of their political existence, appear as most jealous of the privileges of caste, destroying political life in all other parts of the nation. After having enslaved the people or peasants, they deprived the burghers and the cities of their political franchise. In the XVIth century the deputies of cities were finally and forever expelled from the assemblies of the national Diet. By and by the cities fell to ruins; with the loss of freedom life fled from them; neglected by the ruling nobility, the Polish burgher grew poorer and poorer, trade and industry passed away from his hands. Foreign colonists, principally German, began to be introduced, who could lay no claim to the political franchise. Thus the once genuine Polish cities began to be overflown with foreigners and Jews, trade and industry, even the most trifling, disappearing into the hands of strangers. Thus, even now, all handicraftsmen whatever : shoemakers, smiths, carpenters, masons, etc., are still Germans. Burghers could not possess landed estates, neither be admitted to any civil service; in the ecclesiastical hierarchy they scarcely rose above the position of a curate. The Jews were the manipulators and brokers in trade, the nobility selling to foreign exporters the grain and other gross produce of the soil, receiving in exchange the necessities of a luxurious life, and careless of creating any industrial productions at home. Thus disappeared in Poland the national middle class, and all individuality was extinguished in burghers and peasants. The peasant became a poor, soil-tilling, hard-oppressed serf, plucked for centuries by the nobleman, and by his right-hand man, the Jew. Stripped of all human dignity, the Polish peasant never lost, however, in his thus degraded state, his more noble qualities. He is gentle, good-natured, confiding even beyond the limits of reasonable cautiousness, cheerful, patient under ill-treatment, and never revengeful. Originally possessing ability, which long oppression and the absolute neglect in which he was forcibly kept for centuries, have, however, weakened and even partly deadened, he is laborious and hardworking, but scarcely now able to recover from the lifelessness lasting through countless generations. And thus in Poland among the burghers as well as among the peasants, who form the great body of the people, there does not exist that active intelligent class, out of which spring forth mechanics, artizans, etc, on whose shoulders repose the well-being and progressive development of a nation. In one word : in Poland there no more exists a people in the higher social and philosophical meaning of the word. Such a people cannot be created at once, by schemes or abstract theories. Even in the national war of 1831, against the Russians, the nobility did not understand how to be great in their sacrifices and to reinstate socially the patriotic peasantry.*

Russia in her first stage was preserved from any foreign influx to that extent to which it took place in Poland, and in almost all other Slavic regions. Notwithstanding social oppression, intellectual activity, as by a miracle, was preserved in all its vigour among her people, more intensely than in any other Slavic branch, and resisting, as will be shown hereafter, the abnormal deadly action of despotism and caste, grinding all the faculties of mind and intellect. And in this mental as well as in her geographical development, Russia again was left to her own powers and to her own virility. Whatever, then, may be the character of her formation, it bears a peculiarly distinct mark. For centuries she was shut out from any contact with the West, and her early relations with Byzantium were soon broken off by the Tartar conquest and the fall of the Eastern Empire. Notwithstanding that the Slavi did not in any way participate in the overthrow of the Roman world, and did not rise out of its ruins, still many branches of their stock: as the Poles, Tschechs or Bohemians, and others extending towards the south, became at an early epoch, influenced by the western and Roman

* In the beginning of the Polish insurrection of 1830 (for which, to mention by the way, being one of its authors, I was condemned to death), by a legal and official act, in my own and in the name of my minor brothers, I abolished the husbandry service rendered generally by the peasants, leaving with them, as absolute and immediate property, the lands held formerly as farms. Nobody, not even one single nobleman, followed in the track. I mention it here, only "pro memoria."

ideas, in the shape of worship and laws. From the contact with Germany, Teutonic laws, such as the Saxon, the Magdebourg, etc., penetrated, together with that general common law of the whole of Europe, the great *jus civile* But Russia was beyond their reach. In the Xth century, Wladimir the Great, published a book of law called *Prawda Ruska* (Russian truth,) a collection of national legal usages and customs, and this at an epoch when the study of the *jus civile* was not yet thought of any where. The code of law published under the present reign, and known by the name of *Swod Zakonoff*, is a digest of precedental ukases or decrees, most of them based on ancient national ideas enacted by successive Czars according to the exigencies of the time, and of the internal, social or governmental organization and their development.

It may be mentioned as a curious evidence how far no Roman legal notion whatever penetrated into Russia, that even despotism never introduced penal fines. The political offender in Russia proper, when condemned, forfeits all his property; still it is not the government that seizes upon it, but the legal and legitimate heirs. Thus the fortune is never lost to the family. Confiscation exists only in Poland, where Russian law does not yet prevail.

The exterior action of Russia has something in it fatal and unavoidable. Her rapid extension seems directed by a pre-ordained law,—seems to be an effect of more mysterious import than the reason of the time can elucidate. Until now autocracy, Czarism or despotism is the principal agency. How far it is national now, but neither inborn nor indestructible, and thus finally only a transient social and governmental expediency, will be shown in the subsequent pages. Its actions generally do not harmonize with the genuine national character, which often softens the harshness of despotic rule. Thus neither do the Slavi in general, nor the Russian, attempt to violently curb and transform the conquered. This the Slavi have, in common with the French as well as with other races of the south, differing from the German race with all its branches and denominations, all of whom supersede and exterminate the conquered. The Russian, like the Frenchman or other man of the south, absorbs by amalgamation and transforms by a rather slow process, leaving the subdued for a long time in the enjoyment of their distinct social characteristics. Thus the Russian people have neither a hostile feeling nor a craving for the property and the extermination of the Letts, the Finns, the Bashkirs, Calmoucks, Tartars, etc., but once conquering them, allow them to live peaceably at their side. There are small Finnic or Ouralian tribes still leading an undisturbed life, surrounded on all sides by the conquering race. Russia leaves in peace the remnants of a broken people. For the so-called necessities of state, however, and when irritated, the government acts sometimes in opposition to the predominant national feeling.

Each of the primitive races destined to take possession and to people Europe, brought with it a special and distinct language. So did the Slavi. Whatever may have been the cardinal root of all of them, these languages served and serve to mark as distinctly, national deliminations, as could any other geographical lines, set up by nature. One of the most lively, unshaken evidences of a race, of a people, is their language with all its peculiarities. It is the greatest and the highest historical proof—it is the full breathing of the human soul, truer than the testimony of stone and masonry. The Slavic language has the same most incontestable claims to absolute originality, as any other used in Europe by any of the great historical races. In its essence it is wholly independent from any one of them. The primitive Slavic dialect underwent the same process of subdivision and elaboration, as all the other dialects whose nature and historical perfection are already elucidated by scientific researches. As the stem of a mighty tree divides itself into branches and twigs, thus the original language of a race, splits itself into dialects and idioms. And a branch cut off and transplanted, becomes a tree, and thus going deeply back into the past, the now original languages are dialects cut off from a primitive stock. For the Indo-European nations, this stock is the Sanscrit and Zend. Idioms are as twigs; and both idioms and dialects are in the same relation to each other, as are mighty and smaller races and families.

All the dialects and idioms split and unfold progressively, and the farther one can look backwards into history the smaller is the number of subdivisions, less striking the differences, and more positive the proofs of their derivation from one and the same source. This seems to be the law regulating the so-called original languages, as well as idioms and dialects issuing from them. According to the laws of growth and increase, a language can split itself into countless dialects. But to such an almost indefinite splitting, there is opposed likewise a natural impediment. Not all the boughs of a tree become branches, or even twigs. One from among many lives, grows, unfolds and extends itself, while others become feeble, droop, hang, and eventually die.

It would be out of place to enter here into a philological and ethnological dissertation, in order to establish which of the numerous Slavic dialects can claim the legitimate preference, and the right to be considered as having once formed the principal trunk, in this scattered but extensive family. Some eight centuries ago, the Polish dialect, for example, resembled more than it does now, the ancient Slavic, and thus, too, the Russian. This is a proof that the Russian remained more true and faithful to the maternal source. At any rate, the Russian is at present the mightiest tree, not only physically and geographically, but even according to the spirit of the original language. The Russian alone, considered either as a language or as a dialect, is a general key for understanding *all* the other idioms forming the Slavic group. Thus the Russian, by the force of his maternal tongue alone, without the assistance of any study, can at once understand nearly all the idioms spoken out of his country; on the Vistula, the Elbe, down to the Adriatic and to Roumelia, and make himself understood any where through the extensive Slavic region. Neither the Pole, the Tschech, the Illyrian, nor the Serbe, as was proved at the great Slavic congress held in Prague in 1848, can do the like. This special characteristic of the Russian language, in relation with others of its kindred, has already been observed by Adelung, and can again and again be confirmed by every day's experience.

Nearly every language has been developed, perfected and refined, by poets, literati, men of letters, etc., that is to say, from above, from a higher social and intellectual stratum, and consequently, in almost every country, the language spoken by the masses, by the people at large, is more or less at variance with the written one. Not so in Russia, however, as will be explained hereafter, in speaking of the characteristics of the genuine people. True it is, that the poet Lomonosoff, living about the first half of the last century, gave to the language a more precise form, but the pure enunciation and accent pour from the lips of the people, and thence spread themselves over books and literature.

From whatever aspect the Slavic family is contemplated: geographically and statistically, politically and socially, considering the faculty of language, and ascending to the powers of the mind—Russia and the Russian people, form in the present, and for the future, the parent stem of the whole Slavic race; and up to the present time, races have fashioned the destinies of the world, and above all, those of the ancient world. Russia, at any rate, is a huge body. We proceed now to investigate its internal structure.

CHAPTER I.

CZARISM—ITS HISTORICAL ORIGIN.

Various deep or shallow metaphysical and psychological speculations have been laid down upon the reasons, in virtue of which the office and power of the Czar of Russia, with all its criteria of unity, despotism, autocracy, and, very often, of bloody, pitiless tyranny, has taken strong and seemingly indestructible root in the most vivid feelings of the Russian people of all classes and shades. For the solution of this question, how and why Czarism has become thus almost a principal element of the national life and growth, one must look not to abstract theorems, hatched out in the convolutions of the brain, but simply to history. There it stands, a simple, pure historical fact, like many other facts; and there is the succession of events by which this form of absolute monarchy has risen to such eminence, and become, as it were, a religious creed of the people.

This institution, or form of monarchy, which we call Czarism, arose, in its present attributes, or, at least, began to work itself out in Russia during the epoch of Tartar dominion and aggression. Previous to that epoch, and from about the IXth or Xth century, from the Dnieper (Borysthenes), the Dniester, the Carpathian

Mountains, where now extends Gallicia, to the Dwina and the Wolga, Russia was ruled by a number of princes (Kniazia), some weak, others more powerful, who, to a certain degree, were independent, but who all recognized the supremacy of their lord paramount, the Grand Duke of Kiïeff, called *Weliki Kniaz*. These principalities had nothing in them of any feudal origin or principle, but were simply the results of a successive division of the general patrimony among the heirs and children of Ruryk the Norman and his brother, and thus they were all held by kindred and relations. Even the two most ancient Republics since the Christian era—those of Novgorod the Great, and of Pskoff—the historical manifestations of the first, being distinctly visible even in the IVth century, and both of them flourishing by free institutions and extensive trade, when Germany and the north-west of Europe were in utter darkness—recognized the above mentioned Grand Ducal supremacy from about the IXth century forward.

The division of the country into smaller and smaller principalities increased continually, and murderous family feuds were frequent among them. This facilitated the conquest by the Tartars in the XIIIth century. To resist them there was neither unity of command nor of obedience, and thus no unity of action. They accordingly subdued all and established their supremacy. We shall not follow here all the vicissitudes of fortune which the Grand Dukedom underwent. This title passed from one lineage to another, changed seats, wandered from Kiïeff to many other spots, such as Wladimir and others, until in the last years of the XIIIth century it finally found a resting place in Moscow.

The Tartar rule did not change in the least the internal organization of Russia. The Tartar chieftains or Khans did not interfere at all with its internal administration. The Tartars did not spread over the country or settle in any spot whatever in the interior, either in villages or cities. The two races never came into peaceful contact. They did not intermarry or intermingle, being separated *de facto* by immense distances and broad and barren plains. But if they had been thrown together, even then, the watchfulness of the Eastern, or Græco-Russian Church—the intense, vivid religious feeling in the bosom of all classes of the people, the hatred of the conqueror, and of his Mahometan creed—all these violent elements would have been sufficient to prevent any important union of the two races. The family to which descended the dignity of the Grand Dukes in Moscow, and the supremacy over the Empire, proved itself from the beginning of its power, to be inspirited and moved by a statesman like conception. This was by working uninterruptedly, from father to son, to frame out the unity of the Empire, to concentrate all its powers and resources in one hand, as an engine for the overthrow of the hateful Tartar dominion. It was through the Grand Dukes alone that the Tartar Khans communicated with the Empire. The yearly tribute to be paid from the whole, was collected by the Grand Dukes and they alone were responsible for it. Every one ascending the Grand Ducal throne was obliged to seek his confirmation from the Khan, and visit him in his seat or residence at Horda. The Tartar chiefs abandoned to the Grand Dukes the uncontrolled management of all internal affairs. Of this the latter availed themselves during nearly two centuries, in order to absorb and destroy all the petty princes scattered over the Empire. Force and cunning were largely used, the work was a fearful and bloody one; but it succeeded, and the unity of the Empire, under one supreme despotic power, was the result.

Some of those independent dynasties were wholly exterminated, the greater number, however, were forcibly reduced to give up their sovereignties. Such still preserved large private estates by way of indemnity, and retained the title of Prince (Kniaz), taking up their permanent abode in Moscow under the eye of the sovereign. Such is the origin of the countless numbers of princes still to be found in Russia.

In many respects the Tartar supremacy materially aided the Grand Dukes in their enterprise, and thus served to accumulate materials for its own destruction. At last, feeling their strength, the Grand Dukes of Moscow directed their whole energy and weight against the Tartar. This struggle for independence lasted about thirty years. Moscow and Russia bought their liberation by streams of blood. The final battle, called that of the Giants, and lasting for three days, on the plains of Kulikowo, crowned the effort with a complete victory.

In this struggle the religious feelings of the nation were exalted to the utmost intensity. The cross fought with the Grand Dukes against the crescent. It was a sacred warfare. The Grand Duke, the supreme power, the despotic unity, was the soul of the combat. He was sanctified by the Church, and in this powerful moment dawned the identification of the supreme political head of the nation, with its religious worship and sentiment.

The Tartar was crushed. His destroyer—the Grand Duke, the despot, the personification of Autocracy, the Czar, as he began now to call himself—ruled with an iron rod. But as honor and nationality had been vindicated, the grateful people supported rather patiently the bloody lash from time to time brought down upon them. Not a century had elapsed, ere again the nationality of the Russians, their religion, their whole national life and independence, were again brought to the verge of a precipice, and were on the eve of being wholly blotted out, destroyed and changed, by foreign conquest, facilitated by violent internal dissensions.

The direct lineage of the Czars was destroyed by murder. A usurper ascended the throne, and false pretenders, supported by Polish armies, established themselves in the holy City of Moscow, in the sacred Kremlin. Romanism and the Jesuits were to crowd out the Eastern, or National Church and worship. The Czars (Schujski) who had been elected by a part of the nobility and the people of Moscow, after the overthrow of one of the pretenders, were brought chained to Poland, and died in Warsaw in close confinement. It was in the beginning of the seventeenth century. The Poles ruled for several years in Moscow, and the two crowns were on the eve of being united on the head of a Polish prince—which union, if fulfilled, would have absorbed or changed the distinct, genuine nationality of the Russians. All this was the result of the violent interruption above referred to in the lineage of the Czars. Religion inflamed the people—the enemy then established in Moscow was driven out—victory crowned the efforts of the religious patriots, and the palladium of nationality was restored. The whole people, without distinction of classes, now elected the house of Romanoff to the supreme dignity. These events strengthened in the popular mind the belief in the intimate, almost divine blending of religion and of Czarism—of its providential necessity for the life and the welfare of the nation. Czarism, as an idea, is not implanted or based solely on one class of the nation, as were the mediæval monarchies of Europe, or that of Hungary and that of Poland. It is identified with the religion and with the whole mass of the people. This is confessed by the crown in all moments of dangerous crisis, and is evinced by all the imperial proclamations from the time of Michael, Peter the Great, and Catharine, down to that published in 1849, after the conquest of Hungary. All bear nearly the same stamp. Humble in respect to religion, but proud of the Russian nationality, and contemptuous and arrogant with regard to any foreign nation or government, even in regard to the whole world out of Russia. This style of speech agrees with the intimate, vivid feelings of the masses, who are firm in their creed. They believe themselves to be the first people in the world—the only true Christian people—for whom Russia, the fatherland, is the white, or the holy land—all the rest of the world being dark, or black—and the capital, Moscow, most white, holy and sacred. Thus, any foreigner who invades Russia is a heathen, and not a Christian.

The Russian Autocracy shrewdly works out and avails itself of this intensity of feeling and its convictions, in order to maintain and strengthen its unnatural power. By extending the frontiers of the Empire—by conquering other countries, or, as now, pressing upon Europe by a certain moral hallucination, and becoming the supreme arbiter of her destinies; that Autocracy gives nourishment and satisfaction to the unbounded national pride, quenches, for a time, the countless internal dissatisfactions—gives them no time and no breath to combine, unite, and concentrate together.

The parasitic philosophers of the eighteenth century baptized this singular despotism of the Czars with the more civilized phrase of Imperialism, and adulated it accordingly. This, again, to a certain degree, reäcted on the nation, and strengthened in it the power of the Czar, or as we may now call it, the imperial creed. The people believed that from it they received a position in the affairs of the world, a glorious and a prominent place among the elder nations. If the Emperor or Czar tramples under his spurred foot the kings, princes, and nations of Europe, even the poorest serf believes that he shares in the act, and glories in the glory of the Czar. Thus the Autocrat is the great embodiment of the whole Russian nation. *Znaj ruskago*, "*Know the Russian!*" is in such cases the general exclamation of content.

The despotic, all-devouring and absorbing creed which we have called Czarism, is thus a simple result of time and of events. But such results, whatever be their strength, however deep their roots, or however great their duration, are finally undone, dissolved, destroyed by the same elements, by the same agencies which raised them. Time evokes new elements of activity and a new range of events; some of them springing from its own existence, will carry Czarism away with irresistible force into the eternal abyss. The question is, when its knell will sound? That blessed hour is not so distant as some suppose. So much for the historical formation of this Autocracy. In the following chapter is given an outline of the present Czar, showing how Czarism, slowly, invisibly for some, but nevertheless inevitably, is digging its own grave.

CHAPTER II.

THE CZAR NICHOLAS.

"Ein Theil von jener Kraft
Die stets das Gute will, und stets da Boese schafft."

GOETHE.

CZARISM, as an idea in the notions of the Russian people, as well as a fact in the national existence, has reached its zenith in the person of the reigning Czar. Whatever may now be said and wished to the contrary by the enemies of light and liberty, and by conservative owls, according to all the physical laws of nature, as well as to those revealed in history, from this point of culmination, Czarism must begin to decline. These decisive moments are unavoidable, and rule the rotation of bodies, and the destinies of men and nations. The unnatural worship of the Imperial authority begins slowly to die out, even now, in the breast of mighty numbers among all classes of the nation, and the external glitter with which it is still surrounded, depends on the personality of the present Czar, whose successful reign for more than a quarter of a century, has maintained and kindled the flame of loyalty, and has accustomed the masses to believe in his good luck and skilful statesmanship. The like prestige will not surround the brow of his successors. The spell will vanish. No doubt that the cowardice recently shown by the rest of Europe, or rather the infamous treachery of its sovereigns, its aristocracies and conservatives, has contributed mightily to increase the spurious brilliancy surrounding the Czar. However, he has himself thus nearly consumed all the fuel which the faith of the nation can offer him as a burnt offering. The idea is exhausted by him; its extinction has begun; and it is an indisputable truth and law, that what has begun to wither as an idea, cannot much longer sustain itself as a fact.

The present Emperor was born on the 6th July, 1796, and is thus 58 years old. He married on the 1st July, 1817, the princess of Prussia, sister of the reigning king. She was born on the 13th July, 1798. They have six living children—four sons and two daughters. The eldest son, the hereditary Grand Duke, was born on the 29th April, 1818, and married on the 28th April, 1841, a princess from the house of Darmstadt; they have at present four children.

Much has been said about the external personal appearance of Nicholas. He is as vain-glorious of it as any dandy. The glance of his large, blue-greenish, crystal-like, limpid eyes, pierces through and through as with the points of two freezing icicles. A cold pang seizes one's whole being on receiving their full glare.

Nicholas was not destined from his childhood to ascend the Imperial throne; but his education was not neglected. His mother, a sensible, honest, and virtuous German housewife, of the royal house of Würtemburg, directed it, and that of his younger brother, Michael. The two elder brothers, Alexander and Constantine, were brought up under the care of the Empress Catherine, and received from a Swiss, La Harpe, the French encyclopædical, superficial education, at that time in fashion. Among the tutors of Nicholas was the celebrated economist,

Storch; and notions sown by this strong mind took root in that of his youthful pupil, budding forth to a certain degree during his whole life.

The great duel between Napoleon and Russia soon made the mechanism of armies one of the principal pursuits of the young Grand Duke, and other studies were rather neglected. I may observe, here, that there is a kind of mental disease in this family, especially since the unhappy Peter III., *through which they all regard it as their vocation to be good corporals.* All of them have devoted and devote as much time as possible to martyrizing the soldiers with daily exercises and all the petty manœuvres of a parade. But not one in the whole family has ever displayed any higher military capacity whatever. Nicholas, however able he may be, as was his father and his three brothers, to detect a button which is not in its right place on the uniform of a single soldier drawn in line with hundreds of others, or any other fault in the equipment—could never measure by his eye the reach of a gun, or the distance accomplished by a bullet. Thus, during the campaign against the Turks, in 1828, he sought to earn military laurels by the sureness of his eye, in matters of seige and fortification. The Russian troops surrounded the impregnable fortress *Schoumla,* the key to the Balkan mountains. Nicholas pointed out the spot where the heavy ordnance was to be posted to open the fire on the fortress—and the bullets fell half way from the walls. His capacity as commander has never risen above that of directing the various manœuvres of a single regiment of cavalry. The movements of two regiments combined are too much for him. In the sham fights, which every year serve for his pastime, and where 150,000 men are often unmercifully employed in the hottest season, with immense cost and loss of time, the Emperor used sometimes to take the command of one-half of the army, but always to make the most unpardonable blunders, and to be out-manœuvered by his opponent He has even been taken prisoner with his staff at a dinner table; and now, taught by experience, he takes his seat among the judges of the camp. An able general and bad courtier, named Murawioff, who, on one occasion thus took the Emperor prisoner, very soon afterwards fell into disgrace, and is no longer intrusted with any military command. During the above-mentioned campaign in Turkey, Nicholas joined the army, commanded by field-marshal Prince Wittgenstein, interfering continually as we have been told, with its military operations. To this untimely interference the unhappy results of this first campaign were due. The next year the command was transferred to Field-Marshal Dybitsch. The first condition in accepting it was, that both the Imperial brothers, Nicholas and Michael, should remain at home, and keep quiet. Nicholas, grown wise by the previous year's experience, acceded to the demand. The results are known. The army crossed the Balkan, took Adrianople, and there the treaty, bearing that name, was signed. Dybitsch earned the surname of *Zabalkanski* (the Crosser of the Balkan.) Since this lesson, Nicholas has never joined an army, nor appeared personally on any theatre of war, either in Poland or in Hungary. Now he believes himself to be a great naval commander. So much for his military abilities.

From the peace of 1815, to the time of his ascending the throne in 1825, he devoted his time almost exclusively to military exercises, but was known only as the inventor of an ambulatory kitchen-stove, for the use of the camp. But this seems after all to have been a trick somewhat in the way of that practised by Pope Sixtus V., in order not to cause any suspicions in the morbid mind of Alexander, who from 1822 to the time of his death was laboring under the darkest hypochondria. About 1821, the family pact was agreed upon, by which Constantine resigned his right to the succession, and Nicholas was declared to be the heir to the throne. But it was kept perfectly secret, and known only to three or four persons. At that period Nicholas was occasionally present at the sessions of the special ministry, or secretaryship of state, directed by the celebrated Count Araktscheff, into whose hands Alexander, in the last years of his life, totally resigned the reins of Government. So far was this the case, that the Count had in his possession a quantity of blanks with the signature of Alexander, and was thus enabled to decide, publish and execute any law or any other disposition whatever. It seems that the Count, an honest man, and a great despiser of mankind, while wielding this power did not treat the future Sovereign with any excessive deference. After the death of Alexander, Araktscheff, who was at his estates in the country, instantly returned to Nicholas all the blanks of Alexander in his possession. For this the new Emperor rewarded him with the gift of a favorite uniform of Alexander, to be preserved as a relic. A very short time afterward, the Count received orders never to leave his estates without special permission from the Czar. I mention these facts, because they give the best insight into the real character of the man.

History has already recorded the bloody drama attending the ascension of the Imperial throne by Nicholas. It was not, what the French writers call a palace revolution, a tragedy in a closet or in a bed-chamber, performed by a few courtiers and conspirators as assassins, but it took place publicly, before the people, in the streets, and as it were in the forum, and the best, the most intellectual and youthful energies of the nation were among the actors.

It must be mentioned, that as soon as the news of the death of Alexander reached St. Petersburg, where Nicholas resided, he did not at first avail himself of the resignation of his elder brother, but took the oath of fidelity to him, and so did the nation, awaiting the decision of Constantine, who was then residing in Warsaw, and who after some hesitation kept his word.

On that day, so momentous for him and the Russian people, Nicholas gave proofs of great personal courage and of a calm, deliberate presence of mind. The insurrectionary attempt was overpowered, and the first dim aspirations of Russia for a kind of constitutional liberty, fashioned on English and French patterns, were choked. Whether these aspirations were premature or not, and their arrest beneficial or calamitous, cannot be discussed in this brief outline. Among the reasons given by the revolutionary leaders for thus attempting to muzzle the autocracy, or even to expel the dynasty, they pointed to the desolate state of Russia, caused by the imbecility displayed by Alexander in the last years of his reign; to the savage ferocity of his brother Constantine, and to the supposed entire incapacity of Nicholas. Nicholas, who, secreted behind a folding screen, was daily present at the examination of the prisoners, heard all this, and thus received a wholesome lesson.

The accused were condemned, some to capital punishment, others to Siberia for life, or for a longer or shorter length of time. In the execution of these sentences at the time, as well as during the long exile—twenty years for some of the condemned—Nicholas has shown glimpses of a character and feelings—which have more than once come to light during his reign—revealing a cold-blooded heart, and the disposition of a tyrant as far as it is possible to be one in our times, even in Russia. The most prominent and deepest feature in his character, darkening his actions, is an inexorable, unextinguishable rancor. Thus, never, never has he understood how to be liberally, fully merciful. It is more than he can afford. What in the language of monarchies is called granting a pardon, and being magnanimous, he is never able to perform with that grandeur which even the most accursed tyrants have sometimes exhibited. He distils forgiveness slowly drop after drop; never, however, wholly filling the cup of pardon, forgetful thus of one of the most popular Russian adages: *Kaznit tak kaznit, milowat tak milowat,* "Be unyielding in punishing, be grand in pardon."

Capital punishment was abolished in Russia by the Empress Elizabeth a century since, with the exception of the sentences of courts-martial. When the capital condemnation of the perpetrators of the movement of 1825 was submitted to the sanction of the Czar, he for three days refused to sign it, not wishing to be the restorer of such a measure. His councillors urged him to the step. He yielded to their advice. A hangman was imported from Stockholm, as there was none in Russia. The execution of five of the condemned took place publicly in St. Petersburgh. The Governor-General of the capital presided on the occasion. Four were executed one after another. The fifth and last in order was Ryleeff, a beloved and popular poet. The rope broke, and he fell to the ground hurt slightly and alive. The crowd echoed a simultaneous, thunder-like groan. The Governor-General hesitated, and sent for orders to the Emperor. The answer was, to "take a stronger rope and proceed with the execution." In the same spirit, he has never fully liberated any of the political exiles in Siberia, even after long years of punishment; not even when his son humbly interceded for some of them. The immortal poet Puschkine, in his only verses addressed to Nicholas, stimulating him to tread in the footsteps of Peter the Great, admonishes him to resemble Peter in forgiveness, and be of a short memory for wrongs done to himself, as was his great ancestor.

All his qualities for good and for evil, appeared on the surface and shaped themselves out when he ascended the throne. The first steps of the young sovereign were made cautiously, with great circumspection. He tried to surround himself with honest men, rare jewels in Russia, even among those in the highest places. He was directed in his choice by what is there a caricature of public opinion, by the voice of some few saloons, and likewise by the advice of his mother. He thus made some good and some bad selections. He devoted his activity to stopping the disorders which had mightily seized on the Empire in the last years of Alexander; during which time it can be said, there was no government and no administration, and that Russia kept together by an inward, inborn force of cohesion. His primitive tendency was to be a reformer, to give a new and refreshing impulse to the nation, and to awaken its intellect and powers. These first steps were successful. The torpor of the past reign was so great, that the slightest movement in a new direction could not but prove beneficial. The nation saw a new light, a new era dawning before it. Nicholas proclaimed the supremacy of the law over his own will. All seemed to blossom under the rays of success. His star rose and shone more and more brilliantly. The campaigns of Turkey and of Persia were glorious. Then came the Polish insurrection. From this crisis, Russia, after for a moment coming near a new separation from Europe by the possibility of a restoration of Poland through the preliminary success of the patriotic armies—Russia, after the first blow, which was so nearly deadly for her, recovered—and Poland was *annihilated.*

These events, thus happily accomplished in rapid succession, surrounded the brow of Nicholas with a bright halo. The nation believed in him. People always worship the successful. And thus Czarism, degraded by Alexander, was again raised into a higher region. During this time of his ascending movement Nicholas believed that his mission was to be the conductor of his people into light and civilization, that he was to lay a corner-stone for their moral and social amelioration. He believed this to be the mission of an autocrat. *The earnestness of his purpose and efforts at that time dazzled and attracted many generous minds, many strong and active intellects, and they thronged to serve under his banner, to share with him in this laborious but generous toil.* It was something more than a dream—it was a reality of several years' duration. It seemed that in proportion as he rose, his mind extended and purified itself. Under Catharine and Alexander foreigners overflowed Russia, the national genius was crippled, all was imitation in thinking, acting, and in literature. Nicholas put forward the idea of again bathing the Russian mind in the pure life-giving fountain of genuine unsullied nationality—of making it the focus and the compass of civilization. Such is the origin of the so-called Russian governmental Panslavism.

At that time Nicholas was accessible to truth, hearing *remonstrances* patiently, sometimes thankfully. He allowed the criticism of abuses through books and dramatic representations. He combated with all his might, and tried to eradicate the boundless venality and corruption —unconscious, it may be, that they lay at the very bottom of the principle by which he holds his power. In the first years of his reign he several times tried to relax the severity of the censorship for home as well as for foreign publications and newspapers, but he was constantly dissuaded by his advisers. *Very soon he became tired of many good measures that he had attempted.* And he lacks real knowledge of men. Thus he was often misled in his choice even then, when flattery was not yet omnipotent over his mind. In his attempt at reform he stumbled at the above-mentioned impediment. Incontestably he had the power of comprehending a new reformatory idea, and even a deep and broad one; of adopting and giving it form—transforming it into a law. But deprived of the capacity of embracing all the details requisite for putting it into practice, he has had in his endeavors to depend on the good will of his Ministers—who very often, when bowing ostensibly to his will, and feigning to accept the projected reform, have surrounded its execution with countless difficulties, and thus have often succeeded in arresting its action. In this way many reforms projected, and even decreed, have been abandoned.

His mother inspired him with a rigidity of principles, and with a religious respect for his own word. Thus he has a certain scrupulous honesty. He treats with contempt or dislike all diplomatic tricks, or diplomatic tortuosity. He is a good husband, an excellent father; but these qualities do not always indicate a true generosity of soul. Few, if any, have seen a warm tear moisten his eye at a great general and not his own personal misfortune. From the beginning of his reign one can say that he has been generous in his own way, and even lavish principally for ostentation, when in foreign lands, as well as to those who surround him, and whom he believes to be wholly devoted to his person. But such men need kindness less than others, who work hard in the service in lower positions, and to whom he is rather parsimonious. But in whatever manner he bestows a favor, he never does it in a simple, natural way, but always with a pompous ostentation, sometimes painful for the receiver. This leads one to presume that he lacks real benevolence of heart, in which respect he is far below his brother, Alexander, or even Constantine.

These principal features of his mind and character have been his companions, the lights and shadows in the exercise of power, in his progress to its climax. Having reached it, he could not withstand its intoxication. No mortal can; Christ alone, in his God-like nature, resisted temptation. But the tempter, the spirit of lies, darkness and treachery, this father of absolutism, gets control of others. He subdues them all. Thus he ruined Napoleon. On that unnatural height the head of Nicholas soon became giddy. Those regions are frozen, and all generous aspirations die out in that atmosphere. The basest incense and adulation became alone palatable to him. Then struck the hour of his moral downfall, invisible from without, but felt deeply by Russia.

In that part of his reign when his moral influence was in the ascendant, the Czar tried, as we have already seen, to kindle and to spread among the people some sparks or glimpses of light and vitality. But ten or twelve years ago a change took place. His mind faltered, and the downward movement began. The regions of despotic power, limited neither by law nor reason, are like the ethereal space where swim the celestial bodies, in themselves dark, frigid, and lifeless. In that cheerless sphere the Czar lost the perception of light. He became afraid of his own work and learned to dread civilization. He evoked and made a compact with the spirit of darkness, and arrayed him against his own nation. The better germs in his mind withered and shrunk, while the weeds of his character grew exuberantly, poisoning and strangling all the generous pulsations of his heart. The time when he allowed some of his councillors to give him even the most humble advice, came to an end. Now he began to ask for blind compliance, and the most debasing adulation. Once, for example, he had authorized the old Prince Gallitzin, the Governor-General of Moscow, to address him frankly, and to inform him if any of his acts were unpalatable to the national spirit. The Prince enjoying the highest esteem of the public, as well as an elevated social and official position, sometimes, though very seldom, made use of this confidential permission. For a period his observations were graciously received. But on one occasion, when he forewarned the sovereign about a measure which was not at all welcome to the nation, the despot told him: "Prince, you are becoming revolutionary; once I wanted advisers, now I can rule by myself without them."

And so he began to rule. Since the commencement of his reign, the ministers have had stated days and hours to transact business with the Czar, each separately for its own department. They now found out, that the safest thing was to go into generalities only, and, as far as possible, not to disclose any troublesome occurrences, or to let him know the true state of things. All affairs must be represented in the most agreeable colors. Thus, the reports prepared for the sovereign are required, to use the common expression, *to be made sweet as sweetmeats.* The first to introduce this new mode was Count Kiseleff, the head of a newly created Department, that of Public Domains, a department embracing a population of nearly twenty millions. Next to him came the Prince Menschikoff, Secretary of the Navy, and Count Alex. Strogonoff. But there still were some exceptions, and some ministers maintained the old ground. However, the infallibility of the Czar became the all-embracing theme for flatterers, for the intimate court circles, as well as for the debased littérateurs, writers and poets, who principally live in St. Petersburg. Next, they began to offer the incense of praise for his Apollo-like form. Not only the home courtiers, but those abroad, the small German *principiculi* and their pack, as well as other courts—for example, that of Stockholm—burnt before the idol the like offering. The idol believed now sincerely in the irresistible influence and attraction of his personal appearance. In this is the explanation of his unlooked-for visit, paid in 1844, to Queen Victoria, as well as of those made to Vienna, and to the Pope Gregory XVI. in 1846, all of which proved failures.

Once he lighted up the flame of a genuine nationality. Now the nation is embodied in his person. No other utterances of the national spirit are allowed to have publicity. Any scenic representation, criticizing abuses or customs, is prohibited. It is a personal offence. At the same time, the military hobby more and more masters his intellect. Every thing must be submitted to military drill. Thus, for example, the high schools for law and surgery in St. Petersburg are military institutions. The Empire is divided into University Districts, under the Secretary of Public Instruction. The heads of these districts, the directors of the public schools, and those of the higher gymnasia, and of late even the minister himself, are taken either from the army or navy, principally from the latter, as the most fit to maintain an iron rule, and to restrain within just limits the occasional thirst for good information. Finally, a ukase was published, allowing only three hundred young men to receive yearly the higher instruction of the Universities. Of these, there being six in Russia, the total yearly number of their pupils is 1,800, and these are taken from the class of the nobility alone; as another ukase prohibits the burghers, those forming the first and second guild, from giving their children a higher education, because, as the ukase explains, it would contribute to arouse wishes and aspirations not to be reached and realized by that class in Russia, and thus would spread dissatisfaction with the real position of the individuals and the class.

Serious instruction of the mind in history and philosophy is proscribed, as dangerous, and as contributing to give to it loftier and purer ideas and notions than it ought to have. So are classical studies. Not even the shadow of a free, scientific criticism is suffered. All is to be wrapped in the cold shroud of pure, icy despotism.

The genius of Russia will, through eternity, be a mourning accuser before the tribunal of God and of incorruptible, unrelenting history, for the bloody destruction of its most brilliant emanations—manifested in a Ryleef, in a Puschkine, one of the greatest poets of his time—in Lermonteeff and in Bestuschef-Marlinski. Puschkine fell in a duel, a holocaust to the licentious vanity of the Emperor. The Czar, by fostering an infamous scandal which he might have strangled in the embryo, sought for revenge on this independent and unbending poet, who had resisted every seduction. For an offence against a piece of court gossip, and at the same time for an action proper to a high-bred and high-spirited man, Lermonteeff was exiled to the Caucasus, and found there a premature death. Marlinski was also sent there to atone for his liberal opinions. The fate of Ryleef I have already told. All these lyres and many others have been crushed and stifled by Nicholas. Among many whom the Czar has vainly tried to muzzle, is Chomiakoff, who was treated by the despot with an affected contempt, because this versatile genius sings Russia; because he feels deeply that her sublime destinies are independent of Czarism; and because the poet and the thinker never bent his knee, or debased his inspirations and his pen with official adulation.

Thus Czarism levies war against every genuine impulse and idea of which it is not the Alpha and the Omega. As for the Panslavism which would emancipate itself from governmental tutorship and become a truly national conception, full of life, bearing in its womb the future free destinies of Russia and of the Slavic race, the Panslavism blended for life and death with the loftier vitality of the Russian people—the Panslavism which would clear off the rubbish, heaped by centuries of abuse over the roots of the national growth of freedom, and the internal independence of the whole population—the Panslavism which has reminded and reminds the nation that the bigotry of Czarism is comparatively modern, and that communal equality was the cradle and nursery of the Slavi for uncounted centuries; even the mentioning of its name is prohibited to all those engaged in the public service. For officials, professors of schools and universities, it is outlawed by the most severe penalties, such as expulsion from the service or imprisonment. The name of Panslavism is never to be used in speech or print. A similar proscription and similar penalties are imposed on the writing of the history of modern times, or the reign of the Czar. Any publication on this subject is to be submitted to the censorship of the Minister of the Household, or Major-Domo of the Palace, a General-Field-Marshal of the Russian army. And every year brings at least one new measure designed to blot out light and life, and covers Russia with ukases concocted in the workshop of darkness. And thus the Czar fulfils the prophecy flashed but by Lermonteeff shortly before his death :

Skazal umu,	He said to the mind :
Jdi wo tmu ;	Go into darkness ;
J podpisal ;	And signed it ;
" Byt po siemu ;	" Be it so,*
" Czar Nikolaï."	" Czar Nikolaï."

All branches of the internal administration have been treated in the same manner. Every where prevails the most blind and dirty favoritism and falsehood. Corruption and venality have thus reconquered the ground they had lost. Men of the most impure character—deprived of any, even the smallest glow of honorable feelings, as, for instance, Count Kleinmichel and General Dubellt, are the almighty favorites or the informing souls of the ruler.

Thus disorder and oppression gnaw again the marrow of Russia. Advancing in years, the Czar hates to see around him new faces, or to admit them to his cabinet, and especially those who might exhibit independent tendencies, or straight-forward, honest veracity. This has above all been shown by him in selecting Secretaries of the Treasury or of Finance. The old Count Cancrin who was named to this post shortly after the ascension of Nicholas—introduced therein some order, some economical notions—restored and replenished the cash-box, which remained empty after the fatal disorganization, disorder and plundering that flourished openly during the last years of Alexander, and the secretaryship of Count Gurieff. Cancrin knew how to resist the lavish exigencies of the young sovereign, and Nicholas often thankfully yielded

* These are the sacramental words by which the Emperor signs the laws and ukases.

to the adviser. But when after the death of the Count the vacant post was to be filled, the Czar very carefully looked for a man who would obey blindly, without making in any case the slightest remonstrance. Such was the Count Wrontschenko, such is his successor Brock, a servile German.

The financial state of the National or Imperial Treasury grows worse and worse every year. However, no confusion ought to be made between this and the real resources of Russia. These are, in themselves, inexhaustible, and on them is based the credit which the Empire, on the whole, justly enjoys. But notwithstanding the apparent state of things, the productive powers, which yield such results even under the most unpropitious conditions and the most unfavorable circumstances, are really as yet only in a latent state, and cannot be evoked into growth and true activity without order and liberty. On the other hand, the fever of lavish wastefulness increases in the Czar more and more—and this fever must be gratified at any cost. Thus the finances become more and more embarrassed, since not all the resources of the nation and of the soil are within the greedy grasp of the Imperial Treasury. Direct taxation is not known in Russia. The nobility cannot be directly taxed, neither can the soil nor the serfs. The latter pay only a small capitation tax of about a dollar a head, which income is destined to maintain the local administration of the different provinces, or governments, as they are called. But millions of this tax remain for years and years unpaid—and this arrearage increases and extends daily. Whole provinces must sometimes be exempted on account of real impossibility, resulting as well from drouth or storms as from a bad, oppressive, disordered, unprincipled and irrational management of the genuine riches of the nation and of the soil. Thus many begin already to foresee the not distant hour when the actual financial resources will give way to that extent that the internal service will remain unpaid.

The principal revenues of the Empire consist in the monopoly of the sale of all kinds of liquors—the product of the custom-houses and the rent paid by the crown domains. Other branches, as stamps, mines, &c., are comparatively rather insignificant. To increase the income from the custom-houses a duty is laid on exports of the national products. The whole revenue may amount to 125 and 130 millions of dollars. Of this amount, nearly the half is yielded by the liquor monopoly; the custom-houses give about 26 millions, the crown domains about 34 millions, as far as any faith can be put in official publications. But, above all, official statements concerning the finances should be mistrusted; and in Russia every thing is official. Nearly two thirds of the entire revenue is absorbed in the maintenance of the immense army and navy. However small the real pay of the soldiers and officers, the plundering in this branch of the service is beyond calculation. The remainder of the revenue, after deducting the arrearages of several departments, but principally of the crown domains, has to maintain the general administration, pay the interest of the public debt, support the large imperial family, and finally supply the expenditures of the emperor upon his favorites and his lavish extravagance otherwise, for which his private personal income fails by many and many millions to suffice.

A great deal of talk has been occasioned in the newspapers by the investment which the Czar made some years ago in the British and French securities. This was nothing but a master piece of vanity and bragging, and it was really curious to read the incongruous speculations of journalists, economists and statesmen, such as M.

Thiers, for example, in regard to it. This puzzling investment was made after a year of a general failure of crops through the whole of Europe, with the exception of Russia, which thus exported wheat to the value of more than eight millions of dollars. The above-mentioned philosophers unanimously discovered that the money invested by the Emperor was nothing else than that paid to Russia for her breadstuffs. Happily for the pockets of the Russian land-owners, this was not the case. That money went directly to them. Some few hundred thousand dollars only paid by the buyers went into the custom-houses in the shape of export duty. Thus this celebrated investment had nothing to do with the result of that year's wheat trade. The truth is, that the Treasury and the public banks could at that time easily command the required sum of money, and thus rendered easy of gratification the vainglorious egotism of the Czar. Financially speaking, this investment was nonsense. Russia has a public debt, and pays for it a rate of interest far superior to that paid by the Bank of France. If, then, the Imperial Treasury possessed these superabundant millions, the best possible investment would have been in the national debt at home. Shortly afterward, the same Minister of Finance who sent the imperial millions to Paris and London had to make a loan for the Petersburg and Moscow Railroad. This offered another occasion to invest profitably the surplus funds of the Emperor, as the interest paid for this loan exceeded that received from France. We must add that the whole of this noisy financial operation was duly appreciated by the sober part of the nation, and by no means excited their admiration so much as it did that of foreigners.

The wants of the treasury increase almost daily, and to meet them taxes are levied on the citizens or burghers, the peasants, and the serfs of the crown domain. The approximative revenues of the Empire amount, as already stated, to some $130,000,000. The national debt is nearly $320,000,000. The yearly interest thereon is more than $20,000,000—a little more than 6 per cent. on the whole. The war of Hungary contributed mightily to drain the already depleted treasury. This war, and all the military manifestations since, outrun considerably the current revenues—the real official resources of the Government. It is true, that in case of need, extraordinary measures can be resorted to. The banks and their deposits are within the grasp of the needy rulers, who resort to them, and will do so more and more, whatever may be officially said to the contrary. There are no accumulated savings in the treasury, no possibility to make such, and no thought of it.

Every year there is published a pompous announcement of a deposit of bullion from the mines, made in the presence of an official deputation from the merchants of St. Petersburg, in the vaults of the fortress of Peter and Paul. This bullion is announced as representing or giving security to the paper currency in circulation. But this circulation is perfectly arbitrary, and the Government, in putting it forth, is entirely free from control. The proportion of bills to the deposited metal is, at least, as three to one. This bullion deposit was used for the war of Hungary, and thus reduced to a great extent; but the emission of bank-bills was proportionally augmented. This fact, without being publicly spoken of, is well known in Russia. As to the confidence enjoyed by the bank-bills, it has its source in the confidence of the nation, in its own vitality, as well as in commercial exigencies. The colossal internal trade throughout the whole Empire, extending, as it does, from the frontiers of Germany to Kataï, and from the frozen ocean to the boundaries of Persia and Arabia, does not receive the aid of private or public bank-drafts, or of bills of exchange drawn by merchants and serving as a circulating medium, but is almost exclusively carried on either by barter or for ready-money. The banking-houses in the several cities on the Baltic, and those in Moscow, Odessa, and Petersburg, are rather for the convenience of the foreign trade. A wealthy merchant, for example, from Moscow or Petersburg, making purchases of breadstuffs, flax, ashes, tallow, hides, etc., in the interior of the Empire, must carry with him, or through his agents, hundreds of thousands in money, to pay instantly on the spot to the smaller merchants in the interior. When he has brought his merchandise to the place of exportation, he sells it to the foreign exporter mostly again for ready money. Few, if any, Russians are themselves exporters.

Now, it is easy to conceive, that when travelling, the carrying about one's person of such considerable sums is easier, and above all safer, in paper money than it could be in coin. Here is the great arcanum of the credit of the bills notwithstanding their excessive emission in proportion to the basis on which they are issued. At all the great internal fairs at which tradesmen meet together, from all parts of the Empire as well as from the far East —as, for example, at that of Nischneï-Novgorod—no drafts, no bills of exchange are to be seen; and yet, notwithstanding the imperious necessity of a paper currency, the moment may come when the trade will be unable to uphold the credit of the bills, and bankruptcy will ensue, morally as well as financially.

Czarism, or rather the Czar himself, pushed on by unavoidable fatality, has sown mighty germs of disorder in the nation. He was the first to raise the *spy system* to the supreme honors of the Court, and to introduce it into the Imperial Councils. Alexander looked on it and treated it as a shameful necessity. Never until now was it spit forth so directly into the face of the nation, or in so offensive a manner. In fact, since the time of Basil the Bloody, no such institution had been directed by the sovereign himself. This was left for Nicholas. He believes that the secret police and the spy system are the principal securities, the main props of his reign. Thus he has rendered the Police an elevated branch of his Administration. Its commander, its chief, is the most intimate favorite and the inseparable companion of the Czar. So was Count Benkendorff, a German by birth, and the original founder of this infamous system. And it may be observed here, that Germans and Jews are its principal agents and directors, and that very few true born Russians seek for that distinction. Unhappily, the present Chief, Count Orloff, is one of these. Even Napoleon did not make out of a Fouché, a Savary, or a Regnault de St. Jean d'Angely the first men of the Empire, or his nearest confidants. Nothing of the sort—not even the shadow thereof—darkened the lofty and pure mind of Peter, to whose footsteps Nicholas believes he adapts his imperial feet.

Once the Czar believed that there was a nation for whose welfare God had sent him to work and to care. Now he seeks to establish and to raise to a creed the idea that Czarism is the generator of the nation—that Czarism was made first and the nation afterward. But the traditions of the ancient national life are not yet extinguished. Thousands and thousands, full of hatred against the wily debaser, against the group of rampant abettors who surround him, and against his thousands of spies, silently but surely kindle the glowing sparks of these sacred recollections.

In relation to Europe, to the outward and ultra-Russian world, Nicholas firmly and absolutely believes that he is predestined to maintain the ancient tottering order, to shelter and restore legitimacy, to combat and conquer the forces of hell, represented by progress, light, and the emancipatory revolution. He is a true believer of the school of Alison, Haller, De Maistre, and Bonald. This faith in his vocation explains the generosity of his conduct toward Austria after the affair of Hungary. He even—for the first time in his life—forgave, on that event, the house of Hapsburg for the most cruel, the most deadly offence which could have been inflicted on the heart and feelings of a father, and on the honor of a man.

Once he recognized the idea of the supremacy of the law. This was something. It was a recognition of the *persona juris* in his subjects. But now the law is himself, his will, his wish. Thus he is the only *persona* in the empire—others are in reality merely things—and *persons* so far as his will allows them to be such, so long as they submit to move within the iron limits of his whims and of his narrowing notions. Intellectual life—even physical life—can be allowed to exist only so far as they assimilate themselves and support the control exercised by Czarism. But Nicholas has stretched the reins to such a rigidity that every body is hurt and wounded, from the magnate down to the serf. Every class feels the debasement—feels that by him all vitality, all individuality except his own, are absorbed or annihilated. Nearly seventy millions of human beings are, after all, mere chattels, living only for him and through his imperial concession. It is so now—but last it cannot. This tension will break the reins, if not in his own hands, in those of his successor. Those who pronounce his name with a curse are numerous, and belong to all social classes—and more numerous are they who are choked by the words "Czar" and "Nicholas" —and never stain their lips with them. These unyielding elements I will hereafter point out and enumerate.

Thus the brilliancy which surrounds this man, and which is admired from a distance, and worshipped by the retrogrades and absolutists, is spurious, or at least it is the last glimmer cast by the falling meteor. The body gnawed by consumption corruscates the most brilliant hue just before the knell of death. So it is with Czarism, or else there would be neither truth, justice, nor logic in the creation.

Aside from these explosive matters which are inherent in the nature of Czarism and accumulated by the sombre coarseness of the Czar—by which every slightest aspiration of manhood is maimed and crushed, and the intellectual, the rational, as well as the physical activity of the nation, debased, curtailed, trodden down with an unvarying purpose, —aside from this, there exist still other elements apparently of a less dangerous character—but so new, so unwonted in the political life of Russia, that they are portentous for the future of the system. One of these is the present extent of the Imperial family, which in all probability will, before long, be augmenting continually at a rapid ratio, and this just at a time when the scales begin to fall from the eyes of the nation—when the breeze of thought agitates however slowly the public mind, and when, what is worse still, the people at large begin to ponder silently, to judge, to appreciate, to compare, and even to calculate the cost of maintaining Czarism. The celebrated journey of the Imperial family to Italy, in 1846, which in eight months, cost about $8,000,000, occasioned great growling among all classes, and principally among the bourgeoisie of Moscow, and of the cities of the interior. And these expensive journeys are repeated yearly by the whole numerous progeny of the Czar.

For more than six centuries there has not been such an extensive Imperial stock as the present. It amounts to sixteen persons, beside the father and mother. All of them are young, and may thus double in number within the next twenty years. All of them are in the present and in the future, "Grand Dukes," and "Imperial Highnesses," all of them are to be maintained on an Imperial footing—with separate attendants, establishments or small courts—not to mention their rivalries, intrigues, difficulties and hateful contestations, influencing public affairs. Thus it has always been and always will be, when a sovereign family increases, and still is forced to live thronged together. But all are and must be provided for by the nation. For many reasons, such a state of things must become insufferable, and all the more so, at an era when the nation begins to feel its own individuality. As to framing or cutting out distant vice-royalties for these persons, and thus dividing and breaking the unity of the Empire—such a thing is out of the question, now, or in a more distant future. The national spirit, the national genius—will not bend and endure it, and even the present almighty Czar would not dare to undertake such a measure.

Thus escorted, Czarism runs out its course and is dragged toward the abyss. Thus loaded, Czar Nikolai will appear in history, as fatally precipitating into inevitable destruction the power embodied in his person. The growth of the seeds with which he thus abundantly covered the national soil, their detailed action on all the conventional gradations of Russian social life, is already visible. In following chapters they will be pointed out one by one, as well as the capacity of Russia and her people to frame for themselves new and bright destinies, in harmony with the general laws of human happiness.

CHAPTER III.

THE ORGANIZATION OF THE GOVERNMENT.

THE actual organization of the government, administrative as well as judiciary, is the work of Peter the Great. Subsequently to him, however, some changes and modifications have been introduced. Previously to the time of the reforms of Peter the governmental machinery was not so complicated. In introducing the changes, Peter in some instances maintained, however, the old institutions, giving them only a new, mostly Germanic, name.

Anciently the Grand Duke, or Czar, was surrounded by a council called *duma* (which signifies *thought*, *dumati*, to *think*). This council was presided over by the sovereign in person. At that epoch the patriarch could sometimes assist in its deliberations. It was formed exclusively of the principal nobility, and of mediatized princes, that is, of those who once possessed independent sovereignties, with the Grand Dukes as lords paramount, but whose possessions became finally absorbed in the grand unity. Such a councillor was called *dumny boïar*, a boyard of the council, and this was the highest dignity and official title in the state. The provinces were administered most generally by such boyards, having very extensive powers. Their title then was that of *woïewoda*, signifying the war-leader. This name and dignity—used likewise in Poland ever since the close of the tenth century, and introduced by Bolesuas the Great—was falsely translated there into that of *palatinus—palatin*, to which it has no relation. The woïewoda in time of war summoned the people to arms, and led them in person to the place where the whole army of the country was to be united or to meet the enemy. The internal administration of the cities and communes, in the provinces, was made by boards and *dumas*, elected by the inhabitants, under the sanction and direction of the woïewoda. He corresponded directly with the sovereign and his *duma*.

In the *duma* the current business was performed by clerks of the council. Their name was *dumny dïak* or *dïatschek*. They were really the laborious and intellectual part of the council, and thus very influential and much respected, while their hierarchal standing was very high.

Peter the Great principally modelled his administrative reforms on the Swedish and partly on the Dutch standard. He introduced various boards, or *colleges*, for internal inferior administration, and for some offices maintained even their foreign denomination. Thus, for assessor of college, *Kolejskiy assessor*. Nay, even from the Chinese Peter borrowed the official classification of the civil and military service*—imitating thus that of the Mandarins. By this classification the precedency and social superiority was no more lodged in the nobiliar title but became dependent on the degree reached in the public service by this half-social, half-official ladder. Even the inheritance of the nobiliar privilege was made to depend on *the public service, as well as the intitulations:* as, for example, those of well-born, high well-born, excellency, illustris, illustris-

* See Appendix B.

simus, etc., attached to the official dignity, and not to that derived from birth. A prince, *kniaz*, however, and a count maintain their special intitulation, that of serenissime, through all degrees of the service.

Peter did this to force the boyards to go through all the classes of the public service, which from ancient times belonged exclusively to the nobility. Previous to his reign the nobles not only evaded and refused to serve in the lower public offices, but refused to serve or to obey even in war any one of more recent nobiliar title. This struggle, or contest for precedence, is known in the Russian history under the name of *miestnitschestwo.* To stop this Alexis, the father of Peter, had already ordered the nobility to show him all their pedigrees, and had burnt them publicly in Moscow.

By the introduction of this classification every nobleman belongs to the service and to one of the classes whence he derives his standing. Even the right to be admitted to the court depends on this. This right for those who do not belong to the civil or military household of the sovereign, begins with the fourth class, that of the real councillor of state, *dieystwitelnyï statskij sowïetnïk.* Their wives share this privilege, but not their children. The dignity of a *kniaz* or count, without that derived from office, does not open the doors of the court.

All supreme governmental, administrative, judiciary, and legislative powers reside, of course, undivided, and were so for long centuries, in the person of the autocrat. Thus the ancient *duma* possessed no independent attributes. Peter abolished the *duma*, and replaced it by a board called the Senate. This was only a change of a national for a foreign denomination, as the Russian Senate has none of the powers connected with the senatorial dignity as generally understood. Peter often presided in his

Senate—which is a strictly executive and supreme branch of the administration. Its name of *prawitelstwuïouschtschyï Senat* (governing senate) proclaims this. It, in this respect, was, and is the arm of the autocrat.

Under the reign of the Empress Anna a Council of the Empire was formed, and the personal contact of the sovereign with the Senate annulled for ever. The sovereigns now are surrounded by this council, and do the work with the ministers. The council is sometimes presided over by the sovereign, who fills it with individuals according to his personal choice and will. It has a president and a vice-president. It deliberates and decides in all matters whether administrative, legislative or judiciary, which are sent to it by the Emperor. The decisions are by vote. But the proceedings are submitted to the sovereign, who decides between the majority and the minority, or substitutes for both his special personal decision. This becomes law. All the ministers or secretaries of state are members of the council. They form in it a separate committee of ministers, where certain subjects are debated previously to their being submitted to the general council. The council is subdivided into special divisions. In addition to the council and the various state departments, there is a personal Imperial Chancery, divided into various branches. Their chiefs are sometimes ministers; and if not, they take precedence of them. These branches prepare all matters connected with the supreme power, and elucidate and elaborate them for the decision of the imperial chancery. Among the branches of this chancery there is, for example, that of request and grace, where all the petitions directed to the sovereign are referred. Thus even appeals from the supreme judicial decisions come under the attributes of this branch. The judgments are investigated and documents read there, then submitted to the Emperor, who can decide on them alone, or send them to be deliberated upon by the Council of the Empire.

In another branch resides what would be named the legislative power. This branch is called that of the law. There all laws are projected and elaborated, submitted then by the sovereign to the committee of the ministers, and then to the council. Another branch is that of the general police, principally devoted to the espionage or spy-system. This is the favorite one at the present moment. One of the departments of this chancery directs and administers the crown domain with about twenty-two millions of population; another presides over the imperial stud, etc.

The various state departments and those of the personal chancery form in all eighteen branches, all under the personal and supreme direction of the sovereign. To this must be added the separated administrations of Poland, Finland, Caucasus and Georgia, whose chiefs depend directly on the Emperor. The secretaries for these administrations, the directors of the chancery, and the ministers, report personally to the sovereign. Each has special days and hours for this, at least once a week. At a time appointed the special matters must be brought, elaborated, and ready for decision. The minister of foreign affairs, that of the war department, and of the police, have alone access to the sovereign day and night.

It is evident that whatever may or could be the mental capacities of a sovereign, his decisions, concerning very often insignificant and personal matters, as well as others of great weight and influence over the destiny of millions, can rarely be thoroughly and satisfactorily matured. Every subject comes before him, even the drawings and plans of the most insignificant public buildings. Personal punishments and rewards of the innumerable crowds of civil and military officers, are decided by his will. Any public accident in the empire ought to be reported to him. Every member of the chain of the administration evades, as much possible, taking the responsibility of an act which could displease in any way or other, and thus asks the decision of that one above him. Thus the question ascends from degree to degree, until it reaches the Emperor himself. In proportion as the empire extends, the internal administration becomes more and more complex, as new wants start into existence almost daily, and necessarily to be satisfied in some way or other, as well for the sake of the ruled as of the ruler. Whatever may be the magnitude and the strength of the autocratic grasp, it is clear that to encircle every thing becomes more and more impossible. Neither time nor human strength are sufficient for such a superhuman task. Thus the decisions of the sovereign naturally depend nearly exclusively upon the way in which the subject is laid before him. In most cases he either yields or wholly submits to the opinion of the reporting minister. Thus the real power, especially concerning personal matters, is in the hands of the ministers; and this is the source of many acts of injustice, which loudly call for correction.

Next to the Council of the Empire and the ministers come the body of the Senate. Its origin has been already mentioned. Its attributes are various and complicated. It is the chief regulator of the administrative machinery. All imperial ukases and decisions, concerning general as well as special personal matters, are addressed and sent to the Senate for promulgation and execution. The Senate has a president of general meetings. It is divided into several departments, extending its ramification to Moscow and Warsaw, where there are separate departments of the Senate, with judicial, civil, and criminal powers. The Senate forms the supreme court in all such matters, and from its decisions appeal can be made only to the sovereign The Senate is the disciplinary court for all civil officers of whatever rank. The Minister of Justice fills the duty of Procurator or Attorney-General of the Senate. If he finds it necessary, he has the power to reverse the judicial decisions of any department of the Senate, and oblige it to try the case again; and if he still disagrees with it, he can call a general meeting of the whole body to decide the case. Such a decision is final. Criminal condemnations are always submitted to the approbation of the Emperor.

The order to be preserved in the various ranks and degrees, according to the classification of the civil service, is of eminent consequence for those concerned in it, all ultimate advancement and distribution of rewards and favors depending on this classification. The rolls and records are kept by the Senate. It also keeps the pedigrees and heraldic documents of the nobility, so that to be confirmed or admitted into this privileged body its decision is necessary.

The sale of liquors is the exclusive property of the crown in Russia proper (not so in Poland, Lithuania, and other European annexed provinces), and forms the principal branch of the public revenue. This sale is farmed by individuals for several counties together, and forms then a kind of monopoly. The Government farms it out at public auction, before the Senate and the Minister of Finance.

Thus in all its attributes the Senate is an administrative and executive body. It is not even a council. Its name occasions abroad many mistakes on account of its formation and political power. But in its legal action it has now no personal contact with the sovereign, but only submissively and humbly records his decisions. It has no initiative, is never consulted, has no voice, no power or right to deliberate, or even to make suggestions, objections, or representations. The laws and ukases reach the Senate ready-made ; it simply publishes and brings them into operation. In order to do this, the Senate is necessarily in official contact with the special ministers.

Thus, notwithstanding that it is nearly the highest civil dignity, the Senate exercises no influence, and even does not enjoy any very great consideration. To become a senator one must reach the third class of the ladder, that is, become a privy councillor. This requires some thirty years spent in public service. Thus the Senate becomes a hospital of civil invalids, and most of the senators are without any fitness or mental energy for their work. The clerks in the offices, in the bureaus, possess all the influence, and direct the senators. In its action, as the supreme civil tribunal, a wide door is opened for venality, and the decisions of the Senate are often not free from it. They seldom contribute to inspire any respect for the integrity and capacity of this body. The dignity of a senator is never bestowed on military men. But by abandoning the military and entering upon a civil career, one can become a senator.

The whole empire is divided into counties or governments. Some parts form territories with a special administration. Such are Orenbourg and Transcaucasus. Each county has a chief or Governor—*Gubernator*. He is nominated by the sovereign. Such a governor sometimes unites the civil power with military command in the city where he resides. He ought to be of the third or fourth class. The senators are generally made out of these governors. Russia proper, or Great Russia, is composed of about twenty-five such special governments. The provinces annexed since the time of Peter form a kind of satrapies, composed of three counties and administered by a chief called Governor-General. He has more power than an ordinary governor.

A governor directs the administration and the police of the county. In the administration he is assisted by a college or board of councillors, called the government of the county—*gubernskoë prawlenïe.* This board dispatches the current administrative business and all such affairs as are transmitted to it by the governor. It forms a court for disciplinary judgment of civil officers. It puts in execution the judgments rendered by civil tribunals concerning private property. The governor confirms the decisions of the criminal tribunal previous to their being sent to the Senate. The governor is in official relation with the Marshals and the boards of the body corporate of the nobility of the county; he is subject to imperial ministers, but in certain cases receives orders, and reports directly to the Emperor himself.

Each county is divided into districts, whose police and administration are superintended by a civil officer, who, as well as his assistants, are elected from and by the nobility. He is called *Isprawnik* (one who fulfils, carries through). He and his board of assistants judge and decide minor civil and correctional affairs, concerning the peasants, and execute the orders of the governor and of the *prawlenïe.*

Cities are superintended by a kind of city marshals, called *politzmeister* in the larger, and *gorodnitschy* (a Slavic name) in the smaller ones. These are named by the government. The remaining administration in cities is communal and will be explained in another chapter—as well as that of the free or crown peasants.

Thus the power which at the top of the pyramid is absolute, autocratic, and despotic, runs off at the base into the commune. The base is genuine and inherent to general human nature—and at the same time an historical old speciality of the Slavi. The summit is the result of events, accidental, and, notwithstanding its long duration, still transitory.

The administration of civil justice begins for the nobles at the district conciliatory court, then passes to the civil tribunal of the county, and finally to the Senate. The case must be written out by both parties and presented to the courts. No oral pleading exists, and in Russia proper, there is no such class as lawyers.

In criminal cases, the inquest in the country is made by the *Isprawnik*, the district attorney and a deputy from the nobility, if any one of them or of their serfs is concerned personally. In matters concerning free peasants, a member from their administrative board assists. The governor of the county can as he chooses intrust any body with directing or assisting any criminal investigation whatever.

In cities, the politz master directs every criminal arrest, and presides over the preliminary proceedings, assisted by deputies of the classes to which the offender and the offended belong.

The public instruction is under the general direction of a Secretary of State or Minister. The whole empire is divided into districts corresponding to the number of universities, which thus form the centres of such districts. These are: St. Petersburg, Moscow, Kazan, Charkoff, Kijew, the German or Baltic provinces and Finland. Districts without universities are: Odessa Wilna, White Russia, and Warsaw or Poland. For a long period the last has had the greatest number of public schools and gymnasia, open to all inhabitants without any distinction whatever, either of class or religious creed. This equality was introduced into Poland by the Prussian government, and subsequently maintained by the institutions given by Napoleon, and are respected by the present rulers. Thus the number of youth receiving public education in Poland nearly equals that of the whole remaining empire.

Each district is under the direction of a tutor, *popïet-schytiel*, chosen by the sovereigns, generally from among the higher nobility. The district tutor depends upon the minister, and has under his care the university, the gymnasia, and all other public schools in the towns, as well as all private male and female establishments—and at the same time the private tutors of both sexes who are employed in families. In each county and district the nobility elect tutors for superintending the respective gymnasia and schools.

The government names the chiefs or directors of the gymnasia.

Such is the general outline of the administration of this immense empire. More minute details will present themselves when the rights and privileges of the various classes into which the population is divided are described. The internal sections of this administrative network, subdivide and complicate themselves beyond measure. Each successive acquisition made by Russia, as well as the increase of population, creating new wants and relations, activity and extension of industry and trade, the continual increase of manufactures extend and multiply in proportion the administrative entanglements. It is almost impossible not to admit that in the course of time this complication will become unmanageable—and that the loops of the network will slip, under the action of the slightest internal commotion.

CHAPTER IV.

THE ARMY AND NAVY.

The present unparalleled influence of the Czars on the internal questions of nearly every European nation, and their haughty bearing with immediate neighbors, like Austria, Prussia, Sweden, and Turkey, as well as with other more distant states, like Spain, England and France, result partly from a position, which geographically and strategically is nearly inexpugnable, and partly from the maintenance of a numerous well-drilled and well-equipped army. There are only two sides of Russia's immeasurable borders which she needs seriously to defend. These are the western, through its whole length, and partly the southern, from the Dniester to the Caucasus. Along these two sides is raised, so to say, a wall of bayonets, guns and pikes, and these moving machines can be precipitated, by the nod of a single will, in a certain direction, or as far as humanly possible, concentrated on any special point. If attacked, only the extremities of Russia, and above all, the unhappy kingdom of Poland, will be ravaged and destroyed. There she will have to defend herself. Finland is easy to be defended, especially as there is no probability of an attack by Sweden; and Finland being maintained in all her ancient laws and privileges, and not incorporated legislatively with Russia, prospers more than she did under the Swedish rule, and is thus not at all disaffected. Maritime cities and harbors may easily be burnt and destroyed, but after the experience of Charles XII., and of Napoleon, there is but little reason to presume that any invading army would cross the Vistula or the Niemen, the Dnieper or the Pruth. Russia has no militia of course, with the exception of that organized among the subjected populations of the Caucasus and Georgia. Her force consists in an organized army and navy. The army, with its various arms, is divided into corps, divisions, brigades, regiments, battalions and companies; the cavalry into squadrons, etc. A corps on full active footing is composed of three divisions of infantry and one of cavalry, with sometimes a division of reserve. The artillery of a corps consists of 110 to 115 guns of various calibre. A division is composed of two brigades, a brigade of two regiments. A regiment in full *ought* to have four battalions, a battalion four companies, and a company *should* have between 170 and 200 men. All these numbers are seldom complete except in the Guard and a few of the other corps.

According to the official reports for 1852, the armed force was in the following state. The corps of Guards, commanded by the Grand Duke, the heir to the Empire, is established in St. Petersburg, and for a distance of 100 miles around that city. It consists of three divisions of infantry and one of reserve, of four divisions of cavalry, a large force of artillery with 120 to 140 cannon, and a special body of field engineers, sappers, and a pontoon corps. Next comes the corps of the Grenadiers. Its headquarters are in the ancient city of Novgorod, some 100 miles on the road between Petersburg and Moscow. Its regiments are established principally in the military colonies. This corps has three divisions in full of infantry, and one of cavalry; the park of artillery amounts to between 115 and 120 pieces. After these two separate corps, comes what is called the active army. It is composed of six corps, or nearly twenty divisions of infantry, six divisions of regular cavalry, with an irregular one of Cossacks, etc., adjoined in time of war, and at least 700 pieces of artillery. This army is at present commanded by Prince Paschkiewitch. Its headquarters are at Warsaw. It faces the western frontier or Europe exclusively. It is quartered from the Baltic, through Lithuania to the Pruth, the Black Sea and the frontiers of the military cavalry colonies in South Russia. A separate corps occupies the city of Moscow and several surrounding counties.

The army of the Caucasus is composed of four divisions of infantry, one of regular cavalry, numerous irregular Cossacks of various denominations, a body of Mussulmen and militia from among the natives. A division of infantry occupies Finland, and another is scattered in Siberia. This active army is backed by a reserve composed of 25 brigades of infantry and 270 squadrons of cavalry. The formation of the reserve will be hereafter spoken of.

The military colonies for the infantry are formed principally in the government of Novgorod, and partly in those of Pskoff and Witebsk. They are divided into 24 brigades. The colonies for cavalry are in Southern Russia, in the governments of Pultawa, Ekaterynoslaw, Herson in the Ukraine, and so forth. They amount to 75 squadrons. To this is to be added the sappers and artillery reserve, with 54 parks of heavy calibre destined for the siege of fortresses, the military engineers, and military workmen, with a numerous train.

Finally, there is the guard of the interior, formed of armed veterans, quartered in all the countries of Russia, and performing in the cities and boroughs, the internal service. It amounts to 50 battalions which, however, are not full. Further, there is a corps of Gendarmes, containing eight brigades, horse and foot, and spread over the whole empire. It is commanded by Count Orloff, whose function answers to that of Chief of the Secret Political Police. The gendarmes fulfil the duties of the police of the army during war, and of a political police through the country at all times. The officers of this corps form in all counties and districts the knots of that vast net of espionage extended over Russia and the continent. They are in close connection with all the agents of the secret police.

The irregular cavalry consists principally of Cossacks. There are several denominations of them, derived mainly from the regions, or the banks of the rivers along which they are settled. Their General and Commander is the Grand Duke, the heir of the empire. They are divided as follows: 1. The Cossacks of the Don or Tanais. These are the most numerous, occupying a very rich and extensive country, and enjoying the greatest privileges, and an independent military as well as civil organization. 2. Those on the shores of the Black Sea, called *Tschernomortsy*. 3. Those of the line of the Caucasus. 4. Those of the county of Astrachan. 5. Those of the territory of Orenbourg. 6. Those of the river Ural (ancient Jaïck). 7. Those of Siberia. 8. The Mestcheracks, who are a kind of Tartars. 9. The Cossacks of the region of Azoff. 10. Those of the Danube. The Cossacks muster in all 765 squadrons, each containing a few more than a 100 men, of which more than a third can be mobilized. The Cossacks in time of war are backed by detachments of Baschkirs, Calmouks, Buriats, Tunguses, Mussulmen from trans-Caucasian regions, Lesghians, etc. These Asiatic irregulars form generally a kind of military posts or chain uniting the advancing army with the mother country. Such was the case, for example, in 1813–14, when they were extended across the whole of Europe.

In conclusion the whole bulk of the armed land force consists of 17 corps, with 4,900 companies of infantry, and 1,469 squadrons of cavalry, and 330 batteries of heavy or light artillery. More than a third of this ought to be deducted, as not capable of being moved towards the extreme frontiers of the empire, as well as for incomplete numbers in the various battalions, companies, and squadrons. The remainder makes up the Russian warfaring army, which can be moved and directed by the order of a single will according to its whim and pleasure. But natural impossibilities oppose and impede the concentration in one spot and even in one region, of such masses of men and animals. For instance, it is impossible to feed them for a prolonged term of time, in either a cultivated or in a savage country.

The Navy is composed of three fleets or squadrons. Each squadron has a three decker of 100 to 120 guns, and eight smaller two deckers, of from 70 to 90 guns, with six frigates, and a very few steamers and other smaller vessels, sloops, schooners, etc. Threes quadrons form the fleet of the Baltic, and two that of the Black Sea. Aside from this, there is a small flotilla in the Caspian Sea, and a steamer and a few other vessels in the lake of Ural. In the Baltic as well as in the Euxine and the Sea of Azoff, there are numerous gun-boats. All the vessels are well manned, but the quality does not correspond with the quantity. Russia not having a commercial marine, has no great number of sailors, or of masters and mates. The latter are nearly all foreigners, and the small number of Russian commercial vessels, notwithstanding the existence of a law according to which the master of a Russian vessel ought to be a native Russian. But this law is eluded, as there is no possibility whatever of finding such men. The sailors for the navy are selected principally from among the people living along the shores of the Baltic, the Euxine and the Azoff, and from among the boatmen on the Wolga and on the Don. Greeks and Armenians may be found among the number. All these put together do not furnish, however, a third part of the required number, and the remainder of the crew is composed of men who, previous to being enlisted, had never been on water, except perhaps in a ferry boat. A great many Jewish conscripts are thus employed. The mass of the crews are in a season transformed into sailors by mere drill and force. The greater number cannot even swim. The vessels of the fleets in the Baltic can scarcely be kept 4 months on the high sea, and in the Euxine but 4 or 6 weeks longer. This is the whole time which can be devoted to practising naval exercises and manœuvres. The remainder of the year, the crews are garrisoned in harbors, and trained in military land exercise. Thus, the greater part of the crews are neither real nor skilful sailors or gunners, but form a scarcely second-rate infantry.

The officers are educated from childhood in special nautical establishments, and most of them, at least theoretically, are as able and as well-informed in all the specialities of their duty as those of any other service whatever. The navy is the work of the present Emperor. Alexander neglected it most completely. Nicholas, with great devotion and sacrifice of money, has put it on its present footing, and the naval service is now regarded with greater consideration than it was under Catharine and Alexander. An old proverbial distribution of capacities respecting the officers among the various grades of the service in Russia, assigns—*the dandy to the cavalry*, *the learned man to the artillery, the drunkard to the navy, and the stupid to the infantry.* So it was once, but so it is no longer, at least with respect to the infantry and navy. The infantry officers, though they do not belong to the higher aristocratic class, are for the greater part well educated and tolerably well bred. The second son of the Emperor is the Grand Admiral, and now the Minister or Secretary of the Navy. From childhood he has been thoroughly educated for this purpose. This has given a stimulus to the service. Educated and well-bred youths of higher family connections, enter it continually, and thus its ancient disreputable character is almost wholly changed.

The vessels have no uniformity in their construction. Some are as heavy as old Dutch galliots, some are modelled on English and American patterns. The material, which is mostly oak, is bad; not that there is no lumber in Russia, but the navy-yards and arsenals are under the same principle of venality and theft which pervades all other branches of the administration. Thus the vessels last only from ten to fifteen years. In general, the Russian Navy is to be regarded as a defensive wooden wall, which can never be transformed into an offensive weapon against Europe, or be made to act single-handed against any of the maritime powers, with the exception of Sweden, Turkey, and the like smaller ones.

The Cossacks in time of war are rarely used in masses, in a regular battle-field. Their principal utility consists in surrounding the army as an iron swarm, wholly impenetrable to the enemy. Thus they cover the movements of the forces, prevent desertions and fetch up stragglers. They form the vanguard and the *postes perdus*, generally extricating themselves out of difficulties in which all other detachments of the army or individuals would be lost.

In this manner they serve to keep the enemy on the alert, to alarm him continually, to hold him in restless irritation, and to exhaust him. They are like a swarm of insufferable mosquitoes, which it is impossible to disperse or to get rid of. They appear, alarm, carry off some prisoners, and disappear before they can be pursued—to appear in a short time again. As no other nation has such irregulars, they can never be met on like ground. The French, in 1812–13–14, complained of this kind of warfare more than of anything else. The Cossack is in service the most faithful and the most thoroughly obedient, shrewd, and cunning of soldiers. Thus he is used for missions of trust or danger. Nearly every commander of a larger or smaller detachment has Cossacks about his person, and at his disposal. They are remarkable for great personal courage. They will often penetrate single-handed where no other soldier dare venture, and thus they are of excellent use in gathering and procuring information about the movements of the enemy. They equip themselves, receive almost no pay during the war, with, if possible, sometimes a ration for man and horse. But generally they are thrown on their own resources and industry for their food.

This gives a general idea of the Russian armed force. It is strong undoubtedly for the defensive, but it is utterly impossible to throw these masses on Europe. Without mentioning the penury of the treasury, as on a war footing, the pay is nearly quadrupled—to gather them together at any point within the frontier, would have the same effect as destruction by locusts for many hundred miles. The same would take place if in case of a war between France and Russia—the army of the Czar should enter Germany even as a friendly country. All would be destruction and desolation with friend as well as with foe. The region thus traversed would be reminded, not of Napoleon, but of the swarms of Attila, the more disciplined, but for the sake of existence and self-preservation, obliged to destroy and swallow all the resources within their reach. For such an impossible invasion of Europe, the Russian masses might be divided into two parts, one entering Prussia and the other Austria. But such invasions in the present state of the world are impossibilities. Masses will be raised against masses, the invaded country stripped in advance of all resources to nourish the enemy, and whatever may be the inborn gallantry of the Russian soldier—Napoleon admired it—no army in the world can be for ever invincible.

The drill of these forces is, perhaps, the best existing in Europe. But possibly they are overdrilled. Those acquainted with the mysteries of the military profession, pretend that in the firing of the infantry as well as of the artillery, the principal object is a quick discharge, so quick that neither the soldiers nor gunners are able to take good aim; and thus in a battle, out of the immense number of shots, comparatively few are destructive.

The army is formed by means of conscription, out of the taxed classes of the population: such as merchants, citizen-burghers, artisans, workmen, free-peasants and serfs. From all these the common soldiery are derived, with a few exceptions, of the youth belonging to the privileged class of merchants and others, or who, likewise on account of a privilege, have received a higher education in some public establishment, such as the Gymnasia or Universities. A commoner can rise only to the grade of sergeant. A very extraordinary distinction in time of war may push him over the barrier, and make him an officer with a possibility of further preferment. In time of peace twelve years of service and some capacity can raise the son of a burgher to the grade of an officer. The grades of Lieutenants and Captains confer personal nobility, and with that of Major it becomes hereditary.

As has been already mentioned, the public service is obligatory for the nobility. From it exclusively are derived the body of officers in the army, while the nobility alone have access to the civil service. The choice between the two is free for any nobleman, but the military service has the precedency. A nobleman never begins his career as a common soldier. Numerous and various military establishments for every kind of military education, to which the nobles are almost exclusively admitted, prepare the youth from childhood practically as well as theoretically. The education consists of all the sciences connected with the military art and with its highest branches; the French language, Russian literature, history, national and universal, geography, etc. A cadet having gone through all the classes enters the army with the grade of second lieutenant. Those who have been educated in civil establishments, gymnasia and universities, entering as volunteers, are admitted as ensigns and cadets. They wear the uniform of common soldiers, but with lace; are exempted, as all nobles are, from corporeal punishment, and as soon as they master the rudiments of the service, they become officers. Any nobleman who has once become an officer, is at liberty to abandon the service at his will. For the common soldier, the obligatory time of service is from fifteen to twenty years. Once it was for life.

The age of a recruit is between 18 and 35 years. The mode of recruiting is as follows: An imperial ukase orders, for example, that three souls out of every hundred, according to the last census, are to be added to the army. The general official denomination of the taxed population, in the census, in all administrative, legal, and judicial concerns, is that of souls. Thus, a landed property is valued not according to the number of acres, but according to that of the souls recorded in the census. Not the price of the land, but that of the souls, forms the value. For instance: A man owns 1,100 or 1,000 souls. This is the legal valuation in contracts and all documents. The ukase marks the time when, through the whole Empire, or a certain part of it, the recruits are to be levied and presented in each county to a special official board. Each owner of serfs selects from among them, absolutely, by his will, the number to be delivered by him, and brings them before the board. Free or crown peasants, and all the other rural communities of various denominations, as well as those of townships, boroughs, and cities—in one word, all that enjoy a special communal administration, have boards *ad hoc* elected from among themselves, which boards make the selection of the required number of recruits. The law prescribes, however, that a single family shall not be oppressed by successive levies. A commissioner of the government supervises the whole, and complaints against his decision, as well as against the communal recruiting board, can be brought before the central board. A nobleman, who desires to liberate a serf or any other recruit, can present a qualified substitute, or pay to the government two hundred dollars. The substitutes are generally procured from among soldiers who have served the required time, and have the right to leave the service. The central board is composed in each county of three civil officers, one military officer, and a medical attendant. An aide-de-camp of the Emperor is also sent from St. Petersburg to each county, to oversee the doings of the board, to avoid oppression and venality, as the epoch of the recruiting is the richest harvest for all official rascality. A great oppression is exercised in this way on the numerous dissenters from the State Church, as they are generally rich, and opposed to the military service. The Imperial Adjutant likewise selects the ablest men for the Corps of Guards, and other military officers making a selection each for their special branch. A serf, once given to the military service, is emancipated for ever. When his term is out, he does not return into serfdom, but has the choice of position and occupation, with the obligation to become inscribed in some rural or town community. His wife becomes emancipated likewise. Children begotten before his entering the military service remain serfs, those during it, follow the new condition of the parents. Thus the recruiting becomes an agency of partial emancipation. Owners of less than 100 souls combine together in each district to make up the percentage ordered by the ukase. They also must not levy twice on the same family, and there is in each district a board of noblemen to oversee this special operation.

In Poland, where civil equality before the law was introduced with the French Code in 1807, the recruiting is performed directly by the Government from among the available population, without any distinction whatever of any class or social position. Now, however, this is to be changed, as special privileges for the nobility are to be introduced on the same footing as they exist in Russia proper.

The existence in Russia of various kinds of establishments for the military education of the noble youth has already been mentioned. For the children of soldiers, and, above all, for their orphans, establishments likewise exist, where they are received from their earliest childhood, and trained for the military service. There they are taught to read and write the vernacular language, with Russian history, the general outlines of geography, and also arithmetic and drawing. Then they enter the service for life, or nearly so. They are placed in the topographical and engineer's corps, and at the telegraphic stations, which, in Russia, are exclusively for military use, and under the immediate direction of the Emperor.

The very numerous reserve is formed in the following manner: The time of service for the common soldier is between 15 and 20 years, but if his conduct is correct and he wishes it, he receives what is called an unlimited furlough for the remaining term, and can enter civil life in any way he chooses—remaining still under military control. They form battalions and brigades, having officers and staff establishments, which, in case of need, convoke and organize them instantly. They are also brought together almost every year, or a great part of them, from four to six weeks for drill. Thus they are maintained in practice, and the reserve forms the best drilled portion of the Russian forces.

The military colonies owe their existence to Count Araktcheef, who was one of the most curious phenomena in the history of Russia in this century. He was the favorite of Paul, the companion of Alexander, during whose last years he governed Russia most absolutely, and was rather persecuted by Nicholas. Count Araktcheef took for his model the military colonies established by Austria between the Austro-Slavic' and Turko-Slavic frontiers. But the aim of Araktcheff was not the defence of the borders. He surrounded St. Petersburg with these colonies in order thus to strengthen and render impregnable that stronghold of despotism. The crown-peasants of the government of Novgorod, and partly those of Pskoff, were transformed into soldiers, and their villages into barracks and camps. Out of these colonies, the corps of Grenadiers established there were to be maintained and principally formed. The peasants of Novgorod and Pskoff—

those two ancient cradles of Russian republican liberty, destroyed only in the XVIth century by the Czar Ivan the Terrible—still preserved the sacred old tradition, and were of an unyielding and ungovernable spirit. This was to be broken and extirpated. The military system was introduced with an iron hand, and an implacable rigidity akin to cruelty. Unmerciful corporeal punishments were daily occurrences. In the villages thus transformed, the military officers forming the staff ruled most despotically. Every sort of labor, as well as every movement of the newly enslaved, was directed by an order from above. Thus, an order issued from the headquarters of a district, would appoint for the whole colony—for example, a day for plowing, another for sowing, another for harvest, and all agricultural labor was similarly arranged. The whole rural population was bound under penalties to move on the same day—nay, at the same hour. A peasant could not go to market nor sell an egg without a permission from the officers. At the same time neither his wife nor his daughter was safe from their lust. Assassination and punishments for it happened very often, but the system took root. However, during the Polish campaign, in the spring of 1831, when the colonies became liberated from the pressure of the grenadiers quartered among them, a terrible insurrection broke out. The greater part of the officers were killed. In several cases they were sunk in the earth to the waist, and then mowed with the scythe. Despair and vengeance animated the wronged, the oppressed. These colonial insurrections, and others which will be mentioned hereafter, give a foretaste of the character of a future vengeful uprising of the Russian serfs and peasants.

Finally, the insurrection was quenched in blood, by Count Orloff. Numbers were decimated on the spot, and hundreds of families transported to Siberia. However, less cruel discipline was henceforth introduced, and it would seem that the next generation had become accustomed to the heavy yoke. Things now appear to go on there rather smoothly—but the curse of the peasants is poured out with every breath. The tradition of better times of old, and of ancient liberty, glimmers still at the domestic hearth. The time will come, and is perhaps not far distant, when these colonies, organized to shelter and enforce despotism, will become a deadly weapon in the hand of the avenger.

The maintenance of these colonies, the cost of their transformation, the raising of costly buildings for barracks and headquarters, as well as the unavoidable venality and theft in all administrative branches, make this establishment a burden to the treasury. The revenues of the colonies—the rent paid by the peasants—are not sufficient to cover all the expenses. The Emperor himself directs their administration. Once, in the beginning of his reign, he cursed Araktcheeff for their establishment; but now he is broken in to it, and likes this despotic institution.

The colonies established in the southern part of the empire are designed to be the nursery of the great bulk of the cavalry. The introduction of the military rule was as difficult and as bloody there as in the north. Whole families were destoyed. In several cases a father would embark his wife and children in a boat, and reaching the middle of the Dnieper, would bore a hole in it, preferring to be drowned rather than submit to this new kind of slavery. Still there was no insurrection there as in the north. However, the general rule may now be ameliorated, the peasant of Little or Southern Russia, living, like his brother in the north, on the traditions of a once free existence under the domination of the Cossacks, still submits with rage to this military oppression. In his bosom hides the aspirations for liberty and revenge, and the bosom of a Russian peasant has unfathomed recesses.

The breeding of horses is a principal business with these colonies. The extensive region occupied by them contains the best agricultural soil to be found anywhere. Wheat is the general crop, and hardly any manure is required. Thus to a certain extent they are less onerous on the treasury than the colonies in the north; nay, even profitable in time of war, when the squadrons leave their home; then, each district is to supply its special squadron, with men and horses, during the whole duration of the war. These colonies form the reserve of cavalry.

The maintenance of the army absorbs far more than half the gross revenue of the empire, notwithstanding the very small pay of the officers as well as common soldiers. After various deductions made from the pay of the soldier, as for example: for the common purse called *artel*, for blacking, whiting, etc., he finally receives *less than six cents monthly in cash.* His equipment consists in three shirts, two pairs of shoes, two pairs of trowsers, one full dress uniform, one jacket, and a long military overcoat. The pay of the officers through all the grades, even to the highest, is proportionally as mean as that of the soldier. A lieutenant in the infantry has not even fifteen dollars a month, and so on. A general of brigade has not two thousand dollars yearly. The penury of the superior officers, that is, of the generals, is relieved in some way by extra emoluments, granted to them as a special favor, under the denomination of rents for a certain number of years, or as service money, etc. The pay of the officers of the guards, and generally of those of the cavalry, is a little superior to that of the infantry.

A commissariat is at the head of the general administration of the army. It is as great a den of thieves as any to be found in the world. The present emperor has tried with all his might, and many times, to purify this augean stable, but always without effect. If one thief is kicked out and severely punished, his successor will follow, after a while, the same course. The evil is too deeply rooted in the whole government. It penetrates all branches of the administration, civil as well as military. As we have mentioned already in a preceding chapter, it is inherent and vital to the system. The emperor is sometimes driven mad by new and successive discoveries of peculation, either committed by his nearest favorites, or at least sheltered by their influence. On one such occasion he said to his son and heir; *Sascha* (a diminutive of Alexander), *there are only two honest men in Russia: thou and I.* In this he was wrong. There are some few more, even in the elevated circle by which he is surrounded. Thus Pashkewich, Count Bludoff, Prince Souvaroff, and a few more. The emperor might find honest men, elsewhere, in a small number. But such men once put forward, the emperor has not the character to back and support them firmly against the corrupt intriguers, who unanimously oppose such unwelcome apparitions on their horizon.

The organization of the scoundrelism in the commissariat is so extensive, so intricate, and so well-combined, that no sword of justice or that of the autocrat can penetrate or cut it through. In this general onset, next to the commissariat, come the colonels commanding and administering the respective regiments. Their peculation is generally christened with the name of shrewd *blagorozumny*, economy. It is applied to all the necessities of the poor soldier. Thus the colonel, for example, receives yearly the cloth for the equipment, but the soldiers often wear the same uniforms for two years. The workmen of the regiment are all soldiers; the tailors, shoemakers, saddlers, smiths, &c., must work without any extra pay being allowed by the colonel. In time of peace the regiment rarely contains a full number of soldiers, notwithstanding that the pay and equipment are received for full ranks. A colonel shares a part of these "economies" with his generals, or at least their staffs. In the cavalry, very naturally, such "economies" are more considerable. First are those made on the incomplete number of men and horses; then "economy" made on the prices of the horses, and that of the cost of their maintenance, for all of which high figures are paid by the government to the colonels, who make in this manner immense profits. Further, every year a certain number of horses is reported to be renewed, always more than are really necessary, and the colonel pockets the money instead of buying the required number. Generally the yearly income economized in this way by a colonel of cavalry will amount to twenty thousand, that of a colonel of infantry from ten to twelve thousand dollars. To give an idea how these various "economies" are executed let us suppose the following: A sole for the shoe of a soldier as allotted by the goverment is of eighteen inches length. Before it reaches its destination the commissariat and the colonels clip it each in their turn to that extent that it becomes in fact scarcely six inches long. The same is done with flour and groats, in which consists the almost exclusive nourishment of the soldier. If he should have a pound, for example, of each of them, he receives scarcely eight ounces. The soldiers being generally quartered in towns and villages, have the right to claim from their hosts a seasoning of salt and grease. On the flour and groats the captain of the company, as well as the senior sergeant, realize in turn their profits.

This general shrewd economy is to a certain extent sanctioned by the government. Out of it the musical band of a regiment is understood to be maintained by the colonel, as well as fuel furnished for the adjutant's office, and some other small extras. The maintenance of the musical band consists in the pay of a good director and music master, and in the purchase of instruments—the rest of the band are the soldiers of the regiment, made *by force* to become musicians.

The same principle of peculation extends to the navy yards, and above all becomes very lucrative for the officers superintending the construction of forts, and works. Thus the citadel of Warsaw, the forts of Georgewsk, once Modlin, Ywangorod in Poland, that of Dunaburg in Lithuania, on the Dwina, a special pet of the present emperor, but which never will be finished, like Penelope's woof, disappearing as soon as rising in the moving sands; all these constructions, naval or inland, as well as those of the lines of telegraphs (not magnetic but according to the ancient system,) have cost the government tenfold more than their worth. Millions on millions thus melt in the hands of the myriads of constructors, engineers, officers, inferior as well as superior, directing and superintending the like extensive works.

Among all these birds of prey there appear from time to time exceptions—honest men—but they are rare and few, and in the long run are generally brow-beaten by the others. In justice to the Prince Pashkewich, it ought to be said, that his whole career, from the inferior grades to the present prominent one, has been marked by untarnished honesty. He made no fortune whatever as a colonel. Now he is immensely rich, by the gifts of the sovereign. But he, the all-powerful commander, is powerless to stop peculation in the army under his command. As says the old proverb: *nec Hercules contra plures.* During a war, however, Pashkewich always takes particular care of the soldier, of his comforts, and that his due shall reach him as much as possible in the normal measure. The soldier knows it, adores Pashkewich, and fights under his command as cheerfully as courageously; and if, as some enemies of the Prince maintain, he has often committed in his campaigns strategical blunders, which would have jeoparded their issue, the undaunted devotion of the soldiers has repaired the mistakes, and re-established on his side the fortune of the battle. Such, it is said, was the case in the campaigns of Persia and Poland, under Pashkewich's command.

One perusing a military almanac of Russia—if any way acquainted with the characteristic sounds of the Russian and German languages—will be astonished to find the names of officers, and above all of generals, to be foreign ones, and most of them Germans. They have crept into the Russian public service, during a long period, to the greatest dissatisfaction of the genuine Russians, by whom they are looked on with hatred, as a national calamity. As this admixture of the German element is not without influence, as well on the internal struggles and collisions of parties as on the councils of the sovereign and the external action of Russian politics; and further, as the preponderating influx of these foreigners still pours in upon the army—a brief outline of this subject will not be out of order here.

The principal sources of this foreign element are the so-called Baltic provinces, composed of Curland, Livonia and Esthonia. The land-owners or nobility there, as well as the inhabitants of cities, have been Germans for the last four centuries, descending from German knights and other settlers who conquered and civilized these regions, where the aboriginal Curi and Letti, very likely belong to the Finnic stock. The conquerors belonged to the brotherhood of the Knights of the Sword, called likewise the Knights of St. John of Jerusalem, and were also Germans. In the sixteenth century these Knights turned Protestant, married, and divided the country into individual property. They were never really independent, but vassals of Poland, Sweden, and finally, since the last century, they have been subjects of Russia, maintaining still some distinct privileges of caste, and partly the German language, which they call the hearth of their distinct nationality. Apart from these born-subjects of the empire, there was, during those hundred years, an influx of adventurers from Germany in every form and with every purpose, from men seeking civil or military service, teachers and artisans, down to servants and the commonest workmen,—all of them eager to push their career at the cost of the natives. Numbers succeeded. Thus, for example, one of the greatest favorites of the Emperor Nicholas, Count Kleinmichel, is the son of a footman imported from Germany by the Prince Soltikoff, by whose protection the present Count was placed as a boy in a public military establishment of education. His name, *Little Michel*, bears an evidence of his origin. All these Germans, born or imported, form the principal props of despotism, are the faithful agents of its greatest saturnalias. Russia is no fatherland to them. They have no love for her. The only tie between them and her is the most abject devotion to the master whom they serve. No interest is felt by them in the moral welfare of the country, and less now than ever, as they hate more and more the aborigines, by whom, as civilization and culture extend, these strangers are pushed in the back-ground, and whose efforts become stronger and stronger to get rid of their influence. Generally without any roots in the national element, standing in opposition and hostility to it, their existence depends wholly on the Czars, and to imperial whims they are devoted soul and body. This is one of the reasons for the protection which is bestowed on them by the emperors. Thus, Germans are spread every where; at the court, in diplomacy, in military service. The guards are full of them. They support patiently—nay, cheerfully—the iron discipline, before which the Russian nobility retire more and more. They are even the principal contrivers and executors of it. Their cavilling exactitude in all the smallest and most annoying details of the service is proverbial—in direct opposition with the rather indolent manner in which generally the Russian looks on like small affairs. As the national proverbs say: "Until there is no thunder the Russian makes no sign of the cross," which signifies that he betakes himself to work thoroughly only in great emergencies. All the above mentioned qualities of the Germans contribute to secure to them the favor of the rulers. But this is not all. German blood flows rather exclusively in the imperial family. With the Empress Elizabeth, daughter of Peter the Great, pure Russian blood became extinct on the throne. The admixture of the German became more and more copious by each accession—and now it can be said that there is scarcely a drop of that of the Romanoffs—founders of this dynasty, in its veins. Peter the Third, successor and nephew of Elizabeth, was the son of a prince of Holstein Gottorp, and Catharine his wife, an Anhalt. Their son, Paul the First, was thus almost wholly German by descent. From his marriage with a princess from the house of Würtemberg, issues the present sovereign, united to a Prussian princess, as is his son and heir to one from the house of Hesse Darmstadt. Thus Germans have been grafted on Germans already for four generations, and the pure Slavic element is wholly destroyed, absorbed. If the males by birth become naturalized, Russified in some way or other, the women, continually fresh imported from Germany, prefer very naturally to be surrounded by countrymen. Thus these find access to the court, keep up the interest of their kindred; under their patronage Germans prosper in all the directions—and Russia cannot easily become cleansed of them. The German explanation of their preponderance and utility runs thus: they maintain they have civilized Russia, and have contributed pre-eminently, nay exclusively according to their version, to secure her greatness since the reign of Peter the Great. But this is a fallacy. The eminent individuals at that epoch, statesmen or military, were the Menchikoffs, Sheremeteffs, Shafiroffs, Golowins, Kourakins, Dolgorouckis, etc. During the brilliant reign of Catherine II. no German was specially pre-eminent, and one of her crowning merits in the mind and in the heart of every Russian is, that notwithstanding she was a German by birth, none of her countrymen was either her lover, favorite or councillor. In general, in all the great emergencies of the empire, Russians, not Germans, have rendered the greatest and surest services. Potemkin, Roumantzoff, Koutousoff, Pashkewich, and above all the invincible Souvaroff, who never lost a single battle,—far outshone Münich, Michelson, Barclay de Tolly and Dybitsch. The same is the case in the inferior military positions. Ten years ago, the disastrous campaign in the Caucasus was chiefly the result of German commanders, such as Rosen, Sass, Grabbe, etc. Worontzoff, Baryatinsky, and others of Russian stock, re-established affairs there on a better footing. As an illustration how of old the Russo-Germans were looked upon by the Russians, the following occurrence may serve: At the battle of

Culm, in 1813, where General Vandamme was taken prisoner, the Russian Guards, commanded by Yermoloff, contributed principally to the victory. When, after the affair was over, the King of Prussia and the Emperor Alexander came on the field, Alexander clasped his general, assuring him that in his gratitude he should be most happy to realize any desire or demand of his : "*Make me a German in your service, Sire*," answered Yermoloff, who also belongs to the most eminent men in Russia, and is still idolized by a great part of the nation, principally in Moscow, being of genuine Russian stamp.

The characteristic features of the Russian army are those proper to the general character of the Slavi and the Russians in particular. An indomitable stubborness, an unbroken toughness, and perseverance and endurance almost beyond human limits, are the prominent qualities. A Russian never gives up any work whatever, when once commenced. To attain the proposed aim he will, without hesitation, overcome any difficulties. The word impossible is nearly unknown to the Russian—workman, artisan or soldier. Thus if any new or difficult piece of workmanship is shown to an artisan, and the question asked if he will be able to produce something like it, his ready answer will be, *I don't know, but I will try.* In the same manner, the soldier on a battle-field never supposes that any thing there is impossible. He storms batteries with coolness, nay, even composure, and will stand quite unmoved the most deadly fire of the enemy. He has not, perhaps, the foaming vivacity of the Frenchman or of the Pole, but a peculiar, steady, unshaken way of his own. If overpowered and broken by the enemy, he does not fly in disorder from the field, but remains on it, even with the certainty of the loss of life. During the retreat of the Russian army in 1812 from the Niemen to Moscow for several hundred miles, few, very few, prisoners were made by the French. At the battles of Eylau, Austerlitz, and Mojaisk, Napoleon was puzzled and terrified by the inflexible obstinacy, especially of the Russian infantry, and proclaimed it to be among the best in the world. About ten centuries ago, Leo Diakonos, an Imperial historiographer of Byzantium, speaking of the Ros of that time (now Russians), who several times approached the Eastern Capital, says that *the Ros die but don't run away.* Others maintain this to be the result of a stern discipline. That discipline may contribute to it in a certain degree cannot be doubted—but no discipline can stand against fear.

Whatever may be the external appearances, the spirit among the army and principally among the officers, does not consist in an absolute worship of despotism, as is rather generally believed. An uninterrupted breath of liberal aspirations is active there. Most of the officers feel deeply the iron yoke of despotism crushing them and the country. The number of fanatics and idolators of Czarism, at any price, is rather a minority, and the bulk would willingly assist in getting rid of it. The conspiracy of 1821, and above all that of 1825, was initiated by the army and most extensively spread in it. In 1838 and 1839 more than two hundred officers of one single corps were engaged in a conspiracy. It was discovered, and a number of the officers punished, but the affair was hushed up. *Who knows, whether the present warlike and quarrelsome attitude taken by the emperor in the Turkish question, is not a necessity forced on him by some vast conspiracy or uneasiness in the army, which must thus be kept busy some way or other, and its energy directed or expended in some other channel?* A war with the Turks always has a more national character than any other war whatever, and is exceedingly well calculated to kindle intensely the religious as well as the Panslavistic ardor of the nation and of the army, and thus to curb and subdue its disquiet spirit. Such reason contributed eminently to the war of 1828.

Officers quartered and disseminated in the country are in immediate and continual contact with the nation, the people, and can clearly see where resides the source of the evil. With this, the reading of liberal books when they can get them, forms their greatest relish. They crave for the forbidden fruit, and as far as possible, they try to satisfy this craving. Further, they generally are not at all pleased with the part forced on them, of being the props and knight-errants of despotism in other European countries, of being the extinguishers of light and the owls of civilization. The feeling of a genuine Panslavism, aiming at an internal disenthralment of the fatherland, is more generally alive and spread among them, than is agreeable to the Czar. This Panslavism is for beginning the work at home, previous to attracting and aggregating the smaller kindred Slavic bodies. The existence of a liberal spirit among the Russian officers, was strikingly evinced during the late Hungarian war. Notwithstanding the Magyars showed themselves as deadly enemies of the Slavic element and independent nationality, as the Austrians and Germans could have been, still, as their cause was tinted with liberalism, the Russian officers never missed an occasion to show their partiality for the cause against which they were fighting, and their most decided contempt for the Austrians. They never met socially, never fraternized with these allies. No Austrian officer could show his face among the Russians, under the penalty of being instantly kicked out from any place of public resort frequented by them. This took place continually during the campaign, and it was even rumored that sometimes, on the battlefield, the Russians, drawn up in line away from the Austrians, fired, for the sake of fun, whole volleys into them instead of against the Magyars.

The Russian officers would willingly wish to become the means, even the promoters, of a political—nay, even of a social internal emancipation. But they can neither combine together into unity of purpose and of action, nor even communicate together in large numbers, without running the greatest personal dangers. They are watched over, surrounded by spies, and any attempt on their part will always be thwarted by the treachery of some individual among them, or wrecked against the impossibility of acting united. The dawn of emancipation will not rise in those quarters, but its rising may be accelerated and facilitated through their interference. When that blessed hour appears on the dial of time, their duty will be—and many already understand it so—not to oppose the rising of the peasants, of the people at large; not to quench, but to extend the action of the purifying fire.

The most conspicuous mark of the Russian army in general—that of the officers as well as of the soldiers—is, that they never consider themselves as any excrescence in the nation, distinct or superior to the bulk of the people. They do not look on the quality of a citizen as something below them; quite the contrary. This is in itself a mighty pledge for the future. Officers and soldiers both, anxiously look for the moment when they can get rid of the thraldom of the red collar, and return to private life, as citizens or laborers. Officers, if they cannot help themselves otherwise, prefer to change the military for the civil service. They do not share the mean and contemptible notion of the officers of other European armies, as, for example, the Prussians, French, etc., that the red collar and military coat, is something superior in position and honor to the common existence of the rest of the nation. We mean by the above, principally officers of pure Russian blood. They know themselves, as well as those of other armies, to be the trustees of what is called falsely the national honor, but this feeling is intimately blended in them with the love of country, of which, for many of them, the Czar is not the personification, but only a temporary and transient particle. When the time will come, this distinction between Czarism and the fatherland will become more clear and prominent, and then despotism will stand powerless and abandoned by the majority. Sustained now by cowardly conservatives of both hemispheres, its much admired discipline will then be of no avail.

If the officers thus preserve the feeling of citizenship, much more is it the case with common soldiers. More miserable, more oppressed by the drill, the discipline, and crushed by it, living in poverty and destitution, their position is far more helpless than would be that of a serf under the most reckless master. For the soldier the long years of service are but a daily, nay, hourly, iron servitude. Thus nothing separates him from the destiny of the peasant, of the serf. He remains always the serf's brother, and both, however in a different way, bear on their necks the heavy pressure of caste and despotism. And the change is not for the better for the soldier. His feelings remain exclusively with the people. Thus even when brought into foreign countries, the Russian soldier is the least unreasonable in his claims, the easiest to be satisfied, and if he remains for even a short time in the same place, he identifies himself instantly with the poorest classes among whom he dwells. During the occupation of France after the battle of Waterloo, the difference between the good-natured kindness of the Russian and the particularly arrogant manner of the Prussian or the English soldiers was felt by the French. The Russian was easily satisfied with the commonest fare shared with the host, whose labors he also shared sometimes in the fields, but most generally about the house. Often it happened, that mothers going to work in the fields, left the house, the children, and nurslings under the care of the northern barbarian, who turned a faithful and careful nurse.

At home, the soldier is, soul and body, the brother of the peasant. In the military service, the pressure of caste weighs upon him more strongly than in his former state. The common soldier knows well he does not carry in his knapsack "*the marshal's staff*," as the military French proverb says since the great revolution. Nay, he does not even carry in it the simple epaulette of a second lieutenant. No bright horizon opens before him in becoming a soldier, except an exuberant number of corporal punishments. As a soldier he is hourly reminded that he belongs to the oppressed, and the line between them is not broken. Having common misfortunes, he shares their hopes for a better, if even a distant future. Thus their mutual destiny is inseparable.

From this brief but true outline of the characteristics of the Russian army, of its officers as well as its soldiers, it can be conceived that in relation to internal questions, the army has a wholly different bearing from that generally attributed to it out of Russia. In the eventuality of a rise of peasants, burghers, or serfs, the army will not so easily become a tool for depression as those of some other countries have proved themselves to be. With the exception of a party of guards quartered in St. Petersburg, and mostly in barracks, and where the relations between the inhabitants and the soldiers cannot be of the same confidential nature as are those in the country, there is little doubt on what side the soldier will be found in case of any general insurrection. Neither the Emperor, his councillors, nor the nobility at large have any doubt about it. And the more distant comparatively that moment may be, the more assured is the co-operation of the soldier with the people, for in the same proportion the anti-Czarian spirit of the officers will increase or extend. Each successive generation becomes more and more saturated with healthy opinions and discerning love of the fatherland. Thus despotism as well as the privileges of caste, become more and more undermined. Even in these latter years there have been cases where the soldiers refused to fire against partially revolted serfs. From their consciences they could not condemn them, and they could not become murderers. And further, every time when the officers and soldiers come in contact with Europe, they bring home notions not at all congenial to despotism and to the social relations existing there. They become infected with poison. The officer, like the greater part of the nobility, wishes for so-called constitutional liberty as a relaxation and shelter against despotism; the soldier wishes for the more simple and natural liberty of emancipation from the overburdening privilege. Both of them return dissatisfied with existing institutions, and crave for a change. Thus, after the campaigns against Napoleon in 1813–14–15, all the conspiracies were spread by the army. The masses which served to crush the Magyars, traversed such regions as Gallicia and parts of Slavonia, inhabited by kindred tribes, speaking a similar dialect, and nearly connected by the religious tie. And in 1849, there they found the peasants newly emancipated from a kind of serfdom, the *robot* or villainage of varied and more or less oppressive nature. All the dependence between the nobleman or master and the peasant was annihilated. The

Russians saw there the peasants enjoying political liberties—electing members of the general diet, and participating thus in the general legislation of the country, courted by the Government as well as by the nobility. Can it be believed that such an example could be lost, and that the Russian masses on their return home were not living bearers of a new creed, or at least narrators of new and joyous stories, at the hearths of the oppressed serfs? The like things and events once seen can no more be eradicated from the recollection, nor their propagation stopped by any earthly means.

The ways and means of the genius of liberty and emancipation are numberless and various. The army, looked on to-day as the most powerful engine of Czarism, will sooner or later burst in its hands, and turn against it and against the pillars by which it is supported. Hope is not only not lost for Russia, but on the contrary, it is rising—it is on the increase.

CHAPTER V.

THE NOBILITY.

NEXT to the Czar in the social scale stands the Nobility, the strongest prop of the absolute throne, and the immediate instrument for the execution of the imperial will. They form a more compact body in Russia than in any other country whatever. Nowhere else is the aristocratic class so separate and distinct from the mass of the nation. Endowed with numerous privileges that utterly hedge it off from the people, at the same time that they firmly unite its members to each other and to the throne, its destiny is fatally blended with that of Czarism, to whose debasing, annihilating, destructive influence it is more than all other classes exposed.

In the legal meaning of the word, the Nobility form the only class enjoying the *jus personæ*, or personal right. This, however, it enjoys only with reference to the so-called lower classes, while with reference to the Czar, it is nothing more than a chattel. No privileges shield it from the unlimited, autocratic authority of the throne.

Whatever laws are enacted, or even temporarily observed, the Czar is above them. He is the living law, and observes the written one only as far as he condescends to do so. In principle and in reality he possesses more absolute, unbounded, uncontrolled power over the whole nobility, as well as over any separate individual noble, high or low, rich or poor, titled or not, counting his ancestry by centuries of pure succession, or new-made yesterday, than the same noble possesses over his own serf, and even over his real property. But Czarism sustains the nobility in its position respecting the rest of the nation; —and by oppression, the throne and the aristocracy are fatally, unremittingly wedded to each other.

The whole body of the nobility is either hereditary or personal. Hereditary nobility has six divisions (rozriad). 1st. Those descending from a line of illustrious ancestors, without possessing written documents, and those ennobled long ago by the sovereigns. 2d. Military nobility, or those who acquired their title in military service. 3d. Those deriving their rights from the eighth class or *tschin* in the public service. 4th. Foreign families whose nobiliar rights are recognized in Russia. 5th. Titles, as princes, counts and barons, bestowed by various sovereigns, without reference to the antiquity or recent origin of the family. 6th. Old well-born noble families who can prove their rights by documents.

If any one be raised to the eighth class of the *tschin*, and continues to serve, he acquires the rights belonging to hereditary nobility; if he gets this *tschin*, however, when leaving the service, he then enjoys the rights of personal nobility, which is not transmittible to his children. With equal classes, the holders of a military *tschin* take precedence of civilian.*

Foreigners whose rights of nobility are admitted, cannot, however, rank among the Russian nobility without having rendered some signal service to the state, or reached the eighth *tschin* or class.

* See Appendix B.

If any one belonging to the class paying capitation, that is to the bourgeoisie or peasantry—through military or civil service reaches the class bestowing hereditary nobility, all his children born since this epoch inherit the same rights—those born previously do not enjoy this privilege.

An hereditary nobleman can marry a member of any other class, even a serf, the children always inheriting the privileges of caste.

A woman of noble descent marrying below her caste, preserves after marriage the privileges derived from birth, but does not bestow them on her husband, nor transmit them to her children. The same is the case with widows.

Roman Catholic clergy enjoy the privileges of personal nobility, as well as some members of scientific and architectural boards.

The children of a personal noble (by personal noble we mean something similar to the English rank of Knight, which, as is well known, is not transmittible to children), enjoy the rights belonging to the class of respectable citizens (see next Chapter).

Noblemen can erect every kind of manufactory on their estates without being obliged to enter a guild; they can carry on trade freely, and export the produce of their own manufactories. A nobleman establishing a manufactory in a city, and who devotes himself there to general commerce, is obliged to become a member of one of the commercial guilds, without, however, losing the privilege of caste.

The mines, the produce of fisheries, and water-power on the estates of a noble, form his absolute property, without any royalty attaching to them.

Noblemen can erect boroughs with periodical fairs and market days.

Those from the lower classes who have reached by service the position of hereditary nobles, cannot buy and acquire these landed estates, where they or their ancestry have been serfs until the third generation. Personal nobles cannot possess landed estates with serfs.

The privileges of nobility once lost by a judgment or pre-emption, cannot be re-acquired, except through military service.

The following are the principal rights and privileges of the nobility, as a body, without distinction of rank: They alone can possess real estate and own serfs. They alone can hold offices, civil and military, which gives to them the general administration and government of the empire. Only the children of noblemen, male or female, can be admitted to the public civil or military establishments of education at the cost of the state. They alone can enter the universities. The noble is exempted from corporal punishment, and from every other infamous sentence. If any civil or military court finds a nobleman guilty of a crime, and condemns him penally, previous to the execution of the judgment, whatever it may be—whether death or condemnation to Siberia, for labor in the mines—the noble is *disnobled*, and expelled from the caste, after which the sentence is executed. In justice to the new criminal code, published a few years since, it must be observed, that it treats with more relative severity the impeached and criminally condemned nobleman than it does the member of any other class; taking the ground that, as the noble enjoys exclusive privileges, he has thus within his reach all the means of education, and his criminal conduct ought to be more rigidly retributed by the law. Finally, no direct or personal taxation can be imposed upon the nobility or their estates.

The public service being preserved exclusively for the

nobles, it is a matter of peremptory obligation that they should enter it. Thus, if the members of a family shall for three generations fail to fulfil this duty, the third generation falls back into the ranks of merely personal nobility, which is not hereditary. Persons of this class are called *nowodwortsy*, new manor-men, in whom the aristocratic privilege becomes extinct with all its boons, as, for instance, the right to own serfs, etc. Abstractly, and as a matter of principle, the Czar is supposed not to possess any power to hinder in any way the liberty of a nobleman, in respect to his movements in or out of the Empire. But, as nearly every nobleman is, in some way or other, engaged in some branch of the public service, they come to depend on superiors and chiefs; in a word, on the ruling power; and thus they are obliged to ask for permission to go, and for leave of absence. Aside from this, the Czar, who is the living law, may at his pleasure prohibit any individual not only from travelling in foreign countries, but even from circulating in the interior of the empire, if he supposes that the individual is guilty of any political contamination.

The greater part of the internal administration of provinces or governments, as they are called, and of districts, cities, townships, and communalities, as well as that of civil and criminal justice therein, has for its basis the communal principle of election. The boards are nearly all elected by the respective social classes, though most of them are presided over by a member named by the general government. The nobility as a body has the greater share in the boards. In each province the nobility forms a distinct, compact, social, and official corporation, to administer its special affairs and to watch over its general interests. They elect a head, called the county marshal, and a board of councillors. As every county pays separate taxes for its own internal administration, of which, however, the expenditure is in the hands of the governor, and of his board named by the crown, he is obliged to give yearly accounts thereof to the marshal and the board of nobility. The marshal has the right to send his complaints against the governor to the minister of the interior, or even to the Czar himself. Each district in a county elects likewise a district marshal, a justice of the peace, for judicial and not for police duties, an administrative and police chief for the district, corresponding somewhat with the position of a *sous-préfet* in France, and his adjuncts, a council to administer the estates of minors, as well as the real estates of those who are deprived of them judicially, or for tyranny and misdemeanor toward their serfs. The persecution of the like cases belongs to the district and county crown attorneys. In the general elections the nobility of each county select presidents and members for the civil and criminal tribunals—three for each, and a tutor of the high school or gymnasium, with whom the director named by the crown ought to consult in all administrative and disciplinary matters, as nearly all the pupils are nobles—and finally, the like tutors for the district schools.

The nobility elect the judiciary for each county, composed of the presidents, and three members or judges for each civil or criminal tribunal; the district judges, and their assessors or assistants, a conciliatory judge, called the judge of conscience, and a board to keep the heraldic records of the county.

The meetings are triennial, being summoned by the governor. Such ordinary meetings make the necessary elections of the various boards enumerated above. An extraordinary meeting of the nobility can be called together by the marshal of the county, with the permission of the governor, who in his turn obtains that of the minister of the interior, and through him that of the sovereign. At any such meeting, ordinary or extraordinary, only the wants of the respective county can form the subject of deliberation—and about them only petitions can be addressed to the sovereign.

Hereditary nobility only takes a part in such meetings. A woman possessing in her own right landed property, can bestow her elective rights on her husband, son, or son-in-law. To be elected, a nobleman must possess one hundred serfs with the requisite quantity of soil for each, or three thousand desiatin, or about eight thousand acres of land. He must be twenty-one years of age.

The elective principle for the nobility was introduced and regulated by Catharine II., who bestowed on Russia many of the blessings of a wise government. Catharine even intended to inaugurate a kind of deliberative assemblies for the nobility, where matters concerning the internal interests of the empire would have been discussed, and the results of deliberation submitted to the judgment of the sovereign. She called together notables from the nobility to Moscow, but having soon discovered that their deliberations did not throw any light on the subjects submitted to them, she dismissed them with great official encomium.

The nobility holds, or at least shares, if not the power, at least its administration. But in this way also, as depending on the Czar and his special tools, the nobility is the most exposed to the deadly malaria of despotism. Notwithstanding its privileges and standing, it enjoys no real independence, less even in a certain degree than the class of burghers.

Holding as they do all other administrative offices,—which are not elective,—at the pleasure of the Czar, and depending on them, not only for social position, but often for maintenance, individual nobles are often compelled to bear patiently, and with mute submission, the most galling wrongs and insults. An outraged noble, if his family has not any very prominent position at court, is sure not to find any redress, and to be abandoned by his kindred, as nobody will dare to oppose the wrath of a powerful minister or favorite; every one being in turn dependent on the good will of the clique surrounding the sovereign. The burghers, who expect nothing from the direct action of the government, and are not linked with it as office-holders, have more *esprit de corps* in such emergencies, and exercise it more boldly. The public service contributes generally to the financial ruin, or at least the embarrassment of the nobility, who labor under the general disease of their caste throughout the world—that of lavishness and of dissipation.

Thus, the nobility is in a false, abnormal position, privileged to be sure, but without enjoying an independence, and without dignity or freedom. And add to this that its numbers increase rather rapidly by the mechanism inherent in the organization of the government. Thus increases the number of social drones, and worse yet, that of bloodsuckers, and men dissatisfied with their position. The whole service civil, as well as military, is divided as it was said in a preceding chapter, into fourteen classes of ranks. The five lower classes (Nos. 14 to 10, inclusive) are open to those who are nobles, or the sons of personal nobles, of higher burghers, physicians, professors, or priests. The principal privileges of these classes consist in being exempt from corporeal punishment during the period of service. The next superior, or ninth class, gives the rights of personal nobility—as for example, that of owning serfs, without, however, transmitting them to successors; and of the admission of children into public establishments. The eighth class bestows hereditary nobility, with all its general privileges. Thus, the daily extension of all the branches of public service, backed by favoritism and the protection of powerful and influential men, fills the empire with swarms of nobles—espousing all the stupid prejudices of the class into which they come, and shunning no immorality and venality that can procure means to maintain the newly acquired position; and masterly teachers enough they find among the older occupants of the privilege.

This union between despotism and the nobility is far from being a happy one. The links uniting them are not of roses—and mutual distrust, suspicion, and sometimes hatred prevail. Debased by their dependence, the nobility feel their contemptible position—but still they are obliged to live and lean on the power of the autocracy, and to soothe it by flattery and submission. All the oppressive measures toward themselves or the other classes pass through the aristocracy before reaching the others. On it the heel of despotism more violently presses, and if there be in its ranks some slight breathing of better aspirations, Czarism strangles it at once. At present the autocrat restricts even the means of education. The ukase allowing only three hundred youths to each university yearly, we have already mentioned. Thus is blocked from the nobles all possibility of receiving a half-way independent education. The object of this ukase is to force the youth into the army and the military drill, as less dangerous. From among the military, the civil officials are afterwards to be appointed; by this means despotism expects to have more mute and docile tools, though the country should be administered by incapable persons. But in the long run the Czar will find himself baffled in these expectations. The iron rod of military discipline wounds more deeply—

and evokes silent thoughts, preparing, however slowly, a final reaction.

The nobility at large preserve much of true national feeling. They wish for an amelioration, and very often look for the possibility of relaxation in the present hard and crushing system of government. But their position is exceptional and abnormal, notwithstanding these better feelings, and renders them wholly unable to remedy the evil, and to be the harbinger of a better future. Thus in their ranks the sparks of the so-called revolutionary fire is very often kindled, but these attempts remain fruitless. The country's redemption will not come from that quarter. The nobility for centuries have contributed mightily to enslave the people at large, to depress the burghers, to fetter the peasant to the soil, and to rivet his bondage as a serf. Thus the aristocracy shares with Czarism the malediction of history. Vainly will it attempt to free itself from the deadly embrace of the Autocrat. He drags and keeps it attached to his destiny with the bonds of unchangeable doom. Both are gnawed by the same cancer—both devoured by the same rust of decay. Both will finally be called to give a bloody account of their doings. The nobility at large already have a gloomy presentiment of their destiny, and dread both the Czar and the people, of whose real confidence they are deprived for ever.

Whatever the so-called liberal or constitutional reforms wished or attempted by the nobility may be, if ever carried through—which we judge to be a perfect impossibility—that class will never wholly resign its various privileges. It will never put itself on an equal footing with the remainder of the nation. It will grant voluntarily this or that concession, of more or less value, but that is not enough.

The so-called liberal nobles are no rarity in Russia.

There is a certain party, especially among the higher nobility or aristocracy, endowed with pure oligarchical appetites. This party, notwithstanding an external varnish of liberalism, is as hostile and as dangerous to the real liberties of the nation, as is Czarism itself. Its aim is to raise a certain number of families to a dignity equivalent to that of the English peers, and to make them independent of the despotic will of the Czar, but to maintain the existing oppression towards the rest of the nobility and the people. The great fomenters of this scheme are the families of the Strogonoffs and some others, as Kiseleff, Menschikoff, etc. The Strogonoffs are the descendants of wealthy merchants of Moscow, who, in the 16th century, made a compact with Ermak, a celebrated chief of robbers, and, through him, conquered Siberia, but have never since that time rendered any other prominent civil or military services to their fatherland.

Uneasiness, dissatisfaction with the existing state of things, and fear of the future, whatever it may be, are the predominant feelings in the breasts of the greater number of the nobility. In common with that class in other countries, they are overwhelmed with debt and unable to keep pace with the material progress around them, which requires order, intellect, capital, and hands. Commercial and industrial enterprise is of course open and accessible to the nobles. Many of them farm from the crown the monopoly of the sale of liquors. But with rare and very few individual exceptions, trade, industry, or manufactures, form rather a costly pastime when indulged in by a nobleman, aside from his other occupations and pursuits. The spirit of caste is likewise an impediment. Finally, the nobleman cannot cope with men for whom commercial and industrial enterprise is the sole and exclusive aim of life, and who, excluded by the nobility from other more easy social positions, and prevented by the laws even from freely enjoying and making in their turn an *ad libitum* use of their wealth, look on a commercial noble as on one who encroaches on their ground, and accordingly never sincerely fraternize with him. Serfdom is likewise a moral and a material burden for the nobility, and all the more so since the majority of them possess small or reduced fortunes. It is an element financially ruinous, and socially menaces explosion. In truth, numerous nobles revolve in their minds the idea of giving up their estates to the crown for the payment of a perpetual rent. Thus distant clouds gather dark and heavy from all directions around this caste.

The position of the nobility is to be sincerely pitied. They wish and aspire for something better, and still are fatally condemned to the worst. They are continually placed between two fires. That of Czarism it receives in full, while it is loathed by the other classes. Among the noblemen many are sincerely ashamed of being the scourges of despotism, and the extinguishers of light, the propagators of darkness, and the principal tools for the destruction of liberty at home and abroad.

Half willingly and half by fatal compulsion, the nobility shares in the saturnalia of despotism, still receiving the master's first lashes on its humbled head. Before history, and the genius of humanity and of Russia, it stands impeached for having with its own hands worked out the moral and intellectual debasement of the nation. The burghers, the peasantry, the serfs see and feel in it their immediate oppressor. They see, feel, and experience that malversation, venality, corruption, and all the most abject impurities which still stamp the government and the administration, are the exclusive doing of the nobility, she being the exclusive holder of all higher and lower offices.

The real genuine people find their caste every where in the way. It surrounds them as by an insurmountable wall, compressing pitilessly their practical every-day life, as well as every better, loftier impulse of the mind. The nobility have even drawn a line of separation in the social intercourse between themselves and the clergy, who to a certain degree form a separate class, but who on account of their calling, have some approach to education, not only clerical, but partly of a more general kind.

As we have already observed, the caste of nobles has almost exclusive access to the existing means and resources of education; the admission to them of other classes is exceptional, and, on the whole, rather accidental. Thus the nobles have absorbed for their own benefit all the means and rays of the civilization existing in Russia, and they alone enjoy the possibility and the right to give utterance to an intellectual life. They have possession of the arena of culture, and they are presumed to represent it—to hold and to spread the light from the sacred beacon. But the glimmer in which they shine is a cold and blinding mist, or a deceiving mirage. It is superficial, swimming on the surface, like a will-o'-the-wisp. What the real, genuine manifestation of Russian civilization may or will be, can only be appreciated and fairly judged when the whole people shall be admitted to the sanctuary, when the now latent intellectual powers shall blaze in their genuine warmth and brilliancy—when the concrete Russian mind will conquer activity, life, and boundless development.

Suspended between good and evil, between light and darkness, between life and death, irritated and exasperated by the feeling of their social annihilation, by that of moral nothingness, and by the certainty of material and financial exhaustion, the greater part of the nobility are torn inwardly by violent and desperate, but impotent rage. They cannot unite with the people against the common oppressor, as the people distrust and even despise them, and would neither answer nor follow any appeal they might put forth. Full of hatred for Czarism and the Czar, they still uphold him with one hand, while digging with the other their common grave. If the social existence of the class is not to expire contemptibly, it must finally light the purifying flame. Thus it will open up the future, but, at the same time, will itself be consumed by the sacred fire, and perish socially in *the work of initiation.*

CHAPTER VI.

THE CLERGY.

IN treating of the Eastern Church or Greek Church, we shall discuss no theological, dogmatical, or liturgical questions. This church, at the present day, may be said to be eminently Slavic, since the Slavi constitute by far the greatest and most powerful portion—two thirds, at least—of the orthodox or true believers. Thus, the Slavic dialect is heard more than any other in the sacred services of the Eastern Church; and among the Slavic race, and principally on Russian soil, has the independence of this church, from all foreign, hostile, or heathen influence, been secured and maintained.

We now proceed to state the social position of the church and the clergy, their relation to the state and to the people, and the influence they have exerted and still exert on the latter.

Christianity was introduced into Russia from Byzantium, and principally by the action of the Byzantine Emperors and their daughters, who, by marrying the savage Ros (as the Russians were called by the Byzantine historians), tried to soften their dangerous neighbors. Generally, it was through the women that Christianity was introduced, and spread among the northern races. Being a daughter of Byzantium, the Russian Church very naturally held under the patriarch of Constantinople, and was at that early period wholly independent of any action or interference of the civil power of Russia or of the power of the Grand Dukes. After the fall of Constantinople into Turkish hands, one of the patriarchs fled to Moscow, in the sixteenth century, and thus a Patriarchate was established there. From this epoch, the Russian Church, sheltered by the national independence, has looked on herself as being at the head of the Eastern religious family. The patriarchs of Moscow long contrived to preserve the independence of the church from the encroachments of the civil power, not, however, without serious collisions with some of the Czars, and especially with Ivan the Terrible (*Groznoï*), who even imprisoned and nearly put to death a patriarch.

After the death of a patriarch, Peter the Great entirely abolished the whole institution, allowing no new election to be made; and thus assumed a part of the power for himself and his successors. He instituted a board, under the name of the Sacred Synod, formed out of metropolitans, archbishops, bishops, and some lower members of the hierarchy, and appointed this Synod to attend to ecclesiastical affairs of every kind. The decisions of this body, in spiritual matters, are understood to be wholly independent of the influence of the Czars. As to the administration, the power of the sovereign is supreme. In the Synod, it is represented by the procuror, or imperial attorney, directing the deliberations and the administrative labors of the Synod. The Czars nominate the hierarchy, and the Synod gives them consecration. Peter the Great, and finally Catharine, took away from the clergy and the monasteries all their property, which was very large. The whole hierarchy is now supported by the government.

There are two classes of the clergy—the white, or secular (so called from the color of the dress they wear), and the black, or monks. Of the last the Eastern Church has only one order, instituted by St. Basil the Great, one of the primitive fathers of the Œcumenic Church. From among the white clergy, who must be married, the curates are taken, as are the other ranks of the hierarchy below the rank of bishop. All bishops must be unmarried and monks. The members of the white clergy must be married, or at least engaged, before receiving the final consecration. But they cannot marry twice, and on becoming widowers are obliged to enter a monastery, or, as the phrase is: *postryjon w monachy*, be shorn into a monk—as the white clergy wear their hair and beard long. Thus a priest takes most devoted care of his wife to the utmost of his means and power. It is therefore proverbial among the people, to be as happy as a *popadïa*, or the wife of a pope, which is the title of a priest, and is derived from the word *papa*.

The white or married clergy form, in reality, a distinct caste; the male children following, generally, the condition of the father. This is, however, the result of usage rather than of law. Nay, they even intermarry among themselves. Thus the clergy form a class somewhere between the nobility, the bourgeoisie and the people—less than the first, and superior to the two others. As a class, the clergy cannot enter the nobility on an equal footing; and that very few marriages between them take place, is, perhaps, principally on account of the poverty of the priests. For the children of the clergy to enter the body and share the occupations of the burghers would be looked on as a loss of caste. Few, therefore, of this class enter the public service, civil or military, and on the other hand, no nobleman ever takes "orders," with the exception of now and then an old military veteran retiring to monastic life.

The code of law, the *Swod Zakonoff*, gives the follow-lowing definitions of the position of the clergy: The monasteries and convents are divided into three classes, and the dignity and precedency of their respective Abbots and Abbesses accords with this arrangement. The higher clerical hierarchy, formed from the monks, consists of the Metropolitan, the Archbishop, the Bishop, the Igumen, or Abbé, etc. The titles of the white hierarchy are: Protopresbyter, Superdeans, Deans, Presbyters, Protodeacons, Deacons, Subdeacons and common Priest.

Any one who takes monastic orders must receive the permission of the Synod. The men must be thirty years of age—women, forty. If the candidates belong to the taxed class, that is, if they are burghers, peasants or serfs, they must produce a permission from their special superior.

Married persons, or those not divorced, cannot take orders unless both parties do it, and when there are no children under age.

One can leave the order by permission of the superiors, and return to the social class to which he belonged before. For seven years, however, he cannot live in the country where he was a monk, nor in either of the two capitals.

Monks are not exempted from military service, from the capitation tax, and from corporal punishment. They cannot own villages of serfs, or carry on trade.

The order of the white clergy can be entered by any one, with the exception of serfs. The wives and children of the clergy enjoy the privileges of this class, though they may personally belong to a lower order. Thus the children of priests, with few exceptions, are not obliged to look for another social position. They are exempt from military service.

A priest can abandon his vocation and return to worldly life by the permission of the Synod. (A Roman Catholic priest never can.) Such a one returns to the social class to which he previously belonged, but he cannot enter the public service until ten years after his renunciation.

In all religious and disciplinary affairs the clergy are subject to and judged by their own hierarchy. In civil matters the case comes before the civil court, assisted by a deputy clergyman. Deacons and common priests are not liable to corporal punishment. Clergymen cannot own estates or serfs except when they are born nobles or are decorated with a distinction bestowing nobility. They can own houses in cities, and farms in villages, but they cannot carry on trade. If the children of clergymen enter the military or civil service, they enjoy the privileges conferred on the children of personal nobles.

The Roman Catholic and the Graeco-Armenian clergy enjoy the same legal privileges as the orthodox. Each possesses its own special hierarchy, whose decisions must be confirmed by the sovereign. The Protestant clergy, which consists principally of Lutherans and Calvinists, have a hierarchy according to their own special organization. Those wishing to be ordained are obliged to go through a whole course of Protestant theological studies, in one of the Russian Universities, and then to pass an examination before their own superiors. No one can be a preacher under twenty-five years of age. Exceptions are allowed by the special permission of the Minister of the Interior. It is under the control of this administrative department that all the denominations, not orthodox, or Graeco-Russian are placed. Individuals subject to the capitation tax must be furnished with an exemption from it before their ordination. Foreigners must have the permission of the minister to preach, or to be settled over parishes.

The affairs of the Lutheran Church are administered by consistories, all of whose members take the oath of fidelity to the sovereign. Though a Protestant clergyman be not noble born, yet as long as he remains in this vocation, he enjoys the rights of personal nobility, and thus is exempted from the capitation tax. Houses in cities, owned and inhabited by them, are free from military quartering and from taxes. The Protestant clergy have the right to organize a fund for their widows and orphans, with the permission of the respective consistories and of the minister.

They cannot carry on trade or be artisans or mechanics. They cannot be attorneys in lawsuits, not their own, or those of their wives and children; neither can they be guardians of orphans without a special permission of the consistory. In matters concerning their clerical condition, they are subject to the discipline of their hierarchy; in all others they are under the action of the general laws. When in a criminal affair an arrest of a clergyman is to be made, the consistory is to be instantly made acquainted with it. They cannot be subjected to corporal punishment. The widows and children of the Protestant clergy enjoy all the privileges of personal nobles, with the exception of those born after the father has renounced the order. Widows and children enjoy for one year the income of the departed clergyman. One abandoning the order, and not being either a hereditary or personal noble, is obliged to select a new mode of life, and become inscribed in a coporation according to his choice. A clergyman can be dismissed and degraded by a criminal verdict, as well as for the transgression of his duties, and by the judgment of his special hierarchy. A clergyman, condemned to death, or to an infamous punishment; as for example to the *pletnia*, (a kind of whip which now generally replaces the *knout*), or to the mines, or to be branded—even if afterward he should be pardoned, cannot recover his clerical standing, or the privileges connected with it.

The clergy of the Greek or Russian Church are educated in ecclesiastical schools, kept by monks, in monasteries, to which schools children of all other classes have likewise access. The regular theological instruction is given there in separate classes. Children of priests can frequent other public schools—the Gymnasia and Universities, and generally, next to the class of the nobles, they have the easiest access to the means of instruction and education.

The number of dioceses of the orthodox church amounts to nearly seventy, and that is also about the number of Archbishops, Bishops, and Suffragans.

The orthodox clergy, both the white and the monks, exert a powerful influence on the minds of the people, and principally on those of the burghers and peasants. This influence has its principal source in history and in the nationality of the church and of the clergy. The church has more than once raised the spirit of the people in epochs of national distress, and has preserved and nursed, the feeling of nationality during the centuries of foreign supremacy. During the Tartar domination of nearly three centuries, the church rendered to the nation not only the spiritual service of comfort and consolation, but to a great degree preserved the national tongue from the impure admixture of the foreign dialect. Whatever may have been, at that time, the mental activity of Russia, it was limited, and exclusively concentrated in the church. In these labors the Russian church, quite differently from that of the whole of remaining Europe, did not use a foreign tongue, but that of the people. Thus, it not only preserved the national language from deterioration, but the church alone contributed to give to it a higher development and life. All the writings of the fathers of the primitive church were, at an early epoch, translated into the Slavo-Russian, and thus its inborn elasticity was developed. From the time of the introduction of Christianity, the churchmen and monks wrote their records and chronicled events, in general, in the vernacular. Thus Russia, *alone*, has ancient chronicles in her own tongue, a fact of which no other nation can boast. To-day even the purest, the most vigorous language is that used by the church, and no one can know well its powers and flexibility who has not studied it at the above mentioned sources.

In the great struggle to overthrow the Tartar supremacy, the church powerfully inflamed the national feelings, amalgamating them with those of the religion. In the wars with the Poles, the clergy, the monks, often contributed to stir up the people and to repulse the invaders, as in the siege of Wielkie Luki, Smolensk, etc. During the epoch of the pretenders in the beginning of the seventeenth century, when Moscow and nearly the whole of Russia, was conquered and overrun by the Poles, and when thus, for some time, they ruled the country, the clergy stimulated the people to oppose the menacing foreign domination, as aiming to introduce Roman Catholicism; and when Minin, the butcher, and the Prince Pojarski, raised the cry of independence in Moscow, and in Nijnoi Novgorod, the clergy were foremost to echo it, and again contributed mightily to the reconquering of the national independence.* In these events, and in the exclu-

* The thankful people offered the crown to the liberator Pojarski. He refused it, and pointed to the Romanoffs as the nearest kindred of the extinct lineage of the Czars. The chief of the Romanoff family was forced by Gudenoff, the usurper, to enter a monastery—but was carried off with the Czar Schujski, as prisoner

sive nationality of the church are the roots of its influence over the people.

The nobility at large, though externally respectful toward the clergy, yet keep them at a distance, and there exists no intimate intercourse between the two classes, The contrary is the case with the bourgeoisie and the peasants. At their hearth the priest, the monk, is treated with cordiality, and meets with respect. The religious as well as the national tie unites them strongly. In the clergymen, the people at large have entire confidence—but not so in the nobility or in the officials. With the clergy the people live a common life—with the clergy they share sorrows and sufferings, and bear a common oppression.

Like every thing else in Russia, the church is oppressed by despotic power, and the clergy by the social strata overlaying it. Peter the Great annulled the independence of the clergy; and since this first stroke, the all-absorbing action of despotism has pressed down and crushed the church more completely. It must be said, however, that the influence of the sovereign exclusively concerns temporal matters, and, therefore, the Emperor is in nowise the spiritual chief of the church, nor can he in any way decide or interfere with spiritual, dogmatic, or strictly ecclesiastical disciplinary affairs. In this respect, a sovereign of England is more a chief of his church, than a Russian autocrat of his. For instance, the Gorham case, lately decided in England by the sovereign or her council, in Russia, could never come officially before the Emperor. With his power, notwithstanding its intensity, he can not touch spiritual or theological questions. But in all other matters, the clergy and the hierarchy are wholly reduced to nothingness, and are totally subject to the will of the

to Poland. His son was elected Czar, and began the reigning dynasty, whose first founder was thus a monk.

Czar. The common disciplinary decisions of the Synod must be submitted to the soveriegn.

To avoid what the jealousy of despotism calls a scandal, or rather to cut off a contaminating influence which might extend over other subjects, no free discussion of any matter is *really* allowed to the church. The bishops must be very circumspect and cautious in their spiritual and administrative action. They, too, are subject to the investigation of the secret police, or spies, and may thus easily be ruined. Salaried by the government, they are kept in absolute subjection, and those who are too spirited, receive, either directly, secretly, or officially, through the synod, friendly or emphatic admonitions. Any discussion, about the moral power and influence of the church, is looked on as too likely and too easily susceptible to go beyond bounds; thus it is suspected, or rather prohibited, in writing as well as speech. Even the pulpit, that scanty resource of the church, is jealously watched over. Thus, neither the supreme metropolitan, nor the humblest parson, can move freely in his own element. The monasteries are under the same pressure. The choice or selection of the abbot, (*Igumen*,) must be made by them, agreeably to the whims of the government. They are under control, as is every other corporation, and are sometimes treated very roughly and with great severity. With all this the sovereign, and the whole official swarm, show all the external signs of deference to the *Pope* or *Baituschka*, as a priest is commonly called.

We have said above that none, or scarcely any social intercourse exists between the nobility and the clergy. The priests select their wives from among their own class, or from among the lower burghers or peasantry, who are not admitted into the society of even the lowest nobility. Thus the clergy, being both in the city and in the country excluded from the palace and the chateau, very naturally fall back upon the other classes, by whom they are treated with respectful deference.

The clergy are far from being satisfied with forming such a limited caste. For their children they wish, very naturally, for a more enlarged horizon, from which they are crowded out, as much by the institutions of the country, as by its conventional usage. They are, very naturally, disaffected and dissatisfied, and this dissatisfaction with the existing state of things, grows stronger and stronger in proportion as their oppression and the aspiration for emancipation increase.

The only full liberty, protection and firm support enjoyed by the clergy under the government, is in the persecution of heretics and dissenters from the orthodox church. These various sectarians have a strong vitality, notwithstanding the pressure exercised upon them. They are equally obnoxious to the church and to the crown; they form various sects, composed of burghers and peasants, with very few nobles. Some of them do not believe in any regular clergy at all, and these are looked on as the worst; others have no higher hierarchy beyond their parsons; these are called *storowiertsy*, old believers, others are iconoclasts, and still others have various names, as *duhobortsy*, inspired, *malakany*, *skoptsy*, etc. They are most generally quiet and active people, but very fanatical. Temperate and abstemious—most of them use no spirituous liquors whatever—they are thus in good circumstances. By the law they are excluded from holding elective offices in the municipal or rural communes, where they live mixed with the orthodox They really must be looked upon as forming the only true Independents in Russia, since to their religious ideas they join those of political independence. Their political notions are republican, and the Czar, as well as the nobility, is odious to them; they are principally averse to the military service. Dispersed and scattered through the empire, they find the people more tolerant towards them than the government. They thus maintain a continual social fermentation, whose activity is increasing, and may acquire a high importance in future emergencies.

From all this it results, that neither religion in itself, nor the state-church and clergy, form such strongholds and props of absolutism, and of the division into castes in Russia, as is perhaps the case in other countries of Europe. On the contrary, the clergy, and above all the monks, are rather a menacing cloud on the autocratic horizon, and the autocracy is aware of this fact. Not that it can be expected that the initiative of general emancipation will ever issue from the order of the priesthood; but whenever it shall come, the clergy will rather foster than oppose it, provided that it bear, what is beyond a doubt, a national character.

CHAPTER VII.

THE BOURGEOISIE.

THERE is a current and rather wide-spread fallacy, propagated by writers belonging to various nations, about the absence in the Russian social system of a bourgeoisie or *tiers-état*. This misrepresentation is based principally on the erroneous notion, that whoever is not a nobleman, is, *ipse-facto*, a serf or slave. As to such persons being slaves, we have shown in a former chapter upon the nobility, that notwithstanding their superior social position, and the privileges and distinctions enjoyed by them, and by which they are surrounded, in their real relations with the autocracy, the nobility finally share the common lot, and join with the other classes in dragging along the iron yoke. The Czar is, in principle, an absolute unaccountable master, as well over the person of a nobleman, as over that of a burgher, a peasant, or a serf. His power is far more absolute over the nobility, than that of the nobility over their peasantry. The bourgeoisie in Russia are also subject to this power in the same way as the nobility, who precede this class in the social scale. But the class of citizens is circumscribed by the nature of this descending gradation, and thus crowded into a closer and narrower arena, and is more heavily shackled, and to a greater degree oppressed and deprived of individuality and liberty, in body as well as in mind. In a social order, founded exclusively on the complication and combination of what is called privilege, the pressure becomes more and more galling as we descend to the lower grades.

Thus to a certain degree the position of the bourgeoisie in Russia, as will be shown hereafter, differs somewhat from that of the corresponding class in other countries. But still it is of the same kind, though in a more depressed state; sharing partly the common deficiences, but endowed with other different characteristics of its own, which render it superior to the narrow and contracted spirit so deeply rooted in the European bourgeoisie generally.

In Russia, therefore, the bourgeoisie forms a middle class, just as it does elsewhere. It stands there between the nobility and the peasantry. In this central position, through its well defined, well circumscribed corporation, called legally the merchant class, the bourgeoisie touches slightly the heights of the reserved privileges, proper to the nobility; while on the other side it mingles and almost disappears in the genuine people. Thus, if by some restricted privileges it is a little raised above the latter's fortune; on the whole, it supports, in common with those beneath it, the social and moral pressure weighing down upon both from the crushing superposition of a higher caste, and from the all-stifling power of despotism.

In the official language the whole class is called *citizen burghers.* They live in cities, towns, and boroughs, all under similar organizations; devoted exclusively to trade, manufactures, and other working professions. There they are governed by institutions of a communal nature as respects their fundamental organism and structure.

The legal or civil position of the bourgeoisie as a whole,

as well as in the parts into which it is legally subdivided, is as follows, according to the definitions of the law by which the bourgeoisie is pieced out into many and various classifications and subdivisions :

According, then, to the law, *swod zakonow*, the citizen burghers of any city, town, or borough, are : 1. Those born in it, or those who have settled there, established in any business, as tradesmen, artisans, etc. 2. Persons possessing houses, lots, or any description of real estate in the locality. 3. Those registered in one of the three guilds, or any other local corporation. 4. All those who in the city where they live, have fulfilled duties of personal service, who are recorded in the general register, and have accordingly paid the communal taxes.

This body of citizen burghers is divided into various classifications, as follows, thus : 1. The class of the corporation legally called merchants, *kupetscheskoe soslowie.* All of them must be inscribed in one of the three guilds. 2. Respectable citizens. 3. Citizen burghers not inscribed in any of the guilds ; artisans, mechanics, belonging to special handicraft corporations. 4. Freemen, such as discharged soldiers, emancipated serfs, and all others of free condition not belonging to any special corporation, but registered in the general one of the city inhabited by them. 5. Workmen, and all other inhabitants owning houses in cities, but not registered in the general, or in any of the special corporations, can, if they choose, be called citizen burghers, without, however, losing their privileges, if from the order of the nobility, or acquiring those of burghers, if still belonging to rural communes.

The three guilds into which the merchant class is divided, are formed according to the amount of capital employed and declared by those wishing to get an inscription, on which an interest of about six per cent. is to be paid yearly into the treasury. The sum necessary for an inscription in the first guild is about twenty thousand dollars, for the third or lowest, about six thousand.

Aside from this order of merchants, all other burghers form a general body, whatever their trade or occupations. A handicraft corporation is formed of masters, foremen, and apprentices. The members of such a corporation are either for life or temporary. To the first belong those born as citizen burghers; to the second foreign artisans, free peasants, as well as serfs who have learned the special handicraft or are received among the masters in the corporation, being thus inscribed for a certain time, without, however, belonging to the general class of citizen burghers. The body of workmen is composed of all registered in the records of the town, and not belonging to any of the above-mentioned classes, of men unfit for the military service or those having finished it, of foreign immigrants, artisans, or apprentices, but excluding those of bad character, and all those expelled for bad behavior, or for the non-payment of communal taxes, or the evading to fulfil personal duties.

Any one enjoying the right to make a selection of a corporation, trade, or occupation for life, can enter the class of citizen burghers, abandoning thus his inferior position and passing over to the superior one. For this he must be legally and officially accepted by the community which he wishes to join. Exceptions exist for some artisans where the legal assent of the community to the act of admission is not necessary. Thus, for example, cloth-weavers, dyers and dressers, and machinists, can join a general city corporation or community, without obtaining the formality of its assent.

Free or crown peasants can join the corporation of burghers individually or with their families, and so can rural communes, if they are traders, mechanics, artisans, or manufacturers, but not as agriculturists. Individuals passing thus from one state to another, must obtain the assent of the commune which they abandon, as well as the acceptance of that which they enter. When this is to be done by a whole rural community, the permission of the government is necessary. Widows and daughters of free peasants can, under certain conditions, become incorporated among the citizen burghers.

Independent agriculturists (a kind of free yeomen), as well as emancipated serfs, can join a city corporation with its assent.

Jews, as well as seceders from the state or the orthodox Greco-Russian Church can only join corporations in transcaucasian cities. Asiatic nomades, of all races and kinds, Kirgises, etc., can, at their choice, enter any city corporation whatever, and no objection can be raised to this by the commune.

The following are the rights and the composition of a municipal commune. Its members can hold legal meetings for the debating and settling of objects of general interest, necessity, and utility. So says the code of law, *swod zakonow.* These meetings are either general, formed collectively by all the various members of the general city corporation, or special, for each special corporation; as, for example, for merchants, burghers, or workmen. A general meeting is held every three years, being called together by the governor of the county, and presided over by the mayor, who is called *golowa* or head. The legal age for the exercise of the right of voting is 25 years. At such triennial meetings, the community elects members for its internal administration—as the mayor, the common council, called *duma*, the magistracy or board of aldermen, a special board for affairs relating to artisans, a board to superintend the recruiting of soldiers, and a board of depu ties to look over the administrative accounts.

The community of any city can erect a communal bank according to the prescriptions of special laws.

No citizen burgher can be deprived of his standing or special privileges otherwise than by the verdict of a criminal tribunal. In all civil as well as criminal matters, if both the parties are of the same class, the case comes first before the board of magistrates.

Merchants of the first guild, or their children, when the parents have belonged for twenty-five years uninterruptedly to the guild, have the right to enter the civil or military service under the same conditions as the children of personal nobles. Merchants of the second guild, or their children, cannot enter the civil service at all, and the mili tary only as volunteers; that is, with the right to leave it again at any time. All other merchants, citizen burghers, or their children, are not admitted into the civil service on any condition whatever, and when they enter the military, do not enjoy any privilege whatever, but are treated like all the common recruits. A citizen burgher registered in one of the three guilds is free from the general recruiting to which all other burghers are subject. He also does not pay to the state the capitation tax, called *poduschnoe* (from the soul), as he already pays an interest on the capital for which he is inscribed in the guild. All other commercial taxes are paid by the burghers in common with the rest of the inhabitants. Any citizen burgher can own houses or other real estate situated in cities or villages, or lots of naked land—that is, land without serfs. Citizen burghers not inscribed in any guild, but owning houses in cities valued above $5,000, are obliged to register their names at least in the third guild, and pay the interest on their capital. Such houses can be owned by widows or unmarried daughters of the class of merchants, but on condition of registration in a guild. Merchants can belong to and be registered in rural communities according to certain prescriptions of the law.

If a merchant, or in general any citizen burgher, inherits landed estates with serfs on them, the serfs are to be sold immediately to the crown domains at the average price of from $150 to $200 the soul—the right of owning serfs being reserved exclusively to the nobility. The citizen burghers can be deprived of their property only by the judgment of a civil tribunal.

No citizen burgher registered in the general, or in any of the special corporations, can step out of it, and abandon the city where he is incorporated, by settling in another, without the assent of the community or the permission of the government. Any citizen burgher can pass into the close corporation of the merchants, on declaring the amount of capital required to be inscribed in one of the three guilds, and paying to the treasury the interest thereon.

Each community can exclude any member under criminal condemnation, or of notorious bad character. The city of Moscow has alone the privilege of giving up such individuals to the government, either as recruits, to be reckoned as furnished in any future levy, or for the colonization of Siberia. Children of such convicts, above fourteen years of age, have the option either to follow the father or to remain in the community. Minors not having a mother, never follow the parent when sent to Siberia.

Above all the subdivisions of the bourgeoisie, and thus above the close corporation of the merchants—even those of the first guild—rises the legal privilege of the respectable citizen, *potchotnoi grazdanin*. This is a privilege, either enjoyed for life or hereditary. Children of personal nobles become hereditary respectable citizens.

One who, in virtue of the social position of his father as a merchant of the first guild, or as a savant, a physician, etc., has acquired the right to complete a course of studies in one of the universities of the empire, can petition the government to be included in the class of respectable citizens, on producing testimonials of having finished the higher studies, and of good conduct during his stay at the university. The same is conceded to artists when they produce testimonials from the national academies of art; to children of merchants of the first and second guilds, who have passed with special distinction through the studies of the universities, to pupils of special commercial schools, to artists who are foreigners by birth, etc.

At first sight it would seem laudable, that laborious and well accomplished studies, as well as artistical distinction, should open the door to a higher grade in the social scale. But on more close consideration, this apparent liberality loses greatly in its character. It is deprived of the lofty spirit of universality which alone makes such distinction praiseworthy. It has the narrowness inherent in exceptions and superpositions. It is a privilege conceded to one already privileged. It excludes here as it does every where, the man of genius, who by accident is not born in a certain privileged cradle. It reduces to some few what ought to be accessible to all. It is thus restricted, narrow, and exclusive. Vainly is it represented as being a stimulus to the acquisition of social distinction by intellectual labor, by mental accomplishments. It is so but partially in a very limited way. It has the whole smell of caste instead of having the elevated character of being for the benefit of the whole people. It shuts out the poor, the unprotected by purse or patronage. It is stale and musty in its nature, rather than bright and serene as ought to be a genuine incitement of true civilization, securing well-deserved social superiority and consideration.

Members of the merchant class, on whom the government has conferred the honorary title of commercial or manufacturing councillors, if they have never suffered any criminal indictment, and never failed in business, can themselves, as can their widows, rise into the class of hereditary *respectable citizens*. So can merchants, who have belonged uninterruptedly for ten years to the first, and for twenty to the second guild. Any one who has obtained the diploma of doctor or of master from any of the Russian Universities, can petition the government to be included in the class of hereditary respectable citizens; artists and special pupils of the Academy of Arts, have also this right on presenting their diploma of membership. Foreigners living in Russia, if they are savans, artists, merchants, or owners of extensive manufacturing establishments, if they become Russian subjects and have already belonged for ten years to the class of personal respectable citizens, have the right to petition for admission into the hereditary class of the same title. The rights and privileges of respectable citizens consist in liberating them from the capitation tax, *poduschnoë*, from the recruitment, from corporal punishment by either civil or military judgment, from having their head shaved during arrest and pending trial. All the rest of the bourgeoisie, in criminal as well as in police affairs, are subject to personal punishment, inflicted by rods, *palki*, or the cat-o'-nine-tails, *pletnia*.

Below the bourgeoisie with all the above enumerated subdivisions and various special corporations, from that of the merchants, down to that of the workmen, there exists a still inferior class called that of the suburban inhabitants, not separately incorporated, but administered

7

by the boards of the city to which they belong. It is composed, principally of agriculturists or day laborers, who thus form the last link between the bourgeoisie and the peasants. All other persons living in any city by special permission, and devoted to trade, or artisans, are called simply inhabitants or citizens, *zytel*, *obywatel*, from *bywat*, to frequent.

This is a condensed outline of the legal and social position of the Russian bourgeoisie. In surveying the whole, some more minute and less interesting details have been omitted. Being a distinct body, the bourgeoisie form their own boards or committees of internal administration. But these committees are under the direction of the government, exercised by the governor of the county, by the chief of police, who is generally a resigned military officer, and in judicial affairs, by the government attorney and his assistants, *striaptschi*. The recorder of the triennial meetings is elective. By the nature of the above enumerated divisions, into which the inhabitants of every municipal community are cut up, and as a result of the existing numerous classes and of the minute definitions of the position and of the rights of each—from all this arises the obligation to keep up a kind of precise heraldic record for each special corporation, nay, even for each family; and such a recorder, called *starost* or elder, is elected by the community. The inhabitants of the larger cities elect for their internal administration of justice, a kind of arbiter, as well as judges in each ward; likewise a board for directing and distributing the quarters for garrisoned or transient soldiers. In such cities there are architectural boards, elected for directing the construction of new houses; guardians and superintendents of public municipal buildings, as well as of private ones. Further, there are members and directors of the establishments of public credit and of banks, where they exist. Thus, for example, in Petersburg, there being a special commercial bank, issuing bills, its operations are directed by a special board elected by the merchant class, but presided over by a nominee of the government. In large commercial cities, special commercial tribunals are likewise elected, as are the members of the boards of quarantine, brokers, notaries public, auctioneers, assayers, and, in Petersburg, a committee to direct and watch over the public exchange; there is, however, not much jobbing, as foreign stocks are prohibited from being quoted, and the domestic ones are not so numerous and fluctuating as to attract and stir up the gambling passion. The operations on the exchange are, for the most part, purely commercial.

In all these general as well as special elections, nobles owning houses in cities, which they generally do, but not inscribed in the guilds, can participate only by fulfilling the formality of entering one of the guilds, and then they can be elected to any office within the range of the bourgeoisie. But no public functionaries of the government, even if owners of houses, can be elected to any municipal office. In this sort of official contact with the noblese the bourgeoisie maintains its ground rather proudly and haughtily. As the class of citizens are not admitted to enjoy any right or privilege of the nobility, and cannot meet the nobility any where on equal footing, they do not feel at all honored, as do generally the bourgeoisie of other countries, by this participation of the nobles in the special rights reserved to the burghers. Accordingly, though a nobleman may have the right to be elected to a municipal office, he is pretty sure to fail in his attempt. Such things have been tried, and almost always unsuccessfully. Even in St. Petersburg, under the immediate pressure of the supreme government, nay, even under that of the personal interference of the Emperor, exerted to secure the election for the municipal board of a Naryschkine one for the grandees of Russia, and a distant relation of the Imperial family—as the mother of Peter the Great was a Naryschkine—the bourgeoisie resisted, all answering directly in the face of the sovereign, " That as the nobility did not admit them, they would not admit the nobility."

In all these internal elections for jurisdiction and administration, the exclusion from any participation in the general government, or any common action with a superior class, is strictly maintained. The bourgeoisie are surrounded with a fence which they cannot legally pass. In one case only the bourgeoisie partly participate beyond this circumscription, and in an official capacity thus meets the nobility. It is in the *partial* administration of civil and criminal justice. The first Judicial Courts are composed, as we have shown, of specially elected municipal magistrates. The second, or Courts of Appeals, are the tribunals in each county, formed from members elected by the nobility. To each of these tribunals, the citizen bürghers of the city where the tribunal is situated, elect one member to the civil and another to the criminal jurisdiction.

This is the only case where the bourgeoisie reach beyond the borders of a close corporation, and participate in something legally superior. But not even in this case are they put on equal ground with the higher class. Each of the tribunals is composed of a president and of three members elected by the nobility—of a vice-president and a recorder, named by the government, both of whom are of course, noblemen. To them is added one burgher only, and one free peasant, both of whom have scarcely a voice in the council when the pending suit does not concern any member of their own class.

The above succinct sketch of the various shades and subdivisions into which the Russian bourgeoisie are divided, is sufficient to give an idea how complicated, circumscribed and cut up in parcels, how cramped and surrounded with iron bonds, is this numerous and eminent body in the Russian social order. Obstructed in any free movement, heavily chained by laws based on the spirit of caste, they can by no means move onwards, but are forced to labor for ever in the same arena as in a tread-mill, fettered perpetually to the same spot. If the citizen burgher wishes to change his legal domicil, to remove his establishment from one city or region to another, he is obliged to go through the narrow pass of various oppressive formalities. Impediments meet him at every footstep; permission, assent, admission—there is nothing like freedom. With the exception of a very small number among the whole, who reach the region of special privileges, the vast majority of this class, are by the law of caste, almost absolutely prevented from giving a substantial, mental and intellectual development to their children by a thorough education. The impediments thrown in their way extend almost equally to both sexes. Thus woman may be said to be subjected to a mental stupor. The limitations, or rather exclusion by the law of the male from the pale of higher culture and attainments, so penetrate and pervade the customs and the practice in common domestic life, as to cast a heavy and lifeless cloud around the household hearth. In the primary or elementary common schools, established in large cities, districts, towns, and smaller boroughs, the teaching is limited to the first rudiments, such as reading, writing, arithmetic, and occasionally to burning incense at the altar of Czarism. In such schools the girls of the burghers can be taught. But there is no possibility of any further education, no opening whatever for an onward progress. With the exception of St. Petersburg, Moscow, Odessa, and a few other cities, there exists no public boarding-schools where young girls can be instructed. St. Petersburg, Moscow, and some other places have large establishments, where the daughters of the nobility are brought up and educated, or at least varnished. These establishments are under the superintendence of the Empress, and of the great ladies of the Court. For admission therein, the daughters of military and civil officers and their orphans have the precedence over others. The great number of the daughters of nobles receive their education at home, by the means of private governesses, who, by the law, are subject to the ministry of public instruction, and are to be licensed by it. Wealthy burghers resort sometimes to the same expedient for educating their children—but it is as a drop of water in the ocean. The great bulk have within their reach no resources for becoming educated. They can find around them no remedy for this evil. The government holds all in its grasp, and regards it as an axiom, "that the higher branches of education are not only unnecessary, but a nuisance to this class." Thus for the children of common burghers, neither high schools nor universities are accessible. They are doomed to eternal intellectual depression and ignorance. And even if by receiving elementary instruction, they are, so to say, put in the possession of the keys to the sanctuary, still no kernel, no pure seed, is planted in the youthful mind; no corner stone is laid by thorough mental discipline, and by really beneficial studies. Thus reading in after life is limited to indifferent if not bad works, and to a few national poets. The press, crushed as it is, cannot exercise any beneficial stimulus on the general spirit. There is no impulsion from within, as there is no attraction exercised from without. No craving for diversified knowledge, or even information, there being no arena in which to display the acquired powers, no congenial atmosphere to breathe, to live in. A dull, leaden pressure grinds and destroys every intellectual germ. No career opens freely, easily, before the burgher, even if well educated, even if his intellect be well stored with knowledge, science, acquirements. Thus the higher powers of mind, if even laboriously developed by him, cannot be freely exercised; and if accidentally they find a sphere, very soon they become productive only of disappointment, mortification, disgust with the existing state of things, and finally they open to him the road to Siberia alone. All these reasons account for the still apparent indifference of the great number of men and women, of fathers and mothers, of the class of the bourgeoisie, as to the mental improvements and accomplishments in their children. By the unavoidable influence of caste, and of the governmental legal impediments and restrictions, which are transfused, helplessly for the present, into the national manners and notions of every-day life, the sober judgment becomes altered, perverted, and higher studies are looked on rather as a heavy burden, and a nuisance in the smooth current of existence by those from among the body of citizens who might be devoted to them. Such persons lose ground on their own special soil, without being able to ascend easily, or pass over to another higher one. Unhappily, this apathy is fostered not only by the action of the government, but very often by the influence of the numerous white and black clergy, or monks and priests—an influence quite preponderating over the burghers.

Few, very few at present, can shake off these leaden weights thus heaped upon them; and very few are actuated strongly enough by an inward energy, to devote their time to mental acquisitions.

Thus the so-called self-made men are extraordinary apparitions in Russia, and very few names break through the gloom and shine in the records of the national literature. Such a name, for example, is now that of Polevoï, who, being by trade a bookseller in Moscow, devoted his time to studies, to national historical researches, whose result was not quite orthodox concerning Czarism, the privileges of the nobility, the oppression of the burghers, the establishment and the legality of serfdom. Aside from this, he edited one of the best periodicals in Russia, and shunned not to open its columns to more daring spirits, nor, as far as his means allowed, to stand by young, enterprising and spirited writers. As a literary man and historian, he was attacked by more orthodox writers, principally by those of St. Petersburg, influenced by their contact with the ruling power and with the aristocracy. Caution and even silence was advised by the police, and finally as a business man he was ruined, by standing nearly alone among his class. Not, however, that the citizen burghers turned against him. They only mistrusted his capacity for business, diverted as were his thoughts by higher and different pursuits.

From these facts we ought, however, not to conclude that the Russian bourgeoisie are wholly dulled as to the value of mental superiority. Bereaved of the possibility of finding from it any immediate benefit for themselves, they notwithstanding feel and recognize its worth in others. Thus, professors of universities—above all if Russians by birth and in genuine Russian cities, such as Moscow. Charkoff, Kasan and Kiiow—are generally surrounded with respect, and enjoy great consideration among the citizens, wealthy or poor. There they exert an influence upon the bourgeoisie unequalled by that in any cities of other countries. These Professors might easily make themselves the absolute masters of public opinion, as far at least as concerns the less privileged classes, the burghers, and the people. And this above all is the case in Moscow. The bourgeoisie in Moscow and in the other cities of the interior named above, are likewise imbued to a great extent with national panslavistic ideas. All this forms a consolatory indication for the future.

In any legal action, in the pursuits of business as well as in the intellectual pursuits, wherever a burgher turns his path or directs his views or aspirations, he is swaddled in restrictions which affect his mind, his body, his way of life. The thorny barrier of privilege bristles in his path, staring fiendishly at him. By every action, by every movement, by every pulse of time, he is rudely reminded of his humiliating subjection, not only to Czarism and its minions who manipulate the reins of government, but also to the nobility.

By nature active and industrious, and thrown by the social organization into an exclusive area, reduced, so to say, to a special pursuit in life—it would appear that the Russian burgher has before him inexhaustible means for increasing his wealth, and for bettering his condition. Undoubtedly, a very large amount of accumulated or moneyed capital is possessed by the middle classes. But in proportion to the vitality and the impulse which a free use of this capital could give to the internal movement and the development of the inexhaustible resources of the country: most of these invigorating sources once accumulated by individuals, remain barren to a great extent in their hands when compared with their large amount.

The same impediments, surrounding as they do, the every-day life of the burgher, prevent the free use of the means at his disposal. Whatever he undertakes, a concession, a license, a permission is necessary. Every commercial and manufacturing enterprise brings him continually in contact with the officials, and he has good reasons to avoid the like conjunctions. No real liberty exists for this class, even in the exercise of occupations to which it is exclusively reduced. In every respect the burgher is either tutored, lead by a string, or carefully watched over. When in a legal or commercial business he falls into the hands of functionaries, high or low, he is considered as a fair prize, as a pigeon to be plucked to the last feather. The law obliges him to petition to different authorities if he wishes to pass from an inferior to a superior corporation. But if such obligatory petition is not backed by a greater or less gratification to the referees, all will be useless to the applicant: even when he has right on his side. For every step in his business or his career, the burgher is obliged to secure patronage, paying a higher and higher price for it. This is not all. Wo to the enterprising and wealthy man,—whose activity and extension of business brings him, in various respects, into contact with these governmental birds of prey. It is useless for him to try to escape their clutches. The greater the wealth, the larger the enterprise, the more will he be fleeced. If he contracts for any work connected with the government, as construction of public buildings, roads, farming of spiritual liquors, or the furnishing the army or navy: he is obliged to divide his profits with the greedy jackals around him—happy if he escape with a whole skin—if he be not entirely ruined. Hence springs up a mistrust, crippling any large enterprise, the more so where the government assumes the direction or co-acts, as in railroads, steamboats, etc.; the burgher, the capitalist shuns all these generally. In this manner, notwithstanding the moneyed wealth accumulated in the empire, which is far more than sufficient to construct railroads in various directions, foreign loans are necessary, as the home capitalist has no wish to share in an enterprise where the government is the exclusive manager. There is no country where the construction of railroads could be made cheaper than in Russia. For there are few, if any, considerable inequalities of the ground, the land is cheap, indeed may be had nearly for nothing, the wages too, are low, and the masses of the army are able to supply thousands and thousands of good laborers. And yet, after all, there is but one line finished as yet, and that, too, at an immense cost—as it was worked nearly twice over—the levellings and embankments having broken down the first time.

Foreigners, travellers, writers, seeing how little is done, and being unable to account for the cause, discern only the busy government intermeddling with every thing; they take the glitter for a reality, praise the despotism, accuse the nation of inactivity, and slander the people.

But notwithstanding all the numerous difficulties mentioned above, the Russian burgher has still acquired wealth. He has reached the most elevated summits granted to his class. Another still higher range of privilege rises before him, and impedes the free use of his wealth in nearly every direction. He cannot own and purchase landed estates with serfs. Without them the land is nearly worthless, as the population has not reached that degree to supply hands for all uncultivated lands. In Russia as in all old countries, landed estates are represented by villages together with the inhabitants, the peasants. Thus burghers cannot possess villages. Such absolute exclusion of the capitalist keeps down the value of estates, and hurts agriculture. Generally no fresh capital pours into its channel; no invigorating industry renovates the old, coarse routine. The exclusion, too, of burghers from possessing villages is not limited to Russia proper. The German or Baltic provinces are in the same condition, and here it is the work of the nobility without any interference on the part of the Russian government. Notwithstanding that for nearly half a century serfdom was abolished by Alexander in these provinces—the burgher cannot yet acquire landed estates, called manored (Germanice Rittergut). The nobility appeal to the Russian law to strengthen the ancient feudal privileges, and so exclude the burghers, even of common German descent. In Poland no such exclusion or limitation exists, burghers or peasants can own manors and villages.

Just in the same way as the Russian burgher is prevented from using his wealth for acquiring landed property, he cannot use it to bestow upon his children a thorough education—with a few privileged exceptions. These cases have been already enumerated. Deprived of this advantage at home, he even cannot seek it for them abroad. The law prohibits the burgher from travelling into foreign countries without a permission, which is seldom granted and only for commercial affairs, or on account of health. Besides, an education received abroad is generally a disqualification for a public career at home, and to a son of a burgher this would be more rigidly applied than to that of a nobleman.

But even in the city where he lives, the burgher cannot gratify all his tastes. A species of sumptuary law regulates his expenditure. Burghers or their families are not allowed to use carriages with two horses, but only to drive them with one. To be sure this is not strictly enforced, and at least the wives and daughters use a carriage and pair; but to be able to enjoy this luxury they must be on good terms with the police, and pay for it.

As a trader, or engaged in any business whatever, the Russian is active, shrewd and cunning—a match for any. The intellectual powers of the whole people are acute, and would be more so if they could enjoy fair play, and a field could be thrown open to them where they would enjoy liberty and education. But mind and intellect are depressed and confined as well as the social position. Any enterprise or invention must pass through the governmental seive. Another warping influence is the impossibility of free intercourse and communication with the civilized world beyond the frontiers of Russia. For centuries the Russian people, through their geographical position, were secluded from contact with other nations. Their immediate neighbors were the Poles and Turks, enemies, and, to a certain extent, even inferiors in every stage of culture. Hence arose in the minds of the Russian people partly a contempt for innovations coming from abroad through hirelings, and partly an aversion towards foreigners. This feeling is now beginning to die out slowly, but still there prevails a morbid love of old routine, nourished somewhat by conceit, and somewhat by laziness.

The government dexterously avails itself of this predisposition, fostering it equally by laws and flattery, and encouraging mistrust, principally when it concerns Europe or the West. With Asia the Russian trader of every class entertains a direct and unlimited personal intercourse. The great exporting trade to Europe is principally in the hands of foreigners, above all Englishmen, Dutch and Germans; in the south, in Odessa, in those of Italians, Greeks, Armenians and Jews. It is not probable indeed that there exists a single autochtone Russian house carrying on a trade directly with foreign countries, or having branches out of Russia. Raw produce, as for example hides, grain, tallow, hemp, linen, timber, etc., is bought in the interior by Russian traders from noblemen, peasants and nomads. Agents from Russian houses in seaports travel sometimes into the interior, but principally merchants of Moscow, Astrachan, Pazan, Nijuee-Novgorod, etc., buy, store, and bring the merchandise finally to the seaports, as St. Petersburg, Riga, Odessa, where it is sold to Russian wholesale dealers for cash, bills of exchange or credit being rather unusual in internal trade. The exporter, the foreigner, then steps in, and purchases, so to say, at the third or fourth hand. This explains the reason why the Russian merchant-shipping is nearly imperceptible.

The absence of credit in all mercantile operations is the result of an imperfect understanding, or rather false conception, of its real beneficial nature, as well as of the distorted state of society. Mistrust and suspicion prevail all over, and penetrate every social crevice. Unfortunately absolute mercantile honesty is not a prominent feature with the Russian merchant. But he may be excused, since he does not see it prevail any where around or above him. He acts on the defensive, and enjoys as heartily as that whole class throughout the world, to *take in* others, or, as says the Russian, *naduti*. But this bad faith has not found root in the national character, it is on the surface, generated by the corruption flowing from the classes above him. A general opinion prevails that it is difficult to trade with Russians. Peter the Great commemorated it on the following occasion. It must be mentioned first, however, that the Jews never were, and even now are not allowed to settle in Old Russia, or Russia Proper, that is the parts forming the empire previous to conquests and annexations made by Peter and his successors. They can individually, however, sojourn in cities or boroughs for some time, as workmen, artisans, or mechanics, but this only by a special permission, and when no objection is made by the Christian community or any of its members. But they are not permitted to carry on trade.

During the stay of Peter in Holland, the municipality of Amsterdam requested, as a special favor, that he would allow the Jews to settle in his domains. He refused, saying, "*My beloved Russians are too smart, and would strip the Jews of every cent!*"

As artisan, mechanic, or workman, the Russian discovers, when in good earnest, great skill, as well in finish as in delicacy of workmanship. At the recent exposition in London there was sufficient evidence of this. Still it is asserted that the powers of the Russian intellect are rather imitative than creative; that the Russians have no claims to originality; in one word, that they are apt only to copy and learn from others. Should this really be the case, then the reason ought to be looked for, not in any natural deficiency, but in the accursed tutorship of the government. Permission must be obtained before any one can become creator or inventor. And this can be no stimulant to excite the mental powers, and so inspire a healthful activity. Another reproach is more justifiable, the one accusing the Russian artisans of not bestowing generally any very minute accuracy on their work. This want of exactness is a fitting result from the darkness in which the people are kept, which has ultimately become, so to say, a chronic mental disease, a kind of fatalistic prejudice. *Kak ni bud*, "in any way whatever;" and *awos paydot*, "maybe it will succeed;" are the two sacramental phrases with which the Russian undertakes any work. But we do not wish to say that the Russian mechanic or artisan, when pride, self-love, or interest are at stake, is unfit to finish any work he takes in hand, with matchless accuracy.

The carelessness referred to is alleged as an excuse by the government for introducing numerous foreigners, above all, for the construction of all kinds of machines. But is the education of a Russian artisan or mechanic fostered in any way? Are his natural abilities aided or developed by any scientific method whatever? The fault lies exclusively in the social state, and in the government keeping all in its own grasp—cutting off every means for a real education of the people. Further: foreign contractors, if called into the country by a special arrangement with the government to construct extensive works, do not become so easy a prey to the myriads of lower officials, who ruin the domestic contractor by obliging him to perform the job cheaply, and *kak ni bud*, for the sake of increasing the profits to be divided by them in common, conniving thus to cheat the government which they serve. Let there be the pure atmosphere of freedom, and Russian industry becomes at once creative, Russian contractors honest, while the native workman and mechanic will perfect and improve his workmanship.

In proportion to the population of the empire the bourgeoisie, with all its subdivisions, is rather inconsiderable. Cities and towns are scattered rather sparingly through the extensive country, and with few exceptions they are neither large nor densely populated. In the principal cities, as Petersburg, Moscow, Odessa, and a few others more, there is a very large number of floating population, composed of peasants and serfs. The class of real incorporated burghers, at the utmost, amounts to but few millions in Great Russia, or Russia Proper. It contains, however, the kernel of national growth and development, and in the future this may become the focus, or at least a powerful engine, in the work of national disenthralment. At present this class is sufficiently oppressed to aspire for liberty, and in common with the peasants to find their actual state unbearable. Without being normally educated, it possesses an intuitive perception of the necessity of a change for the better. It is easy to comprehend how the burgher must be dissatisfied with his actual position. True it is, that oppression protracted for centuries is eventually transformed into a chronic disease, to which the organism ultimately gets accustomed. It is like an excrescence on the body, which, though borne for a long time with patience, finally becomes painful, and the organism and the individual consequently tries to extirpate or to get rid of it.

The wealth of the burghers increases continually, and at the same time their consciousness of oppression. The more actively they move in their special and contracted arena, the oftener they are hurt by running against the iron fence. Thus the elements of discontent accumulate, which must finally explode.

In their domestic mode of life, the bourgeoisie cherish all old national traditions, clinging to ancient customs and manners. Few changes or modifications penetrate to the domestic hearth. Even in the dress of both sexes, the woman with her *sarafan*, a kind of long gown, and the men with their *kaftan*, a long, broad overcoat, are still to be seen amongst the wealthiest. The girls until marriage wear their hair in long tresses, cutting them off at the wedding-day; an ancient bridal ceremony prevailing through every class of the people, and accompanied by moving farewell songs addressed to the bride by her former companions.

The men wear a beard, an ancient and still maintained national fashion. The great luxury in which the burghers rejoice is the possession of rich brocade, jewelry, pearls, and precious stones for the use of the women, and to adorn the holy images suspended in their dwellings, in their counting-rooms and shops, as well as in the display of rich, heavy silver plate.

It was mentioned in one of the foregoing chapters that the clergy of both kinds live on the most intimate footing with the burghers, and the reasons and the nature of its influence over burghers and peasants have been explained.

One of the characteristics of the bourgeoisie is the *esprit de corps* that animates it more intensely than in the nobility, and for obvious reasons. Excluded generally from the public service, the burgher has no favors to ask of the government, who, on account of the wealth possessed by this class, must, after all, be on good terms with it. Accustomed as the bourgeoisie is to extortions, still when sometimes the measure is overdone, and a member is too deeply wronged and ill-treated, the corporations of cities, as Moscow, Petersburg, etc., will rise on his behalf, and oblige the government, or the men in power, to come to terms. The nobility, as a body, can never make such a demonstration of independence.

The bourgeoisie, the population of cities, are very sensible to national glory; not only to that won on battle-fields, but to that purer and loftier one, acquired by the higher order of accomplishments of the mind. If the bourgeoisie, the people, are forcibly excluded from contributing to literary distinction, they render nevertheless a most hearty homage to individuals and names ranking high as such. It has already been mentioned with what deference the people treat the various professors. *Pouschkine*, the great poet, was popular and beloved by the burghers equally as much, and perhaps more than any other man would have been who had become eminent through military renown. When he was killed in a duel by the hand of a French adventurer, in consequence of a shameless scandal perpetrated by the court and courtiers ——, his death, as a national calamity, was mourned by the whole city population, more perhaps than even by some of the higher classes. In Petersburg, where the bloody event took place, the popular exasperation was such that the hackdrivers refused to attend any individual in whose pronunciation they could detect a foreign accent. Without the interference of the police it would have been worse. To avoid a demonstration, the body of the poet was sent out at night, as quietly and secretly as possible, to the country, to his family burial-place. If this tragical event with its aggravating circumstances had occurred in Moscow, the signs of grief would have been more violent, more dangerous for the public tranquillity, for the court, and even for the Czar.

Whatever may be his love of making money, the Russian bourgeois, rich merchant or poor shopkeeper as he may be, is not generally so debased as the corresponding class in other European countries, ready to sacrifice liberty, and often even fatherland, for the sake of saving the business or the shop. No such narrow egotism is to be found among the trading classes of Russia. In case of hostile invasion they would not hesitate for a moment to destroy houses and goods rather than to see them pass into the hands of enemies. The drama of Moscow, in 1812, would be cheerfully repeated throughout the whole country, and every city would be turned into ashes by the act of her own inhabitants. The same devotion will inspire them when the hour of disenthralment shall be pointed out on the dial of time, when the mysterious sound of the belfry of the ancient *wietsowoi kolokol* shall clang again, rousing the people, and calling it together at the national forum to fight out the battle of freedom. No bourgeois will shun the sacred combat, but will dash into it. Although never initiated into the conspiracy of 1825, the population of Petersburg rallied in great numbers, and if the conspirators had acted promptly, popular support would not have been wanting. And the population of Petersburg has more of the shopkeeper spirit than any other Russian city—its only tradition is servitude. The genuine Russian cities have old traditions of the forum called *wietse* or *wietsche*. In the ancient republics of Novgorod and Pskoff, as well as in other cities, the burgher was accustomed to hear the belfry send forth its summons to shut up his shop, to appear for deliberation, or armed with the axe and the pike prepare for defence. The powerful *chime* of the national *kolokol* is now hushed by despotism, but the tradition still clangs through the memory of the people as lively as ever. It may be mentioned here that the use of bells was introduced into Russia from Byzantium at a very early period, and very likely the belfry of Novgorod was older than those which roused the communes of the western world, not excepting even Italy and Spain. Once again the *kolokol* will shake the air, and the Russian burgher will break the manacles from his hands.

We do not mean to say that Czarism has lost its hold over the national feelings, and become generally less popular with the burghers. Unhappily it is not yet so. Its historical roots are loosened, but still hold on. Decay, however, has commenced, or is at hand. The burgher and the people were wont to consider Czarism as their lifegiving sun, as a shield against the nobility. Czarism was never really such an ægis, but oppressing all, it made the people believe that it served to check the noblesse. But now the burgher begins to see through all this, and and to know better. He has discovered that Czarism is principally propped up by the nobles, and for their sake curtails the rights of the people and the bourgeoisie. The ukases published during the last fifteen years have contributed to disperse the mist. Czarism, through the unavoidable pressure of events, must daily become more restrictive, tightening the knot more and more, and in the same proportion the fascination exercised over the feelings of the nation will die out and vanish.

The official legal relations between the nobility and the bourgeoisie have been explained. The one oppresses the other in a twofold way; as the privileged class, and as exclusive office holder. The two classes never associate, less even in private and social, than in public or official life. A broad chasm separates them. Only the very numerous class of lower officials is in social intercourse with the burghers, and even this seldom on an intimate footing, but at feasts and ostentatious entertainments.

In general the bourgeoisie hate and rather despise the nobility than envy it. It seems that if the bourgeoisie felt the consciousness of their strengh and future. Contrary to the habits of the bourgeoisie of all other countries, the Russian does not run, seek after and covet acquaintance, intimacy and close family connection with the nobility. This occurs seldom and is rather exceptional. The bourgeoisie holds itself aloof, and is calm and rather menacing than fidgety, humble and insinuating. It does not struggle for admission into the ranks which, sooner or later, must disappear before the popular pressure.

In the same way as the body of the Russian bourgeoisie never aspire for nobiliar distinctions, it has not the leanings of what is called the *tiers-état* middle class, whose character has revealed itself in the political conflicts of modern times. The Russian bourgeoisie has not the purse-proud and egotistical demeanor, nor the shopkeeper meanness to be found elsewhere. If it forms legally a distinct class from the people below it, it is rather forced into this position, and has not taken it by free choice. The legal denomination of burgher or merchant *Kupets* is imposed by law. By choice they prefer the denomination of *grajdanin* citizen, which is general and not specific, applicable to the nobleman as to the peasant.

Never a toady to the nobility, the Russian bourgeoisie differs likewise from this class in other nations, in its behavior towards the peasants and the people. Throughout almost the whole of Europe there prevails a strongly marked antagonism between the city and the country, between the bourgeois and the peasantry. Every where the bourgeois has used, and uses the people as a stepping-stone to swing himself into the higher regions of privilege. As capitalists, speculators, manufacturers or land owners, they are as oppressive as ever the nobility could be. In proportion as their wealth and respectability increase, their first effort is to brush off all signs of connection with the people, or at least to conceal them. They try to appear different from those among whom they started, and to ape as much as possible those toward whom they approach. And such *parvenus* in Europe, look down on the peasant with as much contempt as could a silly nobleman. There exists no connection, no similitude between the burgher, the workman, and the peasant, either in customs, manners, mode of life, external appearance of dress or in any other characteristic. A large gap separates them entirely. But not so in Russia. Here the two classes forming the real nation resemble each other, in all wherein they are so different in other countries. Rich and poor, burghers, workmen and peasants use the same mode of life, observe the same old national manners, customs and usages. The dishes at their meals are nearly alike, as are the dress of both sexes and their external deportment. Exceptions are rare and on the whole insignificant. The distinction in dress is not in cut or fashion, but in the quality of the material. Socially, both burghers and peasants groan under the same oppression, which strengthens the existing ties of nationality. Both entertain a common hatred against the nobility, or at least are inspired with an insurmountable mistrust in it. The relations between burgher and peasant are on the most intimate and cordial footing. They address each other by the christian name, without adding the intitulation of Sir or Master. Generally it is customary throughout all classes of Russian society to address in the same way. For example, *Nicolaï Pawlowitsch* Nicolas Paul's son, the termination *witsch* giving the last signification. Even the Emperor in the course of a conversation could be addressed in this manner without any offence. When the lower classes speak to one above them, they add to it the title of birth or of office, but more generally the name of father, *baïtiuschka*, *otets*.

The law prohibiting burghers to own serfs, eminently cements the good understanding which exists between the burgher and the peasant. Disabled from following in the track of the nobility, from becoming a master and oppressor of the peasant, the bourgeois is preserved from falling into the common sin of the *parvenu*, and so they remain on good terms.

Moscow ranks foremost among all the cities exercising a powerful influence over the rural populations. Not through the nobility established there, but through the burghers, and thus Moscow is in every respect the heart of Russia. Along the Wolga extend the best parts of the empire, and their inhabitants are the most active, intelligent, enterprising The locality of Moscow, distant some way from this river, is still, however, in its line. The city is, in the feelings of the people, the mother, the white, the brilliant, *swietlaia bielaia matuschka.* Moscow has her own traditions of good and evil, traditions historical, and deeply intertwined with the existence of the nation. Moscow has a genuine population of her own, whereas Petersburg has no tradition except the will of despotism, and a population accidentally agglomerated with an immense military force, and swarms of officials, clerks, etc. Moscow is the centre of internal trade and industry, as the principal manufactories are established there. The country around Moscow is the most densely populated, the peasants, free or serfs, are the wealthiest, and are in their turn artisans, traders, and even manufacturers, and thus in a continual and intimate intercourse with the inhabitants of the capital. Every pulsation of Moscow acts intensely on the surrounding villages and districts, and extends itself in wider and wider circles. The population of Moscow is spirited, and breathes its spirit into the country. This spirit contains to-day indiscernible elements which may soon transform themselves into tornadoes. Moscow has impulses of independence, and shows them from time to time, if not as yet by explosions, certainly by grumblings which startle at times Czarism in its fastnesses of Petersburg. For this reason the emperors always try to be on good terms with the population of Moscow, pampering it during their visits to this second capital, haughty as is their bearing with the other classes.

The burghers form with the peasants a dense unit through the whole empire, whatever may be the artificial classifications dividing them. This mass is opposed and averse to nobility. Thus the Russian burgher is not a *middle class* uniting two extremes. He belongs wholly to the people, to its holy cause. One cannot err in asserting that in any future attempts or struggles for regeneration, the Russian bourgeoisie will stand foremost, strengthening and not palsying the efforts for a large and radical emancipation.

CHAPTER VIII.

THE COSSACKS.

THE population of the Cossacks once formed an independent sovereignty, parts of them, as for example, those of Little Russia, recognizing ever since the XVIth century, the Polish Republic and her king as lord paramount. In their organization, at the commencement exclusively military, the principle of equality absolutely prevailed. As their power extended, that is, when they spread over the lands surrounding their primitive cradle and at that time not subjected to any special dominion—lands known now as Little Russia, they were ruled by free institutions. At the present day they form still an exceptional population, and however deprived of ancient freedom, their position is far above that of the free peasantry.

The positive origin of the Cossacks dates, according to all probability, from the time when southern Russia was overflowed with Tartars, in the XIIIth century, when the capital was transferred from Kiïeff farther north, and the greatest part of Little Russia abandoned to her fate. It may be perchance, however, that previous to that epoch, even centuries before it indeed, in these extensive and unsettled regions, the highway of the inroads of Asiatic tribes, bands made up of all kinds of runaways, existed for self-defence and robbery, over which the power of the Grand Dukes of Kiïeff could not really extend. Notwithstanding that the Cossacks of the Dnieper alone have a positive historical existence, it is most probable that the other separate bands were formed on the Don, along the frontiers of the region held by the Tartars, on the Wolga, then crossing afterwards to Asia, formed there the Cossacks of the Ural, and afterwards those of Siberia. The resistance to the Tartars was their principal aim, and this justifies the assumption that they have been formed every where from the aboriginal, or Slavic and Christian population. Those of the Dnieper or of Little Russia recognized, as was already mentioned, the protectorate of Poland; those of more distant regions fell under the dominion of Russia, after she had broken down the Tartar supremacy. All of them being, originally, rather wandering, restless bands of horsemen, this fact excluded marriage in their primitive organization; they recruited themselves from among fugitives, outlaws and vagabonds of all kinds. When they grew stronger, and their natural enemies, the Tartars weaker, when they began to possess power and dominion over the lands and regions, where previously they roved only, then they mixed with the population and introduced among themselves marriage and the other results of a more settled life. Still for a long time afterwards, however, celibacy was regarded as a virtue in a perfect Cossack hero, since his calling was an uninterrupted warfare—and thus no other softer ties ought to obtain possession of the heart, or the mind of a true Cossack. A kind of chivalrous love consequently runs through the ancient popular songs of these regions. The Cossacks of Little Russia or of the Dnieper became very powerful; extended their inroads and depredations by descending the river in their small flat boats and entering the Euxine, they ravaged the Turkish shores. The fires of their incursions could often have been seen from the Sultan's seraglio, since they sometimes even burnt the suburbs of Constantinople. To fortify themselves against the Padishah's revenge, they submitted to the protectorate of Poland, then the sole great power not only among the Slavic race, but in the whole of Europe, which was continually victorious over the Turks. They were very devoted to Poland, and formed one of the sinews of her strength, principally in the defence of the southern frontiers. In the beginning of the XVIIth century the Cossacks eminently contributed to establish the brief dominion of Poland over Russia. They were, however, devoted to the Slavic or Graeco-Eastern Church, and when the Jesuits crept into Poland, becoming in a very short time influential over the national spirit and counsels, a religious persecution began to be directed against the devoted Cossacks, which alienated them from their protectors. In the first half of the XVIIth century, Wladislas Waza, the last Polish king, of eminent statesmanlike qualities, who, wishing to curb the reckless spirit of the Polish nobility by the rule of law and of discipline, made a secret treaty with Bogdan Chmielnicki the Attaman or chief of the Cossacks of Little Russia; in virtue of which the Cossacks were to support the king in his projects, and the Attaman was to become a Waievode of Kiïeff, and thus have a permanent seat in the Polish upper house or the Senate, and the Greek or rather Slavic bishops were likewise to be put on equal footing with the Catholics, and have a place among the Polish and Roman Catholic bishops and senators. But the king died before the execution of this scheme, and the wrath of the nobility and of the Jesuits together turned against the unhappy Cossacks. A bloody war began, almost a war of extermination. Chmielnicki, often victorious, demanded only from Poland the confirmation of what had been promised and granted to him by the deceased King Wladislas. But vainly he tried to settle the struggle in a pacific manner; finally he invoked the assistance of Russia, by recognizing her protectorate, and the Cossacks opened the doors of Poland to the invasion of Ragotsy with his swarms of Magyars, Wallachians, and Transylvanians. Poland on the north was submerged by the Swedes, in consequence of a war likewise resulting from the instigation of the Jesuits and of their ally the house of Austria; —and the victorious Ragotsy at that epoch—the second half of the XVIIth century—projected its partition. The hostilities with the Cossacks, the unyielding and unrelenting spirit of religious persecution; had already brought Poland to the verge of destruction. After the death of the Attaman Chmielnicki, part of the Cossacks under his son submitted to Russia; the other part remained still faithful to the Polish republic. The war was continued with unabated fury. Sobieski, King of Poland, abandoned by a treaty to Russia, the left bank of the Dnieper, together with the palatinate and the city of Kiieff and several other places. It was the first time since her historical existence that Poland had lost ground before Russia. The right bank of the Dnieper, with the remains of the Cossacks and the population of the Slavic creed settled there, became a prey to the persecuting fury of the Jesuits and the nobility. Instead of their ancient devotion, deep hatred filled the minds and the hearts of the inhabitants of Little Russia. Sobieski's reign was distinguished by cruel and refined executions.

The nobility and clergy raged amongst the populations, and the house of the Polish noble Potocki, the most powerful in those desolate regions, distinguished itself by its unrelenting ferocity. In the portion which had submitted to Russia, the Attaman Mazeppa in the beginning of the XVIIIth century, aimed at reconquering its ancient independence with the aid of Charles XII. of Sweden, and that of Stanislas Leschtschynski, momentarily king of Poland. Mazeppa's project was to reunite the whole of Little Russia, and erect there a wholly independent kingdom. He fell; and with him the dreams of independence were extinguished in blood. Peter I. transplanted great numbers of the Cossacks, partisans of Mazeppa, to the Don, and generally curtailed their ancient liberties. The liberties of the Cossacks remaining under the Polish dominion were almost wholly destroyed. For the most part they became the enslaved property of the Polish nobility—their religion was trampled down, the priest (the *pop*) became subordinate to the Jew—the overseer, attorney, *alter ego*, of a Polish nobleman. Partial insurrections broke out, and the most bloody was that known as the one of Human, a place belonging to the Potockis. The infuriated people murdered nobles, Jews, and Catholic priests. Generally they hanged them together on the same tree, adding a dog for company. It was a terrible revenge for old, unmerited sufferings—Catharine, Empress of Russia, interfered—and shortly after, through the partition of Poland, these regions came under the power of Russia. A very small part of the Cossacks, in dread of Russian despotism, fled to Turkey. Catharine put an end to the independent separate Cossack organization of Little Russia, transferring portions of its population to the Don, others to the shores of the Black Sea.

In concluding this sketch, it must be observed that one of the principal reasons of the downfall of Poland was the hostility, the alienation and the separation of Little Russia and the Cossacks—and of this the Polish nobility and the influence of the Jesuits were the principal, or rather the exclusive workers.

Of these Cossacks, who thus filled some pages in history, there now exist only the bare recollections in those regions where once they acted and ruled; ruins of past glory, freedom, and times gone for ever. These remnants of the Cossacks in Little Russia still preserve some privileges, elevating them above the class of free peasants. The Cossacks of the Don still form a distinct national body, and the quite considerable territory inhabited by them, makes a separate province. They are the most completely organized, the most numerous, and furnish the greatest number of armed men, as has been already mentioned in the chapter concerning the army. The land inhabited by them is reckoned among the best and most fertile in Russia. Such is likewise that once belonging to the Cossacks of Little Russia, as the governments, Pultawa, Tschernigoff, the Ukraine, etc., consisting of alluvial soil several feet in depth, and covered with the most luxuriant and productive vegetation. The Cossacks of the Ural, and those of the Black Sea, the *Tschernomortsy* have likewise separate organizations and territories of great agricultural value. The Ural Cossacks, formerly called Yaïck, keep vast flocks of sheep, and one of the principal sources of their revenue is the almost exclusive right of taking, in the Ural, a peculiar kind of sturgeon, whose spawn forms a delicacy called *Caviar*, greatly appreciated in the whole empire, and throughout northern Europe.

As was already mentioned, there prevailed in the ancient organization of the Cossacks the principle of equality. All the offices were elective, and that of the chiefs, the Attaman, amongst the rest. At his election they formed themselves into a ring and threw their caps at the favorite; whoever was the most covered by them was elected. The Cossacks of the Don still elect their judiciary, civil and military administrative officers, but they no longer elect their Attaman. This dignity is now vested in the person of the hereditary prince of the empire. A daring *udaloi* Cossack has no longer the chance of becoming the Attaman as referred to in their old proverb: "*Suffer Cossack, and thou shalt become the Attaman.*"

In the course of the last twenty years, the Cossacks generally, and principally those of the Don, have undergone a change. They have lost still more of their ancient liberties, and in their new and very restrictive organization they have become more subjugated to the power of the Czar, and depend wholly upon the minister of war. But old recollections are not dead in the hearts of the bulk of the Cossack population—they still linger there most vividly. In the wealthiest portion, counting among the aristocracy of the empire, the sham honors distributed by Czarism have dried up and blotted out the feelings and the remembrance of the liberty of old. But the mass endure the present oppression with curses, and are thus discontented and dissatisfied. Not, however, as many ill-informed writers maintain, that there exists any tendency or wish to detach themselves and become independent of Russia;—their aspirations are directed towards the recovering of ancient internal liberty. This work will be done when once the whole Russian people rise in self-defence against despotism and oppression.

Since the destruction of the schemes of Mazeppa and of the independence of the Cossacks of Little Russia by Peter and Catharine, the most wealthy and prominent families have entered into the imperial, civil and military service obtaining eminent distinction. Thus the Kotsch ubeys, Rumantzoff, Bestuscheff, Worontzoff, Daschkoff Murawioff and many others.

The intellectual powers of the inhabitants of Little

Russia have generally in them a something of southern character—rather perhaps tending toward laziness, but when once awake and stirred up, they prove more quick and elastic than northern men. The men of Little Russia are found in the different governmental and administrative branches, often exciting the grumbling of the old Russian against those whom he believes to be intruders. It is nearly the same as it is in England, when in London the old English John is superseded by the harder-working, canny, and more business-like Scot.

The immunities accorded by law to the mediatized Cossacks are the following:

Lands inherited by them directly from their Cossack ancestry remain for ever their individual property. They are obliged only to perform certain servitudes which burden such lands. Such property can only be sold to a Cossack, never to any body else.

If a Cossack acquires any free lands, he can sell, barter and dispose of them, according to his pleasure by observing the requisitions of the general law. Cossacks alone possess the privilege of selling liquors in their houses. No governmental monopoly can be introduced in the Cossack lands and territories. Each male pays a tax amounting to two dollars. They fulfil military service. In civil suits among themselves they enjoy certain privileges of a special court retained from olden time. In criminal matters they are under the jurisdiction of the common criminal tribunals. If condemned to Siberia, or by a verdict given up to the government for detention in penitentiary establishments, or to become common soldiers, they lose for ever those privileges which distinguish the Cossacks.

They can enter the communities of free peasants, selling, however, previously their Cossack property to one of the same class. They can become teachers, schoolmasters, and under certain conditions, enter public gymnasia and universities, losing by it, however, the privileges of Cossacks.

A recent ukase reduces to nothing this possibility of a higher education for the Cossacks as well for burghers and the other lower classes.

The military Cossacks (such is now the generic legal denomination of all the Cossacks) of the Don elect among themselves officials for military functions, which are to be fulfilled in the district, the community or township, in the village called *Stannitsa.*

The superior members of the military board, of the military civil or criminal tribunal are elected exclusively by the military corporation.

All the officials for every other branch of internal administration, of districts and communes, for the internal police, the treasurers and the tax-gatherers, are elected by the civil corporation, which includes those not immediately inscribed on the military rolls.

Inferior functionaries, as the heads or elders in a village, the Attaman of a Stannitsa, are elected by the special communities, as well as their decurions and centurions, overseers of the studs, etc.

The Cossacks of the Don have their own gymnasia, academies and common schools. The tutors or superintendents of these establishments are elected from among the communities. Each *Stannitsa* elects members for the civil and criminal tribunals of the county and judges for the districts.

The Cossacks can own villages with serfs, and nobody but a Cossack can settle or own lands in the Cossack territories.

All the commanders or Attamans of each kind of Cossacks are named by the minister of war, and confirmed by the Czar himself.

There is a party of Calmucks called the army of Stawropol organized as Cossacks and having the same elective administration.

The Cossacks of the Black Sea, of Azoff, of Astrachan,—few in number and owning a small territory,—have for their administration, boards formed by election and called by the title of chancery, *Kantsellaria*, assessors, judges of the *Stannitsa;* likewise the more numerous Cossacks of Ural. Generally all other Cossacks, as those of Orenbourg, those on the frontier of China, have a similar organization. The Cossacks spread over Siberia are settled in boroughs, where they elect the elders and the whole borough administration.

The Cossacks of Astrachan are Calmucks. Their elective administration is composed of a member called Assessor and two others for the civil court, with four members for the spiritual court of the Llamas, and two members for the court of each colony or settlement, called *Ulus.*

CHAPTER IX.

THE REAL PEOPLE, THE PEASANTRY—SERFDOM.

"——Servi siam 'si!
Ma servi ognor trementi."
ALFIERI.

THE peasantry form the broad and solid basis of the whole social and national edifice. They are the everlasting fountain of national life. All the other social strata superposed on it, issued once from them, and in Russia, as every where else, draw continually fresh germs of life and existence from the mass, from the people.

The generic name commonly used for the peasantry in Russia, is that of Christian, *chrestianin*. The origin of it is very ancient, and lies in the fact that it was borne by genuine or aboriginal Russians, in opposition to the prisoners of war, the conquered tribes, out of whom were derived principally the slaves, the serfs—all of whom in these distant epochs were heathens.

The people, or the peasantry, have preserved the most decided and pure features of the Slavic character. On the shoulders of the Russian peasantry, reposes not only the whole social edifice, but in its hands is nearly the whole material activity. It fills the armies, exclusively cultivates the soil, furnishes laborers to manufactures, and artisans, and workingmen. It has in its hands nearly the whole internal carrying trade, on land as well as on water; from the western frontiers between Poland and Prussia, down to Kiachta, in China, and from Archangel and St. Petersburg to the Euxine, and the Persian shores on the Caspian Sea. The bulk of the genuine Russian population is split into several subdivisions, distinguished by some shadowings in its idiom, in its accent, and in its enunciation; as well as by some mental characteristics. These principal parts are: the inhabitant of Great Russia, or Russia proper, the White Russians, who during a long time, say about four centuries, were under the Polish dominion. White Russia is composed of the governments Witebsk, part of Smolensk, Minsk and Mohyloff, and finally Little Russia, including principally the lands of the Cossacks, and lands where once was the cradle of the present Russian Empire. These are the lands on the Dnieper, the governments Charkoff, Kiïeff, Pultowa, Ekaterinoslaw, Tschernigoff, the Ukraine, and to them may be added Volynia and Podolia—once called Red Russia, and which, like White Russia, was for centuries under Polish dominion. In the lands of the former dominion, the noblemen are mostly of the Polish branch, and generally of the Roman Catholic creed, with some exceptions among the smaller nobility; the people are Russian, and of the Eastern church. The red Russian has likewise more affinity with the Russian, than with the Polish family. The white Russian peasant is the less favored by nature, and the protracted oppression of an unkind, unfriendly master, has left deep traces on his faculties. His language is not the pure Russian, but forms in every respect a corrupt, deteriorated, vulgar idiom. All vitality and originality seem extinguished in him. He is neither as active or intelligent as the genuine Russian, and in manners and mode of life is already slightly denationalized.

As mentioned already, among the southern, or Little Russians, was once the cradle of the empire founded there by the Varagues and the northern, the Novgorodian Russians, until the time of the Tartar conquest, and the removing of the capital to other regions, as to Wladimir, and finally to Moscow. In the lands of Little Russia along the Dnieper, the principal branch of the Cossacks took root. In these regions, the original national character maintained itself pure from alteration, and more energetically resisted the action of foreign, Polish, and catholic dominion. The southern dialect differs from that of Russia proper, but the shadowings are not so strongly expressed as to form a deeply penetrating distinction; it is perhaps more softened to the ear, and has more of a poetical turn. It has its own poetry, and a kind of literature, and is still written by some amateurs. The people have nearly all the characteristics in common with those of Russia proper, though inferior in intellectual activity; nor are they generally, as enterprising or industrious as the former. In the greater part of Little Russia, the people still preserve very lively reminiscences of the ancient liberty, enjoyed under the Cossack rule. The oppression of the Polish nobility, united to religious persecution, has, in some parts, acted with nearly the same results as in White Russia;—in the proper lands of the Cossacks despotism gnawed at liberty, during the eighteenth century, until it finally destroyed it. It was principally the population of Little Russia, which from the commencement of the Russian empire, between the eighth and the eleventh centuries, warred, most victoriously, with the emperors of Byzantium, and by their exploits, even at that distant epoch, gave the name of a Russian sea to the Euxine—*mare Russicum*, as used by the old geographers. The name of *Rus* (Russian) belongs principally to this region, whence it was extended and adopted by the other parts of the empire. Up to the present time the Little Russian bestows on the northern inhabitant the name of a *Moskal* (a Muscovite). Still the greatest affinity exists between both, in customs, manners, and character. Both have a strong rythmical, musical, and poetical feeling, and the Little Russian is of the two, perhaps, the most fond of song. In all other characteristics they are nearly alike, and thus these two branches of the great stem form a well-intertwined whole.

Great Russia, or Russia proper, extends from the frontiers of the government of Petersburg, already colonized by the Russians on the Waldaï, along the Wolga to the Ural and the Don (Tanaïs). It forms twenty-five densely populated governments. It is the true heart of Russia.

From this great focus life pours out, and activity radiates in all directions. From these regions the colonists and settlers extend to the frozen ocean, to the mouth of the Amour and the Northern Pacific shores, and crossing the Aleutian Islands, already push their way into the northern parts of this continent. The whole people of Great, or Russia proper, speak the most pure and correct language, which is no longer an idiom or a dialect. It is not altered in the mouth of the people; and as it pours out from the popular lips, so it is used by the higher and cultivated classes; by the government, for laws; and by poets, littérateurs, and scientific men, for their mental productions. In one word, it is the language used by what is called the common people, which is likewise the language of civilization. With the exception of the Tuscans, no other people or nation can produce any thing like it.

Among the people of Great Russia is the seat of intellectual activity, of national industry; thence it extends itself in all directions; but there it is pre-eminently at home.

There it divides itself in several branches, and for each of them it has appropriated separate regions. Thus not only districts but the populations of whole governments are devoted nearly to one special industry. In one, the carpenters, in another, the masons, the weavers, and so on. All of them give to the general industry, to manufactures, to mechanics, and artisans, the hands, the workmen, who spread in cities over the whole empire. Their organization will be explained hereafter, and how they are attached to special communities, and through them to the soil, and in this respect the same is true of the serf as of the free peasant.

According to a very ancient patriarchal custom, the families do not separate continually, in each generation, but brothers, uncles, and nephews often live around the same hearth, under the same roof. For the husbandry of the land, which the family holds from the commune or from the master, and for the fulfilment of the task of servitude, a few males, sometimes only the women, remain the whole year through at home. The males—under legal conditions, to be explained by-and-by—emigrate to cities in search of work or of any kind of enterprise. In this manner they spread themselves in all directions from one end of the empire to another, and form the immense moving, floating population of large, and even smaller cities, as merchants and builders, constructors, artisans, workmen in manufactures, either on their own account or as journeymen. Those who cannot continue their occupation during the winter return home, to begin with the coming year the same migration.

In some governments, large communities and villages are engaged in manufactures, as spinners, weavers, etc. Among these there prevails (from olden times) the principle of free association. It is the common chest, the *ar-*

tel already spoken of in a previous chapter. Generally, where the workmen or journeymen gather together to a common work of any nature whatever, they instantly form such an *artel*. Applied to industry it animates it, and creates a reserve fund for its various eventualities and exigencies. Each member (*atelschtschik*) contributes according to his means or the amount of the produce of his labor, and an advance in proportion is made therefrom. Thus the association always possesses funds for cases of any emergency. Time and experience will improve this germ, which, in the atmosphere of the hoped-for liberty, will unfold itself, acquire extension, and become a powerful social engine.

The external aspect of the people is generally rather serious, even to solemn formality. But in reality, under this calm exterior, there is concealed an immense spirit of frolic, gayety, and wit. The old, popular national dance, accompanied by an appropriate song, is a perfect dramatic action. It is not inferior to the most celebrated dance of the South, as, for example, of Spain and Italy. The song is the inseparable companion of the whole Slavic race. It resounds in various modulations from the mouth of Cattaro to Kamschatka. In the pleasant evening of summer or autumn every Slavic village or orchard resounds with the clear, penetrating tones of woman's voice, poured out in song, and so it was from remotest times. The Emperor Mauritius relates that in one of his battles against Bojan, prisoners were made, who, instead of weapons, carried a kind of a musical instrument (a lute), very likely the *gensl guzla* of the Slavi. They were of a gigantic stature, and when asked about their country said it was Slavic, and that among them song and music were looked on as the most noble occupations. Even now the Bohemian or the Tschechs, form the best ambulatory musicians in Germany.

The Russian peasant accompanies all his labors with song. With it he stimulates his horse. Whether working alone or in numbers he sings, and marks any heavy work requiring the union of many hands by time, by rhythm. This he does in war or when engaged in rural toils.

In the interior of Russia, in villages as well as in cities, the girls gather on autumn evenings in courtyards, and making a circle around a fire, sing old songs, principally of love. This is called *korowody*. There the youth of both sexes come together, when tender relations have their origin.

With a facility quite astonishing a group of soldiers or peasants will transform itself almost instantaneously into a singing choir, where all the rules and combinations of harmony will be observed, as if in a well-trained operatic chorus. A leader, or foreman, gives the tune, begins, and the rest follow with the greatest perfection.

The man of the people is warm-hearted, polite in his own way—that is, not when he must be servile towards those above him, but when he meets his equals. He is hospitable to the utmost of his means. Hospitality is the general character of the whole nation. The burghers practice it as well as the nobles, and especially those in the country, to an extent unknown in the rest of Europe. The word for hospitality in Russia is *chlebo-sol*, bread and salt, which gives the true and simple meaning of sharing it without any attempt at ostentation.

In business the peasant is shrewd and crafty, nay, sometimes a sharp rogue. But it must not be forgotten that he is on the defensive against an unjust and crushing social order, and that cunning and roguery are the only weapons which he can quietly oppose to oppression. Therefore, in justice, he cannot be censured for it.

One of the prominent features in the character of the

Russian peasant is an inexhaustible patience, a kind of physical and moral endurance of many wrongs. It is carried very far, and seems to justify one of the warmest and most beautiful stanzas from the pen of the Polish poet Mickewitch:

> O biedny chlopie, pocoz mi lza plynie,
> I serce bije gdy mysle o tobie:
> Ah zal mi ciebi biedny Slawianinie,
> Biedny narodzie ah zal mi twej doli,
> Ieden masz tylko heroism niewoli.
>
> O poor peasant! what is the reason that my tears flow,
> And that my heart beats when I think of thee;
> Ah! I pity thee, poor Slavonian:
> Poor people, I pity thy destiny,
> Thou hast only one kind of heroism—that of slavery.

This is the only passage in which this writer, of some celebrity, has sympathized with the social wrongs of a people.

This patience, and similar prophecies, contribute to strengthen the common opinion that this people is doomed to eternal oppression, that they will always bear it quietly, and thus remain the passive tools of despotism in the old world.

But notwithstanding this patient endurance, the outburst of the wrath of the Russian peasantry, when finally roused by ill-treatment, cruelty, wrongs of masters or of officers of the government, will then be inexorable, bloody, and the revenge terrible. Such outbreaks are limited for the present to special cases, but sooner or later they will break out more generally, and settle their accounts with the old and absolute cause of the social evil. Then the people will lay the axe to the root, and then may God be merciful to the nobility and the officials. Pouschkine, the great Russian poet, relating the phases of an insurrection of the Cossacks of Ural or Orenbourg, joined by free peasants and serfs from several of the eastern counties, exclaims : " May God preserve Russia from the seething outbreak of its own people." This insurrection, which took place under the reign of Catherine, and nearly extended to the gates of Moscow, is known in history under the name of Pugatscheff, the leader, who pretended to be the murdered Emperor Peter III., and called himself, "Czar, the avenger."

It was mentioned in the chapter concerning the army, how, in 1831, the peasants in revolt in the military colonies dealt with the officers. In 1838–'39 partial insurrections in the villages and communes of some counties took place, and principally in the government of Saratoff, where the manor-houses were burnt with their occupants, and civil officers (*isprawniks*) thrown into the fire. Such movements occur continually in various places—as the boiling elements and gases in the bowels of our earth, burst out partially here and there, sure forerunners of a terrible and a more general geological convulsion.

The features of the national character mentioned in the chapters concerning the burghers and the army, have a more direct bearing on the peasantry, as forming pre-eminently the people. In its present anomalous state, it is only a wonder that it produces artisans, workmen, and manufacturers at all. Its intellectual powers, in themselves quick, inventive, and manifold, acting thus against so heavy, numerous, and crushing odds, prove their virtuality and intensity. The peasant has in his turn more painful impediments to overcome in any of his enterprises, than even those which the burgher has to encounter. Any instruction is almost unattainable for the Russian peasant. Thus inborn originality has no room in which to extend her mighty wings, and up to the present time the intellectuality of the people has never really and seriously been awakened into life. A normal development is impossible, and thus the higher individuality remains latent, not having opportunity or room to manifest itself freely.

The mode of life of the Russian peasantry, in its various branches and regions, is nearly alike. That of the White Russian is an exception, he being the poorest and most dejected, and moreover settled on the most unproductive soil of Russia. The principal and general food is farinaceous, and no people in Europe consume so much of it. In the northern provinces, rye and oats; in the more southern, wheat, are the staples of food. Potatoes are not yet generally cultivated, and consequently not used as daily food, and still less form the exclusive basis of nourishment, as they do of the people in Poland and through the whole of Central Europe. In general, aside from the above-mentioned exceptions of the Poles and the Bohemians, the whole Slavic family is the best and most substantially nourished in the old world. If the Slavi in general, and above all the Russians, do not consume meat for daily use, they do not live on cabbages and vegetables, but on flour in various shapes, on groats, and animal fats. To be sure, times of scarcity and famine make exceptions, and these are rather increased by the bad state and the difficulties of internal communications. The south of Russia, equal in extent to nearly the whole of Germany or France, would be always able to feed the north in case of a bad harvest, but to carry the breadstuffs there would become far more expensive than to bring them to the English market. Nay, in some cases, it would be wholly impossible. When once, however, a good system of internal communication is introduced and extended in every direction by means of railroads, which are easily constructed in a country where for hundreds and hundreds of miles nothing disturbs the level of the soil, scarcity, or at least famine, will become unknown in Russia. The use of tea is nearly general among the peasants of Russia proper; with many it is a substitute for the use of liquors. Not that the Russian peasants are temperate, but still those of Poland, Germany, England, and Ireland exceed them in intemperance. In Poland, Lithuania, and White Russia, the nobility, in Russia proper, the crown, have the exclusive privilege to inebriate the people.

Cleanliness, especially with the genuine Russian, is more general than hasty and superficial travellers give him credit for. All the population of Russia take generally, once a week, a steam bath, resembling that called "oriental." Every village, every hamlet, indeed, has a public building for this purpose called *banïa*, besides numerous *banïas* of private individuals. The women go to the *banïa* on Friday and the men on Saturday.

The wooden habitation of the peasant, the *jzba*, is kept cleanly, except where absolute poverty prevails, when the miserable huts are disgusting with filth and are wretchedly kept. This is more generally the case among the serfs.

These are the principal and most general outlines of the character of the Russian peasantry, of its life, and its activity. The peasantry, the people in Russia, is most purely preserved as a race, and there is very little, if any, foreign admixture. The historical feeling of nationality is as strong in them as in any of the Slavic tribes, and even stronger and more intense than in many of them. Notwithstanding his oppression and total exclusion from any political action—with the exception of furnishing pre-eminently food for the god of war—the Russian peasant has a strong historical self-consciousness, and this alone would point to him as the bearer of the destinies of the whole race.

The whole number of the people or peasantry exceeds forty-five millions, that is, of the pure Russian stock. This mass forms, legally and socially, two great principal divisions: that of the so-called free or crown peasants, and the serfs. The former are cut up into several subdivisions, according to the rights by which they hold property or soil, and according to the kind and the nature of the servitudes which they have to fulfil.

The code of laws, *Swod Zakonoff*, calls the peasantry rural inhabitants, and divides them, as follows:

1. Those inhabiting or settled on lands belonging to the public treasury, *kazna* (a word of Tartar origin).

2. Those on special crown domains.

3. Those on lands forming the personal property of the Emperor.

4. Those settled on lands belonging to the imperial habitations or palaces, *dwortsowyïe* (from *dworets*, a palace).

5. Those settled on private lands, that is, on lands belonging to the nobility, or the class of serfs.

Finally, a small number of freedmen, freeholders, having lands of their own.

With the exception of the serfs, all the others have certain special personal rights, as well as special duties or services to perform, owing dues, most of them, however, rather communal than personal. Among these communal services the principal are those pertaining to military colonies, already spoken of; others, such as are attached to the imperial or governmental studs; others to the mines of Siberia; others, again, who keep post-horses for public and governmental use. Villages of the latter tenure are called *iama*, and the peasants, *iamsctschik*.* There are

* Foreigners may be struck at the often repeated occurrence of so many consonants, as in the word *iamschtschik*, but in Rus-

several others of a similar kind, of special communal services, to be mentioned hereafter.

To the class of free peasants belong likewise foreign, mostly German, agricultural colonists—a kind of yeomen called *adnodwortsy*, from nobles having forfeited their privileges—and free agriculturists, all of whom possess the soil as personal property.

These last two, *adnodwortsy* and free agriculturists, live scattered in single habitations and farms, all the other peasantry form rural communes, and enjoy the communal franchise. Thus the commune is the cradle of the social organism. The basis of the commune is the land on which the population is settled, and thus is incorporated with it. Every peasant not a serf must belong to such a commune, which may be large or small according to the quantity of land owned and the density of population. There are communes having a population amounting to nearly twenty thousand souls. Such a commune is called *wolost;* it is composed of hamlets, *derewnia*, and villages, *selo;* just as a New England township may embrace several villages. Several such communes form a rural district or canton. A village generally counts between six and eight hundred families.

The internal police, the correction of small offences by short imprisonment or by no more than fifteen blows; the settling of contests among the members; the superintendence of a primary school, whose maintenance is obligatory; the distribution on each member of taxes, services, and duties; the administration of the recently founded communal rural banks; the equal distribution of the military recruits from amongst families; in one word, every thing

sian, the sound composed out of *schtsch* is given by a single sign, or letter.

concerning the internal administration and working of the commune, is done by the commune itself. The commune is responsible to the treasury for the rent levied from each family having a separate communal household; this rent, called *obrok*, generally, through the whole of Russia, even on the estates of serfs, amounts to ten dollars. The commune maintains the highways and roads on its own territory.

The commune owns all lands within its limits, arable or uncultivated, forests and pastures. No member can possess a distinct, separate property therein, with the exception of the dwelling-house. The arable land is divided into equal shares (*utschastki*) among the heads of families. A married couple, *tam* (*tieglo*) is entitled to twenty acres. If the population increases beyond the capacity of the soil to maintain it, the government removes the surplus into another commune possessing superabundant lands. The houses and the land owned in a community can never be encumbered nor sold by the holder. Such a property, held from the commune, cannot be divided between widows and children, but *de jure* returns to the community, which grants it again to the eldest male in the family, sometimes to a brother, and not to the son of the deceased. Communes can by purchase acquire new lands.

A commune can expel from it any member for bad conduct, for not fulfilling his communal duties, or give him up to the government as a military recruit, to be accounted for in the next general levy, for imprisonment for life or even for transportation to colonize Siberia.

A commune of free peasants can be entered, at any time, by burghers, manumitted serfs, free bastards, serfs bought by the crown, or slaves bought by the government from the nomad tribes, by discharged soldiers and their children. The admission of any such new member is to be decided by the commune.

The free peasants can own lands out of the commune, houses in other villages or cities. The mines discovered on such lands are the property of the owners. This is the origin of the great fortune of the Demidoffs, so well known in Europe. Their ancestor, a skilful foreman in a manufactory of arms at the time of Peter the Great, was rewarded by the Emperor with extensive lands near the Ural, supposed to contain only iron ore; but by mining, gold, silver, platina, were discovered, and the family became wealthy but not influential. Still the peasants are excluded from owning houses in the two capitals, St. Petersburg and Moscow. To live out of the commune, each individual must have the permission of his communal authority.

In the chapter concerning the various corporations of burghers, it has already been mentioned that peasants living in cities, as tradesmen, artisans or workmen, cannot be elected there for any town office.

The communal board is called *wolostnoë prawlenie.* All the members of it, as well as those for the details of administration and police, are elected within the commune.

The elections are consequently made for twofold duties; firstly, for the general or public, and secondly, for those specially belonging to each commune, village or hamlet.

The public functions are those of a kind of conciliatory court, members for the rural court of police in the district, decemviri and centurions, *desiastki*, *sotski.*

Only free peasants participate in the elections made for the public or general offices; for the details of a local police administration, serfs in the district can participate with the commune. No Jews or heretics from the Greek Church, can be elected to any office whatever in an orthodox commune.

The elections are decided by the majority; they are mostly triennial, and their mode is as follows:

Five hundred souls as recorded in the last census, all male householders of the community, make choice of an elector who must be thirty years of age, a father of a family possessing a house and land, of good morals, and who never underwent any punishment. The document stating his election ought to have the signature of the clergyman, and of at least five husbandmen. These electors meet in the capital of the district, and elect members for the public offices. The election is made by ballot or by chance, drawing out the names as the lots in a lottery; this last mode being the more ancient usage and still preserved in numerous communities. The person elected ought to be a peasant,—but should there be none qualified for the function, then a nobleman or any functionary of the government can be chosen.

Peasants fulfilling any public official position cannot be subjected to any corporal punishment, except by the decision of a court. They are salaried, and have to wear a particular dress or uniform.

The elections for the special administration of each community, for villages and hamlets, are likewise triennial.

Every hamlet has its elder, *starosta*, who with his assistant decemviri, *desiatski*, is elected by the inhabitants. The starosta receives a salary amounting to thirty dollars, the desiatski serve without pay. A hamlet too small to have a starosta is governed by a desiatski. The individual, thus elected, must be twenty-five years of age, of good morals, never having been punished or under any criminal accusation.

Elections for a village, and for a whole commune are made in the following manner. Every ten husbandmen choose an elector. These meet and elect an elder, *starschina*, and his aids. Such an elder of the village has a salary of about eighty dollars. Further, a collector of taxes and his aids. An overseer of the common storehouse. In such houses, after each harvest a certain quantity of grain is deposited by each husbandman, to form a reserve for times of scarcity. A conciliatory judge, overseers and their assistants of communal forests, the centurions or *sotski*, are all elected, and from each village there are three candidates for fulfilling the public offices.

The communal board, or *wolostnoe prawlenië*, is chosen by the electors, named by the villages and from the number of the above mentioned candidates, who are elected at the primary elections.

The functionaries thus elected are—the *golowa*, head presiding officer over the whole commune, an elected board of administration, and the conciliatory judges. The salary of the golowa is about 120 dollars. The administrative board has a salaried recorder.

The dissidents from the state church, and particularly those who do not recognize any regular clergy, if they live in the same village or communities with the orthodox, cannot be elected to any other function than that of an overseer of the forests. Those among them having a clergy, can be elected tax gatherers. When, however, the whole community is composed of sectarians, then all the offices are possessed by them.

Near the sea shores or in the well wooded regions, there are villages and communes whose service is to prepare timber for the navy, and in them, individuals for directing such labors are also elected.

The rural police, the keeping in order of roads and

highways, the catching of thieves, etc., all these duties are fulfilled in hamlets and villages by the desiatskis and sotskis. As mentioned before, the serfs of the district can participate in such elections, and be elected for these inferior duties if they combine with the free communities. This depends, however, exclusively upon the masters, who at their will can select from among their serfs the members of the rural police.

These are the legal powers of a commune, and the rights of the peasantry—called free, as a distinction from the serfs. All these communes are superintended and directed—and their elective or internal administrative action confirmed, by a special governmental branch having its boards in each county. Their duty is to watch over the interests of the communities as well as over those of individuals, in all their external relations or eventual collisions, or contests with other branches of the goverment or with the nobility.

This governmental branch is the ministry of the crown lands or demesnes, and has thus about twenty-two millions of population under its direction. It has an organic action, as it introduces among the peasantry all kinds of reforms; administrative as well as agricultural. In some respects, its action is beneficial, as when for instance it introduces agricultural schools, rural banks, and other ameliorations, thus making the people acquainted with the results of advancement. But where it is true to its origin, where with all the weight of despotism it tries to transform the people into mere machines, depriving them of free will and action—where it arbitrarily curtails and destroys the scanty remains of individuality, and of human dignity in the people, then it is a curse. And such in many respects, it has proved itself to be, and as such it is looked upon by the peasantry.

The crown peasants, whatever may be the nature of their tenure, have no other special master than the sovereign or the goverment, and never can have another. Once the Czars granted to individuals vast territories of lands with crown peasants or serfs on them. This is the origin of many great fortunes in Russia, consisting in large estates, and hundreds of thousands of souls, as that of Scheremetëff, Naryschkin, the Orloffs, the Branickis, the last of which rose out of the ruins of ancient Poland. Peter rewarded real services, as in the case of Scheremetëff; Catharine was very lavish to her favorites of every kind, and she thus laid the foundations of numerous large fortunes still existing in Russia; and Paul, was most indiscriminate in bestowing his favors. For the glory of Alexander it must be recorded, that in his youth, when under the influence of a generous and humane inspiration, he published an ukase by which it was henceforth and for ever prohibited to any sovereign, to make donations of crown peasants to any private individual whatever, or to sell them, or render them liable to any statute for husbandry servitude. The present sovereign has thus far religiously maintained this ukase. Even in Poland, since the revolution of 1831, the emperor, in dividing numerous estates of the crown, called *starostwa*, among the Russian generals and others of his servants, by a special clause in every grant directed that the statute labor existing until that time should ultimately become extinguished, and the peasant on such lands become the free and independent owner of a suitable homestead. It must be mentioned here, that in the actual kingdom of Poland, slavery was abolished by the last king of Prussia in the year 1800, when this part of Poland formed one of the Prussian provinces. This was confirmed by the Code of Napoleon, introduced after the treaty of Tilsit in 1807, and is still maintained. But neither of these governments secured for the peasantry any homestead on crown or private lands.

The free peasantry in Russia enjoy some rights and privileges, rendering their position by far more supportable than that of the private serfs. It has been already shown that a free peasant can freely engage in any mercantile, manufacturing, mechanical, or other industrial pursuit, and establish his domicil in any city of the empire, if he possesses a permission of his commune, which permission can no wise be refused as long as the individual pays the *obrok* and the taxes in the commune to which he belongs, and fulfils through any hand all other communal duties. Provided with such a permission or certificate, the movements and actions of a peasant are perfectly free; he can make proposals for all kinds of public jobs contracted with the government. In such cases other contractors are obliged to give securities; but a crown peasant presents only the authorization of his commune. He can enter into the class of burghers by abandoning his commune with its consent, passing thus into what is considerated a higher social corporation.

The chains of serfdom do not hang on him—but if he has no special master, he, like the burgher, has still to deal with rapacious officials. What is true of the one is still and even more largely to be applied to the other. Entering the superior corporation the peasant can meliorate his position—but this melioration is very limited. All openings for education are absolutely shut before him. All that he can learn is to read and write wretchedly. If there are exceptions they are very rare—and, so to speak, rather the work of a miracle.

In the hands of these free peasants is by far the greatest part of the internal carrying trade; they furnish the greatest number of hands for artisans and all kinds of handicrafts. Their sole contact with the nobility is with the numerous officials, the *tschynowniks* of infamous celebrity. But this is sufficient to gall them to the utmost, and keep alive in the peasantry the hatred towards the nobility. Then the free peasants dwell and live by the side of the serfs, their brothers, relations, friends, acquaintances, and thus find many occasions to nourish and stir up this feeling of hostility. In proportion as their well-being increases, and by their busy life they come more and more in contact with worldly doings and relations, they feel the more their oppressed and dejected position, and the stronger and more intense becomes the desire for emancipation.

Generally, a spirit of independence prevails among them to a high degree. They learn in their communal organization to judge and act, to be something; to exercise, however feebly, their mental powers; to have the aspirations of a human being. The official pressure aims principally at their pockets, and thus with money they are enabled to come to terms with the officials—still they retain the ever-growing wish to get rid of these officials, and of the whole governmental structure. They have in common with the whole mass of population, an inborn consciousness of the absolute existence of human rights, of human dignity. This consciousness, however dim and feeble it may be at present, will by-and-by grow and transform itself into a social fact.

Not to say that for the immense majority of the peasantry, the Czar *in abstracto* has ceased to be something between Heaven and earth, between God and man,—yet the deputies of the Czar contribute most actively to tarnish the Czarean aureole, reducing by slow progress, the supernatural conception to the most earthly and oppressive reality. The old consolatory feeling and adage uttered by the people at every injustice and oppression: "*If only the Czar could know it,*" dies slowly and slowly away. The people become more and more aware that: "*The Czar knows,*" but turns away and helps not.

The peasant learns, that in his commune he could do well without the official, and that such interference, while it is costly, is always rather pernicious than otherwise. The official strips him of the earnings of his industry, the results of his hard labor. And this official acts in the name of the Czar, and under it shelters his authority, as well as his abuse of power. As before said, the peasantry begin already to perceive the inutility of the *tschynownik*, and in time will see clearly the inutility of the Czar himself.

It has been mentioned, that to the class of free peasantry belong various kinds of freeholders, as well as some others occupying lands granted under servitudes already extinct, reminiscent of a state of things changed wholly by a new governmental organism. Thus the creation of a standing army destroyed the class of the so-called *pancernyie boïary*—coat-of-mail boïars, whose duty was to appear armed in case of war, and who formed the common soldiery of infantry and of cavalry. The legal position of all such free-holders is as follows:

First, are the *odnodwortsy*, one-manored, formed, as stated, from nobles who have forfeited their privilege—as well as from old soldiers colonized by Peter I., in some of the southern governments, and on whom he bestowed that right. The *odnodwortsy* can hold serfs, but they cannot buy them from real nobles, but only from members of their own class. If they have lands in rural communities, in common with other peasants, they pay therefor an obrok. In such communes they participate in all the rights and privileges of the commune, and can be elected to all the communal functions.

The coat-of-mail boïars were once very numerous—but by grants, or mostly by an unlawful appropriation, they became, with their lands, the private property of the nobility, and thus were transformed into serfs. If, however, any descendant can prove his legitimate descent, the government pays about thirty dollars to the owner for his emancipation.

Land held under the like tenure cannot be sold by the holder except with the permission of the Czar. Such lands are transmitted by inheritance in a direct line. It is, so to speak, the only feudal tenure that ever existed in Russia.

These boïars pay the capitation tax like the burghers, but no obrok for the land. As they are not numerous, and rather scattered, they do not form communities, but in some cases, as for example, in that of recruits, or in fulfilling the service of the rural police, they are incorporated into the nearest rural commune or village.

Free agriculturists, *wolnyë chlebopaschtsy*, are principally manumitted serfs, with soil or without, and in this last case, they can buy land from anybody. The manumissions with soil must be made by the owner during his lifetime and not by will.

If they are numerous enough, they form rural communes on the general principle; if not, they are incorporated in the existent ones. They can sell and buy lands and divide them among their children, but in lots not under sixteen acres. They can contract for public jobs, *podriad*, enter guilds, erect manufactories, carry on trade and enjoy all the privileges of free peasantry. There are still some few other kinds of privileged peasantry, but their number is very small and wholly insignificant.

II. The serfs. Nearly the entire half of the Russian peasantry, if not wholly enslaved, according to the absolute signification of the word, are, however, serfs or bondmen, attached to the *soil*, *glebæ adscripti*, rather than to the *person* of the nobleman, and thus they are at least not chattels. The power of the master is not wholly arbitrary and unlimited and unlawless—but the servitude, is reduced to a certain method, regulated as follows, by the civil law.

By usage, the serfs are of two kinds: agriculturists and house serfs, but the *law* does not recognize these distinctions.

An Ukase published by Catharine in the year 1781, prohibited, for the future, the enslaving of the peasantry.

The ownership of a serf or serfs, is proved by the census. The first census was made by Peter the Great, in the year 1714; the next in 1744. In the present century the census is made every ten years. In the territory of Bessarabia, neither Russian nor Moldavian nobility can own serfs from among the Russian peasantry, and other races cannot be enslaved. This law was published to prevent the introduction of serfdom in a newly conquered and annexed territory. It is a kind of Wilmot proviso. The children of a male serf remain in the condition of the father, even if the mother belongs to a better class.

If any nobleman sends, for punishment, his serf to Siberia, and the serf receives there lands from the crown as a colonist, his children, the males under seven years of age, and girls under ten, follow the father to the new condition—colonized exiles in Siberia form successively communities of free peasantry.

A woman from a free class marrying a serf, becomes free again as widow; a woman from bondage marrying a free peasant, becomes likewise free.

When the husband becomes free by law, or by manumission, or by contract, his wife shares his freedom *ipso facto*, but not the children; they must be emancipated by a special act.

If a master demands from his serfs any thing contrary to law, as revolt, murder, stealing, and they accomplish it, they are punished as his accomplices. The serfs pay the expenses of the administration in each county. This is the only direct tax levied on the property of the nobility. In criminal matters, the serfs are judged by common criminal tribunals, before whom, they likewise can appear in the character of accusers and witnesses.

The law makes it obligatory on the serf to resist any attack made on the property of the master, as well as upon the honor of his wife and daughter. The owner cannot force his serfs to marry against their will, or point out whom they shall marry; this provision of the law is very generally evaded.

If a serf makes an unjust official complaint against his master, or if he dares to present such a petition to the emperor: the petitioner, and the writer of the petition, are both most severely punished.

In case of insubordination, disobedience to the master or the overseer, the serfs are punished by a military commission, and pay the expenses thereof. All civil or police and military functionaries, are prohibited to receive any denunciation made by the serf against his master, with the exception of a conspiracy against the person of the sovereign; or when the master tries to make a misstatement as to the census; or when, if a Roman Catholic, he tries to convert his orthodox serfs.

A serf cannot change his master, leave him, or enter any corporation. For all these the consent of the owner is necessary. Without such a consent serfs cannot be received as volunteers into the army.

Runaway serfs are returned to the owners at the cost of those who had kept or secreted them. After ten years a master forfeits the right to claim a runaway. Such claims, supported by proofs, must be made during the first year after the escape, if the master is in Russia, and in the course of two years, if the master is abroad.

If a serf is killed by accident, his owner receives from the culprit the sum of 330 dollars; but if it is a murder, then the murderer suffers the same as if the crime was committed on any one else. In such a case the owner of the murdered man does not receive any compensation.

A serf who is not a house servant, must work for his master three days a week. He cannot be forced to do any work on Sundays or any other church and parish holidays, or on the day of the patron saints of the reigning sovereigns. The master can, at his pleasure, transform the house serf *dworowoï*, into a soil tiller, and *vice versa*. He can hire his serfs to mechanics, manufacturers, and to any other labor whatever. He is the supreme judge in all civil contests between his serfs. He can punish them corporally, but not cripple them, or put life in jeopardy. He can require the assistance of the government for the coercion of his serfs. In case of a criminal offence the master must abstain from any punishment, but deliver the offender to the law. He can send serfs to Siberia or to any other penitentiary establishment.

No serf can live in any city, or serve any person whatever without the consent of the master, and the authorities are to see that this provision be not transgressed—and are severely responsible. The master gives to the serf a passport, and furnished with this, he can move freely in the whole empire.

The master has the power to transfer the serfs individually or by whole communities from one village, district, or county into another. Any nobleman owning serfs of any kind, must have for every one, at least twenty acres of land. Only a nobleman can receive a power of attorney for the buying or selling of serfs.

The master cannot hire his serfs to individuals whom the law prohibits to own serfs, nor let them learn any profession any where else, than from masters inscribed in a guild.

Serfs, either servants or agriculturists, held by those who have no right to own them, become free; that is they become incorporated into the free crown peasantry, and the unlawful owners pay a fine into the treasury.

Families cannot be separated by sale. The family consists of the parents and the unmarried children even if of age. The children form a family after the death of the parents. Serfs cannot be brought to market, but are to be sold only together with the estate. If sold separately the crown takes them as its peasants, and the transgressors of the law are fined. Serfs acquiring their liberty in such a way, can make the choice of a mode of life, and of a corporation into which they will become inscribed.

In cases of scarcity or famine, the owner cannot send away his serfs, but is obliged to take care of them. He is likewise obliged to take care of the old, and the invalids.

If there be any abuse of power by the master, any cruelty or rape, the law takes from the owner the administration of the estate and puts it in the hands of guardians, or of a board selected for this purpose in each district, from among the nobility. Such masters cannot acquire new estates by purchase, and in aggravated cases can be given up to the criminal courts. For this the special decision of the sovereign is required. Likewise the owners cannot live on the estates, whose administration is thus taken out of their hands. The villages or estates are responsible for governmental taxes. If a serf has a lawsuit, his master must prosecute it, and the master is answerable for the results, whenever the serf has had his permission to enter into any civil liability. In criminal matters concerning a serf the interference of the master is optional.

Serfs cannot be sold separate from the soil, or at any public auction in execution of the debts of the master.

If a serf or serfs sue, on legal grounds, their master for emancipation, having been brought into serfdom contrary to the provisions of the law: while the legal proceedings are pending, the master cannot inflict on them any corporal punishment under the penalty of a criminal prosecution; nor can he mortgage or let them out by lease; and if the first court decide in their favor, and the affair goes to the court of appeal, the master cannot give them to the military service pending the final decision.

Serfs carrying on a legal trade with the consent of the master, cannot be given up by him as recruits or for the colonization of Siberia. Serfs cannot own immovable property; all houses and lands possessed by them are the property of the master. Should a serf inherit such property, it must be sold and the money handed over to him. Serfs erecting shops and manufactures, must have a special permission of the master, likewise for entering the guild of artisans, and for selling the produce of their industry in cities and markets. For taking public jobs, *podrïad*, or keeping post-horses on public roads, they must have the consent and the guaranty of the master.

The serf can lend out money on legal terms, but not take mortgages on land in villages or estates. Only with the consent of the master can they buy on credit goods for traffic—otherwise they cannot be prosecuted, and any bargain or stipulation is void by itself.

The master has the right to manumit his serfs individually, or by whole hamlets and villages, with or without giving them lands.

A permission given by the master to his serf to marry a girl, who is a pupil and educated in a public establishment for the children of burghers—is equivalent to manumission.

A manumitted serf cannot be brought again into serfdom. A serf can obtain his liberty by a legal juridical decision. 1. If he proves an antecedent right to liberty. 2. If his master does not belong to any Christian confession. 3. If the master has made a forcible attack on the virtue of his wife or daughter, or committed any other impropriety. 4. If the serf was made a prisoner by the enemy and carried beyond the frontiers of the state—on returning he does not return into serfdom. 5. If by the master he is given up to the disposition of the government.

The serf obtains his liberty if he proves against his master the crime of treason, or a conspiracy against the life of the sovereign.

A serf condemned legally to exile to Siberia ceases to be owned by the master; his wife following him into exile becomes free.

A serf becomes free if sold without lands, or if the buyer does not possess the quantity of land required by law, or if his family is separated from him by sale.

These are the principal features of the legal organization of serfdom. As was said, part of the serfs are agriculturists called *pachatnaïa duscha*, the others house serfs or *dworowaïa*.

The agricultural serfs are settled in hamlets and villages, till their own soil and that of the manor farm, fulfilling there all the labors of husbandry. In more populous villages, and above all in large estates, they are organized in communes on nearly the same principles as are the free peasants. But such an organization depends absolutely upon the will of the owner. It is mostly the case, where the arable land is not extensive enough, or for some other reason is wholly abandoned to the peasants, that they pay for its use to the landlord a redevance or obrok, and in such case they are called *obrotschnye duschy*, renting souls; or the master receives from his farmlands a certain quantity of the produce of the soil. But all such arrangements depend absolutely upon the master.

The house serfs live on the manor and its immediate dependencies. They are often very numerous, and thus a heavy burden to the owner, sometimes even his ruin. They generally refuse to be settled as agriculturists, looking upon it as altogether below their condition. They constitute the male and female servants of the household, stewards, private overseers, household artisans, mechanics, and workmen, sometimes even personal attorneys when by choice or whim the master has given to such one a suitable education. Generally the master takes care to make the males learn some handicraft, and when they are able to earn their living he gives them a permission or passport, and they go over the country in search of suitable employment. They, as well as all other serfs who are furnished with such a passport, can be called home by the master at any time. These wandering serfs are obliged to report to him their whereabouts; and they pay him a rent proportioned to their earnings, or the cost of their education. Others establish themselves as tradesmen, etc.

The serfs compose, to a great extent, the floating population of cities. In the largest of them, as St. Petersburg, Moscow, Nijnei Novgorod, etc., serfs can be found who are wealthy tradesmen. The obrok paid by them to their owner is generally the customary one, and at a rate not at all proportioned to their fortune. But they are completely dependent on the will of the master, who can recall and transplant them to any of his villages and hamlets. There are cases where masters are comparatively, nay even positively poorer than their serfs, and still refuse to sell them their liberty, even for a large sum. Such a refusal is generally the result of an inveterate pride, and of a repulsive feeling concerning emancipation.

In absolute principle, the whole movable property, money, etc., of a serf, belongs to the master. The law is silent in this matter. In practice, however, no owner in this manner robs his serfs. Public opinion would not tolerate it, and above the public opinion there is suspended the dread of assassination.

To a certain degree, the law watches, in a more or less tutelary manner, over the fate of the serfs. Its provisions have been enumerated. But abuse, or evasion of the law cannot be prevented. Its handling, its execution, as well as the framing of public opinion is in the hands of the nobility. Only very tyrannical abuses of power come to daylight. They are corrected either by the law, or by the interference of the sovereign, or in the last and supreme appeal, by the sufferers themselves. It is likewise a great error committed by some eclogical writers who dilate complacently about the would-be patriarchal mutual relations of serf and master. Such a paternal rule may be found by accident, but even such accidents are so rare, that they cannot be looked on as establishing any rule. Neither of the extremes of cruelty and paternal suavity occur generally—and the bulk of the noblemen are neither tyrants nor patriarchs, but shrewd masters—taking watchful care of their own interest. The owners of large estates do not live on them—and sometimes do not visit many of them at all. The task of ruling the serfs is given up totally to overseers—who generally are no patriarchs, whatever may be their nationality, German or native. The small nobility want generally more than their fortune yields, and to get it squeeze as much as possible the laboring serf; and without being inhuman, they will not sacrifice their own well-being to that of the peasantry.

The internal organization of estates and villages is absolutely unconditionally dependent on the owner. He can introduce any form whatever, and as has been mentioned, the communal organization prevails here likewise. The power of emancipating the serfs is absolutely in the hands of the nobleman. No law obliges or prevents him from doing it. Pride, together with economical considerations, embracing that of "to be, or not to be" for the immense majority of the nobility, are the principal impediments. It must and cannot be forgotten, that the nobility, rich or poor, counting their serfs by thousands, or hundreds, or only by tens, all live on the peasant. When the estate is large, or formed of several villages situated together, their administration is easier and thus more beneficial for the laboring class. Worse is it when they are parcelled out—which is very often the case—into small hamlets, scattered in all directions—distant miles and miles from each other. But the worst of all is when a small number is owned by a poor obscure country squire, and of such owners there are very many.

In large estates—the prescriptions of the law to the contrary notwithstanding—the marriages of the serfs are always made with the interference of the master or the overseer, but on such estates, the choice of the serf is generally regarded. As the wife follows the husband, a maiden is seldom taken from a neighboring estate, except where the bridegroom is rich enough to buy his bride. In smaller estates where the choice is more limited, generally after the field labors are over, in the fall season, the master calls the families together and inquires about their mutual inclinations, pays attention to them, and endeavors to arrange things by mutual agreement; but when all is of no avail, then he decides arbitrarily—points out the pairs, and then the ceremony is fulfilled by the parish priest.

Such are the nature, the characteristics and the working of serfdom in Russia. Accursed as it is, it has little or no similitude to that greater curse—absolute slavery. It is neither so cruel nor so debasing, so degrading to both servant and master as the "peculiar institution." Serfdom in many most striking features is wholly different from the slavery of the ancient world, and the modern slavery of the United States, which in their turn differ, and not for the better, from that of the East.

Slavery and serfdom are in nowise autochtone Slavic institutions. Quite the contrary. Both serfdom and slavery were in use among the savage Germans and Celts as well as among the civilized or polished Greeks and Romans. Antiquity as well as Christianity dealt with it. Serfdom disappears reluctantly from modern civilization. The French revolution of the eighteenth century was its death knell. But slavery was unknown to the Slavi of old. Not even prisoners of war became enslaved. The Byzantine Emperor, Mauritius, describing the manners, customs and the mode of life of the Slavi on the Danube and beyond it, says that prisoners of war were detained for a year, and if during this time they did not become acclimated to the new country, they could freely return to their own. The accounts of antiquity concerning the Hyperborei, whose dwellings in all probability were in the northern part of the present Russia, describe their hospitality, and peaceful habits of life—and inform us that their country was a safe harbor for all fugitives. This does not point by any means to slavery. That these Hyperborei were the source, the forefathers of the Russians, could with difficulty be contested. Nothing authorizes us to presume, as there exist no proofs or records, that either serfdom or slavery were used by the two most ancient republics of the Christian era, that of Pskoff and Novgorod, situated in the regions of the Hyperborei. It was likewise unknown in the primitive times of Poland, Bohemia, and all the western and southern Slavic regions. In Poland it was unhappily rather fostered by the Roman clergy, who traced the descent of the peasantry from the cursed Cham; there, as in Bohemia, it was introduced by contact with the Germans, nearly simultaneously with the establishment of nobility; both slavery or serfdom and nobility are thus eminently German and Celtic, and above all Anglo-Saxon institutions, founded among them already by Cæsar and Tacitus. The Slavi from the Adriatic to the Baltic and the Wolga were not familiar with either of them. They had only elders, *starschiny*, or as in the western tribes, the *Zupan*, from whom by the influence of time and of a bad example, arose or was formed the *Pan*, that is the Sir, Lord, Nobleman. In the East, in Russia, the denomination of noblemen, *dworianin*, is derived from *dwor*, manor, a thing anciently unknown among the two republics.

The Slavic region was for the greater part divided into smaller or larger communities—and old legends mention chiefs or princes elected by the people from among themselves; and such chiefs were agriculturists, artisans, as wheel-makers, jewelers, etc. In Russia slavery dates, with the utmost probability, since the introduction of the Northmen, originating with prisoners of war, and being established over conquered tribes of no Slavic descent. This was done when Rurik and his successors descended the Dwina, the Dnieper, and established there new dominions. In the course of time, the conquerors cleared the forests, established villages and cities. As in other feudal countries, the tower, the *Schloss*, was outside of the village or of the borough :—so was in Russia the *dwor* or manor, where the conqueror or master dwelt—and from which was derived his name of *dworianin*. That the genuine Russian of that time, whatever may have been his social position, was free in his village, is beyond doubt, as, according to old records, the boroughs and villages, dependencies of the manor, were settled principally with prisoners of war and the conquered population. It was during the centuries of the Tartar dominion that the people, the peasantry, became nailed to the soil and deprived of the right of freely changing their domicil. Then successively every peasant, that is, every agriculturist tilling the soil with his own hands, became enslaved. Only in estates owned by monasteries and convents, which were very numerous and generally very rich, slavery being judged to be opposed to Christian doctrine, it did not take root at once. Generally monks were reluctant to the utmost, and even directly opposed to the sale of men in the markets, and the dependants of a monastery were never sold in such a manner.

Borys Gudenoff, the usurper of the throne and the murderer of the lawful heir in the last years of the XVIth century, tried to restore to the people their lost rights, at least that of a free change of domicil and of master. But his attempts were unsuccessful, and only served to make him more unpopular with the mighty boyars or aristocracy—which unpopularity facilitated the conquest of the Empire by the false pretender Dimitry.

Donations of estates made by the Grand Dukes of Moscow to the nobility, to the boyars, and to princely families after they had been deprived of their sovereignty—were among the principal means by which free rural communities became private property, and were subjected to slavery, to serfdom. Of this practice, there are traces in the ukases, and it was stopped only by the ukase of Alexander, who also prohibited the sale in the market, the separation of families, and connected the possession of the serf with that of a corresponding soil. This has been already pointed out. It was done in the short epoch of that autocrat's generosity, the brief period of his youthful feelings.

He, as well as Nicholas and many high-minded nobles, wished sincerely and may wish still, to find a clue to this labyrinth, by which to direct themselves in an attempt at emancipation. Nicholas several times stirred up the question, publishing even ukases as preliminary essays for settling the complicated matter. Some accuse him of bad faith, and of trying thus to become popular with the people and crush more the nobility. But this is not in his nature, and on the contrary, in these last years, he rather strengthened the position of the nobles, rendering it more inaccessible. The wish for the peaceful emancipation of the serfs sprung up from a purer motive. He very well knows that the solution of this question is a bloody cloud suspended over the future of the empire, and of the dynasty, and he attempted to prevent its bursting out, giving to it a more quiet issue, and thus to raise for himself a "*monumentum ære perennius*" in the annals of humanity. But now the better inspiration is exhausted and extinct. Among the aristocracy, above all, the Wasiltschikoffs, owners of large estates, were devoted, sincere, and disinterested partisans of emancipation. Stimulated by them, the body of the nobility of the government of Kursk petitioned the emperor, who to this effect, published an ukase; but its execution met with insurmountable difficulties—and it remained a dead law.

However, by far the greatest number of the nobles, and above all the smaller ones, living in the country on their estates, are violently opposed to any large measure, and curse the emperor for having made any attempts, and awakened the attention and the feelings of the peasantry,—for having, so to speak, brought the question again before the people. Scattered as they are, they are afraid to be thus surrounded by menacing crowds. To it must be added the unavoidable material ruin of the nobility, which will result from either a pacific or a violent emancipation.

The population of Russia is neither spread equally over the whole region, nor has it yet reached, so to say, a normal, or necessary amount. In one word, there is no balance between the forces or hands, and the quantity of the soil. Wages differ from one part, nay, sometimes from one county to another. It is feared by the nobility that the peasant if emancipated, would abandon the region where the prices of produce are low and wages are small, or where the soil is poor, and wander to more prosperous sections. Thus the lands of the nobility would become deserted and nearly uncultivated, for want of hands which could not be procured for insufficient wages. Further, the serf is attached, by indissoluble ties to the soil which his ancestors have tilled for centuries, which was their property before both land and men were enslaved. The government and that part of the nobility friendly to emancipation, wish that by a possible arrangement, the soil now possessed and used by the serfs forming their special homestead, may become their conditional property, for which they may pay a rent, releasing them from other servitudes and statute labors; or that to become absolute owners of a homestead, they pay its value in some way, in successive terms, or otherwise. But the peasantry, the serfs, look on the soil on which they live as their immediate property; they are, so to speak, one and the same with it. Thus in the most cases they refuse emancipation without the land, saying: that the soil ought be emancipated in common with them, or that both would remain in serfdom awaiting their time. But such a time will not be the result of a pacific arrangement. The nobility will never come to such terms, will never give up willingly the land and the men. The peasant refuses a partial boon or concession. For the peasantry, emancipation very logically corresponds with complete, absolute independence of the nobility, with the entire secession of all now existing and prevailing ties, nay, with the extermination of the ancient master. Thus, where the rumors of emancipation have penetrated more distinctly to the people, where the matter was only slightly mutually spoken of, it resulted in violent attacks on the *dwor* and on the *dworianstwo*, nobility. For the present, the affair is pending. The nobility are in a state of frightful suspense. Many of them wish to give up to the government their estates, land and serfs, for a suitable rent. The serf waits until he can take the whole as an inherent right, and not get it as a favor distilled in scanty drops. And the serfs are right. Any liberties, political or social franchises, conceded by compact or granted as a favor, are no liberties at all. They have no security, they have the odor of condescension on the part of the donor, and when accepted, they are a recognition of his lawful superiority. Liberty, to have its full worth, to be really beneficial and valuable, ought to put every body on an equal footing, and thus be conquered as an innate property and not humbly received as a grant. It will be shown in a subsequent chapter, what is the position of the non-slavic races inhabiting or scattered over Russia. A cruel anomaly exists between the fate of the real autochtone — or native, and the conquerors; the intruders and the subdued. The master is slave and serf, because even the free or crown peasant enjoys less freedom than the stranger or the annexed. Comparatively, the German, the Finn, the Calmuck, Tartar, Baschkir, the Samojede, the Lap, the Georgian, etc., are more free than the peasants—the serfs; as the German burgher of the Baltic provinces, of Poland, or any of the not ancient Russian lands, is superior in privileges and franchises to the Russian burgher. The genuine people in all their divisions have less individuality, less space for free activity, than has the nomad wandering on the soil conquered by the former. If the peasants, the serfs, shall ever take a cruel revenge, let it not be forgotten, that nothing, absolutely nothing is done for their intellectual, moral and social melioration. If the burghers and the free peasants find insurmountable difficulties in acquiring education, the serf is wholly abandoned, forgotten, and cannot participate even in the wretched resources allowed to the others. His education depends wholly upon the master, and the latter does not much trouble himself about the matter. Thus if a serf can read and write, it is rather the result of an accident, and not a common occurrence among the millions of serfs. But there is in Russia a ministry called pompously that of the national popular enlightenment, *narodnago proswieschtschenia*,— what a heartless irony!

CHAPTER X.

THE RIGHTS OF ALIENS AND STRANGERS.

THE Russian language, as well as the Russian law, have two different and distinct denominations for all those not belonging to the national stock. Thus *inorodets* signifies those born in the empire, or tribes residing from time immemorial in its different regions, but belonging to a different race and stock, and generally not of any Christian religion. [This word is composed from *ino*, different, and *rod*, stock, family.]

Inostranets designates those born in a foreign country, this being the signification of the word *strana*.

Among the *inorodtsy* are reckoned the Tartars and other Mahometans, the aborigines of Siberia, the Kirgiz of Siberia, the islanders of the American Aleutic Archipelago, the Samoïeds in the county of Archangel, the Laps, and the nomads of Asia and the Caucasian territory, the Calmucks, the Baschkirs, and the Jews.

The aborigines of Siberia form three classes: those settled in fixed dwellings and regions; the nomads, or those having flocks of cattle; and the erratic clans, living by hunting and fishing; these last inhabit the north-eastern part of Asia. All of them are free, can never be subjected to serfdom, and are exempted from military service.

They can enter any corporation of free peasants, or burghers, and become inscribed in any one of the guilds, according to their choice.

They are ruled by their own chiefs, elective or hereditary, according to their special custom transmitted from old times. These chiefs receive a small salary from the government.

The hereditary chiefs preserve all their hereditary titles and distinctions, but they cannot enjoy the general privileges of the nobility, except by a special grant. They are nearly all ruled by their traditional customs and laws. They pay to the crown a certain tribute in kind. They can carry on every species of trade, with the single exception of selling liquors.

The Kirgiz have the privileges of free men. They can own landed property and serfs if inherited, but can not make or buy new ones, under forfeiture and severe penalties.

The Islanders are administered by the American Trading Company. They do not pay any tribute whatever to the government, nor has the Company the right to collect any for its benefit. Their service consists in hunting and fishing for the Company, which feeds and clothes them, paying them a small remuneration for the produce of the sport. This service is obligatory for three years for each male; then they can fish and hunt on their own account, but the Company has the exclusive right to buy the produce thereof.

The Samoïeds of Archangel, the Laps, etc., are organized and have the same rights as the erratic tribes. No Russian can settle on the lands occupied by them.

The nomads in Asia and in the Caucasian territory own vast tracts of land for their own use, and no one else can settle on them, or use them as pasturage for cattle.

The Calmucks centered in the government of Astrachan and the Caucasian territory, are divided into seven large districts or Ulusy. Their lands are also protected by law from being used in any way by other inhabitants or tribes. The Calmuck nobility, called *noïons* and *zaïesangs*, have the right of primogeniture, and their real estate cannot be divided. If they enter the army they enjoy the privileges of the Russian nobility.

All the *inorodtsy* enjoy absolute religious liberty; in civil matters they have their own jurisdiction as well as in small correctional offences; in criminal ones they have to submit to the general laws of the empire.

All the nomads of Siberia elect their boards, elders, or have patriarchs of the tribe. They elect the collectors of the taxes or of the tribute, their assistants, the scribes or clerks. The elections are made according to ancient prevailing usages, by general meetings, or by families or clans.

Every facility is accorded to nomads to become fixed in their settlements with their movable property, as inherited slaves, cattle, chattels, and to form rural communities, such as exist in Russia Proper. These nomads often possess houses and gardens, where the family dwells, while the master roves with the cattle on the pasturages. The Tartars, the Wostiaks, Baschkirs, and Mestscheraks, Mordwa, Tschouwasche, Tscheremyss, Tepters, Bobels, and others scattered in the east of the empire—some inclosed by Russian population, and all of them of Finnic or Ouralian stock—when living in villages or rural communes have the rights of freemen, *Selskïe Obywatcli*. In no manner, nomad or settled, can they be made serfs, or be deprived of their property of any kind. The Tartars can make contracts, take farms or estates on rent, buy or sell their own, settle where they please, and dispose in any way of their persons, as well as of their personal and real estate.

Mahometan and other heathen prisoners of war, whose purchase was allowed to the Scotch colonists in the Caucasian territory, cannot be resold by them into slavery. Those bought under the sixteenth year of their age, obtain their liberty on reaching their twenty-third year. Those bought older than sixteen remain slaves for seven years. They have the right to buy their freedom before the lapse of these seven years, for the legal price of one hundred and sixty-six dollars. All the children born in slavery are free.

The aborigines of the Caucasus, of Georgia, and the Armenians are governed by their own chiefs as the other *inorodtsy*. But where the social state is more ordered and fixed, as, for example, in Georgia, Russian civil and administrative organization begins to prevail, still having regard, however, to local laws, customs, and manners. The Caucasian and Trans-caucasian nobility, Christian, Mahometan, or Tartar, are all of them put on an equal footing with the genuine Russian nobles.

The Jews enjoy perfect religious liberty. They are married and divorced by their own rabbis and according to their Jewish laws. In all other civil and criminal matters they are subjected to the ordinary jurisprudence. All their judicial signatures must be made in the Russian language. (The Asiatic *inorodtsy* can sign such documents in their special idiom.) The Jews can send their children to gymnasia, academies, and universities, and thus they enjoy a facility refused to the Russians at large.

The Jews principally inhabit Lithuania, White Russia, Little Russia, and Odessa, generally in those regions which anciently formed a part of the Polish dominions, and where they established themselves under the Polish protectorate. They are excluded from Russia proper. Their number amounts there to more than eight hundred thousand. Nearly the same number are in the present kingdom of Poland. They are likewise very numerous in Gallicia, and the dukedom of Posen, both parts of ancient Poland. It is supposed that their population scattered over the globe, amounts to some nine millions; thus Poland possesses nearly a third part of the whole. Ancient Poland was for a long time their Paradise. The Polish Jews are the most dirty and filthy of all, but they are also the most learned of the race, and most of the schoolmasters and Rabbis in Europe, are Polish Jews.

In Russia, that is where they were found at the time of the conquest, they can own houses and gardens. But they cannot have Christian servants in their houses, but only hire them for daily work, as well as for fulfilling personal, communal and governmental servitudes. They are now subjected to military recruitment.

A Jew who receives a diploma from a University, or an Academy of Arts, has the right to petition for the privilege of a personal respectable citizen. Those who become Doctors, can become hereditary respectable citizens, and even with the special permission of the sovereign, can enter civil and military service. Jews can be teachers and professors. All these services can be entered upon, only in the regions inhabited generally by them, that is in the so-called western counties. Jews entering into service there, can obtain permission to sojourn or live in the capitals and the countries of Russia proper.

Jews can become agriculturists on crown lands as well as on private ones. In this last case they do not become serfs. Those who settle as agriculturists, are, for a certain number of years, exempted from military recruitment.

Jew merchants, burghers, and artisans, in places where the laws allow them to reside, enjoy all the privileges accorded to Russians and Christians of the same social class. They can erect shops and manufactories, and employ Christian mechanics and workmen. They can enter the different guilds. They can neither own nor rent estates with peasants and serfs on them, nor be overseers on the like lands, nor rent the obroks or other payments due by the peasants to the nobility.

The Jews are specially taxed. For the distribution of this tax and its regulation, they have their own board called *cahal*, elected by themselves and responsible to the government. They participate in the general elections for the city and communal functions, and if they master the Russian language they can be elected to any one of them.

Foreigners, aliens (*inostrantsy*), are the subjects of other states, who become Russians. Children born to them in Russia become Russians and belong to that class to which they have a legitimate right.

A woman, being a Russian subject, marrying a foreigner, follows him to his country. But by thus expatriating herself, from choice, she can own no real estate in Russia, and ought to sell the same in the course of the six months succeeding her leaving her fatherland. She pays a tax of ten per cent. on the capital exported by her.

All foreigners can enter, settle, or leave Russia, according to certain special regulations as to passports. Foreign Jews, however, cannot settle in Russia and become Russian subjects.

Foreigners can, in some cases, enter the military service, but not the civil, except by special permission of the sovereign.

Foreigners, even nobles by birth, cannot own serfs, peasants, and villages unless by special permission of the sovereign. But they can own houses in cities. By permission, gained from the authority, they can be teachers and private tutors.

If they inherit villages and serfs, they must sell them either to the crown or to individuals who may lawfully own such property.

A foreigner, naturalized as a Russian subject, can renounce this subjection and leave the country, but he is obliged to sell his real property. If he belongs to any of the corporations subject to capitation, on abandoning it he has to pay in advance the amount of three years' tax, and leave the country in the course of a year.

Prisoners of war, naturalized and married to Russian women, returning to their fatherland, must separate themselves from wife and children, these not being allowed to follow them; and before they abandon their family they must secure for it the means of subsistence.

CHAPTER XI.

THE COMMUNE.

THE communal organization is deeply intertwined in the social life of all classes of the Russian people. All its artificial subdivisions, nay, the differences of descent and race, unite on a general and common social ground, that of communal institutions. Self-administration, through elections, is thus a general, legal, social usage. The elective principle, in a restricted form as used by the nobility, or in the more extensive and genuine form as used by the other classes of the people, forms the basis and the cement of the organic social existence of the whole.

Neither the elective franchise as used by the nobility, nor the absolute commune existing in cities and rural districts, is originally and in principle a gift granted by a power existing out of or above the nation. It is a right inherent in the people, and by far more ancient, than the accidental and temporary growth of autocratic power in Russia. The nobility, using this franchise now, have but diverted a small rivulet from the original, great, popular stream; the nobility itself every where, and above all in Russia and in the whole Slavic family, being an excrescence and not a fundamental element of the historical and social existence. Thus the communal life is not a concession made by any aristocratic or monarchical sovereignty. It was not a lure presented, as in some other countries, by such authority to the people, when in some struggle it was necessary to carry the masses on its side.

It is not necessary to enter into minute and laborious dissertations, based on abstract reasoning as well as on history, and to argue the question of priority in the mode of the primitive life of the human family, between the so called patriarchal rule and the communal action of society in its cradle—the one being the type of monarchy, absolutism, and autocracy, the other of freedom and equality inherent in humanity. It would be a rather easy task to prove to those who believe that the march of civilization or progress moves in a circle, passing through different stages and forms, to prove that as in such a case the process must finish where it began: that therefore the social starting point was not patriarchal, not the power of one over some or over many, but equality in association of those composing the first family, tribe, city, or nation. Our belief is that there can be no well-founded doubt about the social character of the original starting point, and that the further progress of our race is infinite—in every direction—radiating like the light, and not confined geographically, mentally and socially to the direction from east to west, as believed religiously by some pseudo-philosophers.

Every where liberty and equality were certainly anterior to the supreme power of one man, to castes, and privileges. The most striking testimony of a primitive sin, or fall, may be found in the successive establishment of social oppression by patriarchs, high priests, kings, or nobles—and the labor of the redemption may be looked for in the uninterrupted efforts of humanity to disentangle herself from their clutches.

In relation to the Slavic race and family, history confirms the above proposition. It has been already mentioned, several times, that among the primitive Slavi, from Novgorod to the Danube and Cattaro, there are no traces of any privileged, distinct class; that their principal occupation, agriculture, gathered them into villages or large communities, where they were governed by elected elders (*starschiny*) or chiefs. In this state were the Slavi found at the first dawn of history; thus, therefore, they must have lived of old, during the long period that is called ante-historical. If the Kimbri, beyond the Palus Meothides, and those of the Tauric Chersonesus, expelled therefrom by the Scythic invasion, were, as the great Goerres establishes, of a Slavic stock, their disastrous discomfiture on the battle-field ought to be principally attributed to their being led and acting under separate chiefs (each tribe or community), and not under one supreme chief, or king, or sovereign. When afterwards Darius crossed the Danube for retaliation on the Scythes for their invasion of Media and Asia Minor, and the Scythes tried to call to their rescue other tribes living there, Herodotus does not say that they sent their messages to kings or chiefs, but mentions only the names of the tribes. This omission authorizes us to presume these tribes, undoubtedly of pure Slavic and not of Scythian descent, acted and answered for themselves, and not through an omnipotent chief, whose name, if such existed, would not have been omitted by the father of history. Undoubtedly, therefore, liberty and the commune, the organism most simple and most congenial to human nature, is older in Russia than princes and Czarism, nobility and serfdom. The people do not consider the commune as a grant from any one, but as a right transmitted from antiquity, through successive generations. As an evidence that it is so we may take the vitality of the communal usages and the deep roots which they struck into the life of the nation. There they exist by their own strength, indestructible by their most deadly enemies, slavery, serfdom, Czarism, and the despotic centralization; and thus a germ was preserved, a germ full of promise for the future.

Neither was the communal organism borrowed by the Slavi from any other race or nation. If a source may be traced for it, this source is the nature of things, and from this fountain-head each human family might draw it for itself. Admitting even that the father, the patriarch, may have been its first chief, naturally his power descended equally to all his children, brethren among themselves, mutually associated, and thus originated the commune. It is, therefore, the absolute property and attribute of mankind, as association is its most natural state. Treachery, craftiness, and brutal force were the means by which man was subsequently deprived of his inherent social right.

Those who take the Mosaic records for indisputable historical evidence concerning the origin of man and society, find there that monarchy and castes originated in the revolt, and the first man bending others under his will and power; the first monarch, was Nimrod, the inventor of murderous weapons, a savage hunter, and then an oppressor and a usurper.

The Slavi, in their immense plains, appointed by nature and climate to agriculture, are found by history living in villages, that is, in association, and not on separate farms or in isolation, as were most of the German tribes. The same mode of life must have existed before the historical epoch, and prevailed during the legendary one. Everywhere history meets among them elective chiefs of tribes, territories, and nations. If such was the origin of power with these supreme leaders, it follows, logically, that of the same nature was that of chiefs in the separate villages and communes, where they were elected from among the members of the community, to administer but not to rule. No traces were there of hereditary supremacy. When general history shall be more keenly examined and understood, and when a pure, philosophical light shall penetrate more and more deeply its recesses, then it will come out distinctly to daylight, that the greater number of dynasties, oligarchies, and aristocracies are of secondary, if not tertiary, social formation.

The Slavic commune, at any rate, neither is nor was borrowed from the Germans, no more in the legendary times than in the historical ones. The existence of the Slavic republics of Novgorod and Pskoff, at least contemporaneous to any positive, organic social formation among the tribes of Germany, and thus differing in their essence from any found there—this existence is a proof of the communal institutions being of an intrinsic domestic growth. Further: the Slavi do not appear any where in history to have been so continually moving, roving, and wandering, as were nearly all the German tribes. From the like mode of life sprung up by itself the necessity of chiefs or kings, their retinue or companions, and thus the formation of a military or noble caste. The Slavi never were thus pushed hither and thither. From the time of their immigration to Europe, as an Indo-European branch of the human family; or from the Caucasus, if the heights of Armenia were its cradle and nursery; or whatever theory may be adopted concerning the origin of man, since his distribution or dissemination over the earth, the Slavi have always occupied one and the same region. Subdued, conquered, by other tribes and nations, whose waves overflowed them northward and westward, their toughness remained indestructible, rooted as they were in the soil and in their villages. It is more natural to conclude that the Slavi, who instructed the Germans in agriculture, if a transmission is to be admitted, transmitted to them the notion of communal organization.

The existing Russia has thus, in her bosom, an organic force, alive and acting, by which the mass of the people, however abject and oppressed, are still accustomed to take care of themselves. For the eventualities of every day's life, a city or a rural commune is able to take counsel and provide for itself, without the necessity of the spurious guardianship of the supreme, governing power, or of the privileged classes, hovering over it like birds of prey. Should all these tutors disappear, or be driven away together, this would not startle the population, nor find them unawares, or unable to cope with the new emergency. Already accustomed to administer and settle their domestic affairs by the election of the ablest, the people will soon get accustomed to extend the practice, and find means to care for the affairs of the district, the county, and, finally, those of the whole nation. In an area of activity, enlarged through self-consciousness and liberty, the intellectual powers acquire elasticity, penetration, and compass, in single individuals as well as in whole masses.

It is beyond discussion, and does not require any argumentative proofs, that the communal organization is, for every nation, the first condition of practical, political, nay, even of social liberty. Only within its existence the enjoyment of an orderly, peaceful liberty is possible. The absence or the utter destruction of the communal order in France, is one of the reasons why its destinies are thus thrown into the arms of despotism. The people there are not accustomed to decide for themselves in any, the most common or slightest, occurrence. Stating and proving that this germ exists in Russia, and what deep and indestructible roots it has spread there, seems sufficient to justify the hope that, with this incentive, the liberation of the people from the present thraldom is within reach of possibility. To-day the commune is still the corner-stone of social order within this vast empire. It is a finger-post to the future; in due time it will become its keystone. Restricted, cramped now, and denationalized, the commune will reconquer its normal growth and vitality, when the Russian soil shall become moved and turned over by the fructifying share of revolution. Then what is now only germ will shoot out to a mighty social structure. All the abnormal, false, and artificial restrictions, preventing the healthy germination of the seed, will dissolve, die, and fall off; the inborn elasticity of a genuine communal order will no longer encircle small and lifeless corporations, but embrace a people, and give space and air to the culture and practical application of new social combinations; it will be a potent agency, the sword as well as the law for emancipation.

CHAPTER XII.

EMANCIPATION.

The deepest ice that ever froze,
Can only o'er the surface close;
The living stream lies quick below,
And flows and cannot cease to flow.

BYRON.

NOT only the soil and the serf, but the whole nation gravitates, though slowly, towards emancipation. The onward movement of so large a mass, with such complicated internal wheelwork—if indiscernable to many — still exists. The preceding chapters have given an outline of the political and social compound existing in Russia—a mixture of arbitrary will with seeds of free institutions. Complicated to the utmost, yet possessing the normal elements of a symmetrical combination. What there is confused and entangled in it, is a result of the artificial working of the supreme power and government; while what is simple, uniform, self-unfolding, is a patrimony of the people, a product of its ancient social life.

Every year, as well as every new extension, adds new complications and augments the intricacy. New entanglements pour continually out of the autocratical source. The frames encasing a society with so minute an artificiality are surfeited; they overfill and crack, grinding mercilessly the various classes of the nation. From among the particles into which power and the privileged class have shivered the people—the greater number, like the edges of a bleeding wound, try and seek to reunite, to restore, to reconquer the healthy normal state. It seems, beyond any human possibility, that a society thus artificially built up and encircled, could secure to its members—growing in strength and in vital activity—the necessary air and all the resources of a free and undisturbed existence. In the present state they never can live harmoniously or act peaceably by the side of each other. The mass forms a misshaped pyramid, where the superposed press with all their might on those below; all in their turn being pressed down by the key-stone of this anomalous construction. In this, more than in any other governmental formation, the action of the government, instead of being beneficial—must be oppressive. Thus conflicts, continual pulling between the various classes, and with the government, are natural consequences. Outbreaks must follow. Whatever may be the length of time for the existence of such a structure, it can only be protracted arduously, though without hope for its stability.

At present despotism binds Russia awfully in its anaconda folds. Strict restraints, called laws, twist harshly around all the various members of the political whole,—of the nation. Such a state cannot last for ever, nay, not even for a long lapse of future time; more especially now, when the people become more awake to self-consciousness, and are thus wounded to the quick by the diverse agencies that oppress and grind them.

Whatever may be the future revolution of Russia, it will bear a mark of its own, as does every thing connected with this people. The coming revolution will pour out from within, rather than be a result of any outward influence or excitement. To say that an affinity of aims and aspirations having their eternal source in the imprescriptible rights of human nature, shall not exist in Russia in common with other people and nations, would be absurd. Other more positive incentives from without cannot at present, for many reasons, penetrate and spread among the people. But the nation contains fermenting elements in abundance, and their ebullition extends and becomes daily more intense.

Russia hovers now over Europe, luridly clouding the progress of emancipating civilization. It seems that in a twinkling destructive hurricanes can rend the air, hurl upon Europe, extinguish and destroy every light, strangle every hope. Such suppositions may be pushed too far; still it remains incontestable that as long as Russia shall stand there menacingly, instead of being carried on by the general providential current, the task of other nations will remain difficult to the utmost, if not wholly impossible. It will not be so easy for Europe to fling off the decayed crust and establish new and invigorating institutions: whether they be of limited monarchy, republican, or of any higher social order.

By her compactness and force, Russia powerfully supports retrograde opposing interests, which otherwise ere long would have to breathe their last. Every where do exist—and will exist for a long time—various social elements tied and wedded to the past. Doomed by the present, they still possess strength enough from their traditional organization. Common danger unites them in opposition to any effort of disenthralment, and their force increases when backed by such a vigorous ally as they now find in Russia. These breakers, hidden or towering over the surface, exist every where, prompt to wreck and destroy any generous undertaking. A spontaneous and unanimous effort of Europe, divided thus into two hostile camps, is not easy to be anticipated. As long as Russia shall side with monarchs, aristocrats and priests, they will not be hurled out of their seats for some time to come.

There exists a very dim probability, that an evolution, bringing Russia from the wrong to the right side, can be effected in such a short period, as the present eagerly wishes for; but actual sufferings and calamities, however poignant, count scarcely as a moment in the great run of time. The human mind vibrates in Russia as elsewhere, though at present not with equal celerity. Before Russia shall be enabled to accomplish her internal revolution, and enter broadly the apprenticeship of freedom,—she must undergo a rather long process; passing from the stage of fermentation to that of mature action, and then only will she weigh in the right scale. The most ardent wishes are powerless to accelerate this historical momentum. There are certain organic laws for the whole creation, regulating alike the material or physical world, and the higher region of mind and of intellect; the region in which men, nations, mankind find and fulfil the conditions of their existence. Some of these laws are general, others special, appropriate to this or that mental or physical organism. The history of the world is pre-eminently a record of the action, of the development of mankind in the whole, as well as of distinct races, nations, nay even of individuals, under the influence of similar various laws and phenomena. Russia as a nation, as a people, as a social or politic body, is under their action; her history has some common characteristics with that of other nations, again differing from them in some respects. Thus she remained almost entirely untouched by the mediæval element, which shaped all the parts of the social structure in the West, church and state, popes, bishops, kings, barons, burgesses and villeins. But under the Tartar supremacy, her unity was wrought out, nearly in the same way as that of France, England, or as it was attempted in Italy.

Louis XI., some of the Tudors, Cæsar Borgia, or Philip of Spain resemble, in more than one respect, some of the Grand Dukes of Moscow. This unity—by which alone the liberation from the Tartars could have been effected—was only to be obtained through an energetic concentration of power in one single hand. Thus alone, simultaneous and powerful action was possible—and thus originated the despotism still holding Russia. The results obtained by such an agency could not have been obtained by any other; what once was effected in a certain way, could not happen or succeed in a different one. It is useless if not childish to quarrel with facts and with the past. What once took place bears in itself the evidence of its unavoidable necessity, or else it would not have happened at all. Events and results once accomplished could not have taken a different turn. It is therefore of no avail to speculate how a past event was to have come out differently. Every fact and every form which existed or exists, was or is necessary. It had or has the necessary conditions of its existence or else it would not come into existence. For the long run, nothing can subsist by the support of material or brute force; and moreover such a momentary support is in itself a proof that some congenial combinations supply the required elements of strength. Terrible phenomena in nature, as well as in history, are succeeded by others more bright and beneficial. Thus Czarism was a necessity for Russia. It condensed the empire, moulded it into a unit beyond a possibility of dissolution. Its violent cohesive action will cease, but the molecules forming the body will henceforth cohere. In this manner united Russia arose out of scattered parts; it resisted external enemies and became a political and historical individuality. Czarism has accomplished the task of the pioneer towards the unfathomed solitudes of Asia. In that direction, where it is the destiny of Russia to act and to civilize, Czarism has already spread broadcast Russian seeds, has laid down or prepared foundations for the future, and it has in all directions through the country fulfilled the often cruel but unavoidably necessary task of engrafting the dominant nationality on the subdued ones. Among its numerous dark sides it has thus some that are sunny, or at least consoling. But Czarism has nearly run out its course; it has fulfilled its terrible mission. Whatever, therefore, may be its external show, it is on the wane in reality. It was a process of formation which Russia was to undergo for the benefit of the whole Slavic race. Now it will be succeeded by another more congenial to the innate character and life of the people, and to new external and internal emergencies. A transition, an evolution is to be effected. It is already taking place in the conscience of the people; and this being done, it will break out, come to light and become a palpable fact.

In the formation of our planet, epochs of creation succeeded one another. Some of the geological revolutions breaking forth at distant intervals, were previously brewing in the bowels of the earth. The grander and more durable formations in nature, result, however, from agencies and forces working silently but uninterruptedly. The slow process of molecular sediment was more extensive, more general and more creative than any other in nature. In the typical formation and development of nations and people, the slow way may, after all, prove to be the surest. This applies to Russia, accused to-day of backwardness. When the fluid trickling from within shall have silently penetrated all the fibres of the people, then to complete the transformation a commotion, if necessary, will most deeply shake the national base. All that is old, worn out, decayed, will be swept away and engulfed, making place for a new life. Such a social commotion is imminent for Russia, and with her for the Slavi. It will at once be the more beneficial and efficacious, *because* the more it will be the manifestation of the people. It will be primogenial in their history. The emancipation of Russia is an absolute condition of the emancipation of Europe, and thus of the future harmonious and progressive activity of the European or Christian world. Russia can neither be conquered nor partitioned. If in a war successful for the liberal side, Russian armies shall be repelled, the permanent danger will not be averted for ever, but merely hushed for a rather short lapse of time. The Slavic race must participate more generally in the European movement than it does now, being represented there by partial and weak and insignificant branches. Without its adhesion, the universal wheelwork can never turn with ease and security. Russia alone can not only facilitate but decide the peaceful union of the whole race.

And besides, how difficult, even impossible it is to fix with any certainty the epoch when the Russian people will break and throw off the shackles now maiming them, and join in the work of liberty: this hour once arrived, the Russian people will very likely more completely carry out the task of renovation, than it has been done hitherto by any other European nation.

Russia is almost inaccessible to a menacing and destructive invasion; this at present strengthens the power of despotism; but by it likewise the people have acquired a conviction and faith in its external individuality, it has an unshaken national self-reliance. The past, and its historical recollections, teach the people that all resistance to invasions and the conquests of others, have been accomplished by the nation itself, without the friendly co-operation or help of any other state, and this during long centuries and in epochs ominous for the preservation of national independence.

No Russian thinks in any way of foreign help or interference in what he does or may undertake at home or abroad. Never having looked for the assistance or assent of others when once at work at home, the Russian people will not anxiously calculate or ponder what other states or neighbors may or may not do. Neither their political nor material welfare depends on similar combinations. This mental independence will secure the completeness of any internal movement. The French people, at the climax of the great revolution, then inspired by a like feeling, and led on by the immortal Convention, accomplished the more than herculean task of destroying the past at home and of resisting combined Europe. The revolutionary movements of 1848, opening under circumstances incomparably propitious, stranded in a short time, principally because none from among the nations involved in them dared at starting what they ought to have dared. They hesitated, cautiously looking about on each other, losing thus a precious opportunity of success. It is not given to any mortal to accelerate a single minute on the dial of time; but when the hour strikes, when the chain bursts, and the event appears, it is in man's power to seize upon it, and turn it to his benefit. This was missed in 1848, and there lies one of the primordial reasons of the apparently inconceivable failure. The supposition may be justified that the Russian people, once up, will not commit the same blunder.

Nor did the masses of revolutionary Europe show any confidence in themselves. They seemed incapable of acting without the guidance of leaders, instead of acting on their own; impulse, as well as direction, came from the other strata of society. In one word, the masses of people in Western Europe, both in small affairs and in ponderous events showed incapacity of spontaneous self-action. The representative system introduced long ago in some states, for instance in France, but restrictive and one-sided in its application, did not really penetrate any where to the mass of the people. The French people are more tutored and governed in most matters referring to internal administration than the Russian. It has been shown in the preceding chapters, that the communal system leaves in the hands of the people the internal administration. A new emergency will find them capable to take their own counsel. In the European representative system the masses have neither participated, nor were they represented. Men often unknown to them were elected to represent interests they did not feel and wants which did not affect them. The system was not interwoven with the people or evolved from their life; it inspired no confidence, and rendered them indifferent to its restriction or even abolition. The European revolutions of the latter epoch have not been the general work of the masses. The impulse was mostly given by the so-called civilized strata, most of them wishing some little ameliorations and not great fundamental reforms. Nowhere was there an aim at eradicating the social evils which crushed the people proper. The movements originated with politicians, system-mongers, theoreticians, learned professors, as in Germany, who appealed to the popular force to carry through their own special schemes, rather than to account for the immediate necessities and claims of the people. Thus old abuses became continued under new names; the masses relapsed, and submitted quietly to the reaction, returned to the old yoke, and lost again for the moment the confidence in any attempt of reform. Tired and exhausted, they seem not to have any faith in the future, used up and ruined as they are by unsuccessful and oft-reiterated efforts.

In Russia the social upheaving will come from below. The real people will rise, stirred up, awakened by the consciousness of their imprescriptible rights. They will act for themselves. The revolution will be at once social and not merely political. There will be no class to turn the common efforts to its own especial benefit, and there will not appear those locust-like swarms of old respectabilities, political speculators,—that curse of European revolutions. The people, the mass, will find and give its sacramental word, it will find the solution for all emergencies. In Russia neither the people, nor even any class now above it, are entangled in, encumbered with any social or political formulas. This is one of the boons for the future, derived from the now all-crushing, all-levelling, all-stifling and destroying despotism. Common original reason will be enabled to act freely. The Russian, unacquainted with any political systems or theories of foreign growth or elucubration, will not lose time and generations in experimental essays of application. Nobody will look for precedents to imitate them. Nothing will fetter the extant home-materials. In Russia the number acquainted with theories of a mitigated monarchy, of the equilibrium of three powers, *id est*, of a government in government, and of other fanciful unrealities,—is small, insignificant, and scarcely worth mentioning. Such individuals are in no condition whatever to exercise any, even the smallest, influence. These fallacious theories have no currency in Russia, with the exception of few, very few nobles.

This social commotion will crush to atoms the artificial structure now pressing on the people; despotism, privilege, Czar and nobility will be overrun by the same destructive lava; and with them will disappear their accessories. Nothing will be done by halves, that mode being repulsive to the national character, and nowhere known in the history of Russia.

The people and its communal organism will alone remain standing, when every thing else is prostrated, pulverized. This primitive organism will cement and keep together the new self-unfolding society. Not the tension of despotism, but easy and elastic free action will unite the vast country. It has been pointed out that no real demarcation separates the people, the peasants from the burghers, or from the so-called middle class. A still less separation of tendencies and interests will be effected, when, by combined and mutual efforts, the common enemies shall have been swept away. The condition of the Russian people differs from that of any other country in Europe, even from Switzerland. There, when by mutual efforts the patriciate and nobility were overthrown, the struggle for power began between the arrogant middle classes and the people of the country, against which finally nobility and burghers joined together. Nothing like this could ever happen in Russia, as both burghers and peasants mix intimately, forming a compact whole: the people. Once running on the revolutionary track, it will be easy for them to plant real democracy and self-government, being already partly more accustomed to it than other nations of Europe, which are kept more rigorously in the swaddling bands of administrative centralization, than the Russians.

The embryo commune existing now through Russia, will advance with equal steps with the revolution, extend and spread out to a general republican net, embracing the whole state. The revolution will not begin in cities, but in the country, resembling that now going on in China; the flag of emancipation will be raised by the strong hands of the peasantry. Thus again will take place the reverse of what generally occurs in Europe. An efficacious revolution in Russia must originate in rural districts, in villages among the serfs; and there alone it will originate. Contrary to the progress and development of all other revolutions, the rural communes, instead of being new offshoots for the elementary political education of the masses, will form exclusively the fountains and the sources of a new organism. Each commune already existing will extend its action and influence in continually widening circles, all gravitating towards one and the same object, towards emancipation. Thus they will form one great national family. It is the only possible, because the only natural course. A great number of serfs are already partially organized into communes, or at least surrounded by those of the crown peasantry, which either they will join, or they will form new ones, immediately after the destruction of the masters. It will be as easy for the *wolost* (canton) to elect members known personally, and fit for a general council or administration, as it is now to choose the elders, the *golowa* (head) and other boards. This work once accomplished, only then, and not before hand, theoreticians will come forward to co-operate and give it the required finish. Their task will be eminently facilitated, finding materials already vigorous, instead of being obliged to invent them, and to teach their adaptation and handling, to the people. The plain question will be, not to introduce a new unwonted social form, but to harmonize the parts and facilitate the working of an already existing one.

"*Si licet exemplis in parvo grandibus uti*," the fathers of the American republic found on their path many difficulties cleared away by the pre-existence of communal organization. Thus, when the inevitable revolution in Russia shall rise from the deep upon the national horizon, its thoroughness and rapidity will compensate for its tardiness. Every sign points to the approach of such a moment, to such a commotion and explosion as shall surprise the world, alike by its strength and by a peculiar character of its own. The originality of the people will hold out in this new emergency, as it asserted itself in the past, in various terrible complications and catastrophes. Not to say that influence from without must be ineffectual on Russia, the contact with the civilized world may contribute, by a natural and inevitable friction, to set fire to the accumulated elements. But this contact works there differently from its action in other nations. The press or writings are not the channels, they do not penetrate to the people; silent personal observation supplies them already. As was mentioned in another chapter, the hundred thousands of soldiers led abroad by the autocrats, return home so many propagators of a better state of things existing in the countries where they have been. This was partly the case after the occupation of France in 1816–'17, and will be the result of the invasion of Hungary, when, as in Galicia, in Slovakia, the Russian peasant-soldier saw his brother peasant of the same stock overawing the noblemen, and through the election of deputies participating in the affairs of state. Even the absorption of Poland, where no serfdom exists, and where the laboring peasant is directly protected by the government against the nobleman—even this must act as a fermenter with the Russian people. Thus, in the long run, the very acts and undertakings of the Czars will serve the liberation of the nation. And then there are periods in the life of humanity, when, without any direct agency and material communication, a general commotion seizes upon all minds—a spiritual chain excites and links them in simultaneous action, in spite of all barriers raised by the retrograde spirit of the dark. Perhaps we are approaching such a moment; at any rate, not only nature, but the human world also is governed by laws ruling the whole creation, and silly would be an attempt to prevent the sunrise or the advent of the spring. For the spring appears at its appointed time, and the sun rises at his eternally appointed hour, unwelcome to those who delight in darkness, but cheerfully greeted by all who love and bathe in his light. And so with the destinies of Russia, of its people. For a long time the bugbear of civilization, it must, in its turn, enter the common orbit. Then the Slavic race, whose fate is inseparable from that of Russia, will pass under the command of the immortal Genius of Liberty. Many attempts of other nations, failures now, shall then turn out successful by the participation of the Russian people. Not that in the onward march of mankind it should be reserved to any race or nation to solve the problem, to complete the task, and to fulfil alone the destinies of all. Such presumptuous assertions are results of feverish imagination, rather than of a reflective contemplation of the history of our race, and of the laws presiding over its infinite ascension. The productions of mental creation, of various people, conform to the characteristics of species or genera in the world of nature. No single organic being, whether a plant or an animal, represents the complete organism of the whole species. The distinct speciality of each consists in the fact, that in every such separate being there is but one particularity of the general organism pre-eminently developed, while in another the same remains in the background, sometimes even wholly disappears. In the same manner a production of mind or intellect in a single people cannot possess the high and general perfection whose attainment is reserved to the whole human race, in the use of all its powers, which are never within the reach of a single branch, nation, or people.

The Slavic race, as well as Russia, have nothing to atone for in good or evil. This is true of all other nations more or less advanced in progress and development. Every people, every state of the past, as well as those now existing, has its dark as well as its sunny days; it has moments when it serves the cause of mankind and its eternal rights; and others again, when by its institutions and acts, under the pressure of unavoidable events, of transient, if not permanent, causes—it has trodden down and defiles, the same sacred cause. The succession of light and shadow, the mutual action of good and evil, are among the things distributed through creation; the problem is to restrain the one and to extend the other. In Russia the pernicious action of despotism has affected the national character, and thus there are many weeds to be extirpated, before the people will be able to assume a dignified position among the human family. But each nation has such spots in its history, in its character. It is, therefore, narrow-minded, and betrays a want of philosophical judgment, to condemn a race or nation as doomed eternally to slavery, subjection, or despotism, to proclaim it damned beyond the possibility of redemption. This, however, is uttered against the Slavi and the Russian people by many wholly unacquainted with their character or history. This is done daily, hourly, in similar respects, all over the globe.

The dark and gloomy sides will successively diminish in Russia, when the people itself will come to daylight. Human nature and human institutions are purified and washed white in the atmosphere of liberty; it alone contributes more to redeem, lift up, and ameliorate men and their actions, than all ethical catechizing under slavery and oppression. The human mind in all its spheres and attributes, whether in abstract speculation, or in things relating to immediate application in natural or in social science—only when free and unshackled—rises to purer regions, gives solutions for ancient and past, as well as for new phenomena. Liberty is the most powerful dynamic, both in the spiritual and in the material world. When it shall penetrate and move the Slavic race and Russia, then the lightning of animation shall flash and true life begin. The national spirit, once aroused, will grow stronger and stronger; no more secluded, contemptuous, or menacing to others, but elastic, communicative, and susceptible of higher culture. It will flow in a pure and mighty stream when relieved from its corrupting inlets—works of despotism and of privilege. Emancipation, evoking a new life, will strengthen it in all directions. Then only will real culture and civilization begin. Mind and intellect, inspired by freedom, will shape out and improve every object within their reach. New mental powers, streaming broadly from the whole people, and not, as now, from some scanty few, will transform and change the whole aspect of the nation. Then only reason and intellect will have a signification, fructifying every object in their domain. Art, literature, science, will then brightly flourish. Agriculture—that aboriginal property of the Slavic race, now neglected, and generally in the state of coarse empiricism—that inexhaustible source of wealth, that basis of national existence—agriculture, will become an art and science, when the soil and the bondman tilling it, yoked together by oppression, but united in fraternal love—when both, in Russia as well as in the other Slavic regions, shall become disenthralled. This soil, ploughed by a freeman, sowed by a free hand, will yield more and better harvests than when scratched by the serf, than when the seeds thrown in reach the furrow wrapped in the curse of a bent-down, oppressed creature.

Industry, with its unfathomed domain, can only prosper in the air of liberty, and in Russia its flowering depends on general emancipation. All kinds of property must be accessible to every body, and man must be master of his time, and of the productions of his intelligent labor. It has been proved sufficiently in some of the foregoing chapters, that neither the one nor the other exists in Russia. What there is of industry now, may be considered as a dim foreboding of what it may become, when liberated from corporations, official guilds, and the minute interference of the government. From the stand point of political economy, the real interest of the people and the prosperity of its industry depends on the protective principle. To the great market of the west, Russia exports raw products of the soil, viz.: all sorts of grains, ashes, potash, hemp, linen, raw hides, bristles, etc.; four fifths at least of all these articles coming from large estates owned exclusively by the nobility. The imports embrace principally articles of luxury and refinement, for the use of the opulent classes; the tariff forms thus the sole direct taxation paid by the noblesse. Home industry is more than sufficient to supply all the wants of the people, and, to a great extent, those of the burgesses or middle classes. Asia, opening daily more and more its markets to the Russian trade, receives principally the same products as are consumed by the great home market, consisting chiefly in woollen cloth of all qualities, ordinary cotton goods, common silks, etc. Emancipation, raising higher the national faculties and energies, industry, will grow powerfully under its shadow, multiply its activity to the infinite. The dull workshops, filled with ignorant serfs, will be transformed into illuminating piles, warming the intelligence; enterprise and industry, united by freedom, will attain in Russia the lofty position which belongs to them in the development of human destinies. When the national mind shall become elevated, purified by a truly progressive and popular education, daily life will brighten, and the part which the Slavi and Russia have to play in human affairs, will become significant and noble.

CHAPTER XIII.

MANIFEST DESTINY.

THE Slavic race with Russia its mightiest branch, by its geographical position, extends in an uninterrupted line over the greater part of Europe, covering daily with its roots, the North and a great part of Central Asia more and more. This long chain is broken by no nationality of distinct origin, nor indeed by any state whose influence could finally become dangerous to Russian and Slavic autonomy. Uniformity and fraternity of language strongly cement the whole, as the dialects and idioms clustering around the Russian depend rather on it, being insignificant in themselves, and at any rate unable to influence or disturb the process of fusion continually operating through the central or dominant one. Dominant not so much on account of its being the official instrument of the power, but because it is used and spoken exclusively by the people numerically forming a great compact mass, and which alone has an independent national life. There the Russian language rises like a mighty tree from among shrubs and underwood, overshadowing them all.

Religious unity, still one of the great cementing elements of ancient society and of the ancient world, binds together not only the genuine population of Russia but by far the greater mass of the whole Slavic blood, as the Roman Catholics count no more than one fourth in the whole family, and western Protestantism, with the exception of a few nobles, has not penetrated under any denomination whatever, any where among the Slavic nations. For those attaching a special worth to it, it may be mentioned that the Eastern church generally allows the reading of the Bible in the vernacular language. The translation for the use of the people of both the Old and the New Testament, is older in the Slavic than in any other language of modern Europe.

The soil and the region on which the whole race is implanted, between the Adriatic to the mouth of the Amoor or Shika, emptying into the Pacific—this whole space is rich in all the climatic varieties of fertile productiveness on its surface, and with inexhaustible metallurgic wealth in its bowels. The statistics, whatever may be their fluctuations, give the number of the whole Slavic groups at about eighty millions, of which Russia's genuine population makes about fifty-seven or fifty-eight millions. Add to it, on the Slavic domain, the scattered Roumans, Letts, Arnauts, Moldavians, Armenians, Greeks, etc., numbering between eight and ten millions, tribes which never can assert or maintain a distinct and independent nationality, and who are bound to the Slavic by the conformity of creed, and to a great extent by that of customs and manners of daily life, then the whole Slavic element reaches more than ninety millions. By the natural increase of population of one and a half per cent. yearly, this mass will in a short time nearly approach the population of the remainder of Europe, which is almost over-populated; the Slavic region being, on the contrary, able to support three times the present number, without any signs of surcharge.

This Slavic and Russian colossus solders Northern

and Central Asia with Europe; it is a channel to convey in the future, an easy, peaceable intercourse, furthering the final ends of civilization

Whether a higher will has assigned this eminent position to this race from the time of the first and primitive peopling of that part of the world, or it was directed and led there by the successive development of events beyond the reach of explanation: there it is indestructible and unchangeable, not a result of an historical accident; therefore with a task to fulfil, with a destiny to unfold. How far, then, is this destiny already a manifest one?

Manifest destiny of a nation, a lift of the curtain veiling its future! This axiom, bearing on the present and future, and not merely an explanation of a past: an axiom for life and not for the definition of bygone historical relics; was for the first time boldly uttered by the great vivid spirit of democratic America! And no wonder; only where the human mind and intellect pulsate freely and invigoratingly through the whole people, where all act, think and participate in the national life; there the mental powers acquire the elevation, intensity and clearness necessary to cast a keen look into the coming destinies of a nation; to unravel in the dim future and point out luminously the course which it has to follow for the good of the human family. Only where there is a people and no classes, where education and all gradations of life are freely accessible to all, does self-consciousness kindle in every breast the lofty feeling of being a man, and of fully enjoying all the rights of man. There each individual aims to ameliorate, to perfect, in one word, to ascend into the higher region of moral civilization, whose pure light radiates over the whole nation, illuminates the path opening into the future, and to those inspired with its sacred principles, points out moral duties and obligations as well as lands and regions where to carry them, and to implant these precious seeds for the benefit of the human race.

This is the flash of revelation. But aside from it, by the slow but uninterrupted working of science and reflection or of philosophy, the sanctuary containing in its recesses the destinies of nations can now be more easily approached than it could have been in times closing behind us, and its secrets become at least partly deciphered and manifest to the eye of the mind. Almost every scientific sphere brightens more and more; discoveries widening continually, set all knowledge on more firm and fixed bases. Reason more matured and clear illuminates the thorny path of researches in the regions of matter, as well as in those where lay heaped up by uncounted centuries, the annals of nations engraved by the burin of time. Our epoch recasts history. The past is better appreciated at its real value; without a mean and humiliating worship, and without presumption trampling down all. From the work partially accomplished by preceding ages, by various states and peoples, from the extent and the brightness of the track left by them on the orbit of civilization, it is possible to draw more positive conclusions as to the future of the existing nations. Thus the past is now better understood and explained; the purified reason—that high and exclusive attribute and instrumentality of the mind—is enabled to assign with less difficulty the positions, and to outline the future signification and destiny of a race, a nation, a people.

Civilization is now laid on broader foundations. It enters the epoch where every science combines more and more with the daily life, and thus the horizon before individuals as well as before nations, extends and clears up; the activity of the mind and of the intellect becomes daily more enlarged and easier; material ameliorations, inventions, and their large applications in subduing nature and her elements—reducing time and space through navigation, railroads and lightning-like communications: in one word, all the powers of action on the material creation immensely augmented, serve not only to master and utilize the material world: they likewise eminently contribute to smooth away the various difficulties in the region of thought and of reflection. They put easier and more various objects within the reach of the mind, thus enabling it to vary its observations and researches, to ascertain more precisely by comparison and combination the value of notions and ideas, to discern better, to find out more clear and positive analogies, to operate in a broader and clearer space—without groping painfully on the way: and therefore to deduce more positive conclusions, and establish laws strictly harmonizing with the world of facts. With them are closely connected the destinies of nations, which thus for the eye of reason are no more a book with seven seals.

Whatever misty exhalations may still cloud the beacon of pure and impartial reason, it is incontestable that its light penetrates more keenly, and illuminates more distinctly our epoch, and our generation. We understand ourselves better than our forefathers did, and the past likewise is no longer for us a dark and inextricable labyrinth. Centuries and centuries elapsed before one of the greatest historical events became understood and explained. It is, by many called the providential appearance of the races and tribes which crushed the decayed ancient or Roman world, with its worn-out, exhausted refinement, rather than vivid civilization, with its narrow notions and ideas in relation to men, void of any higher spark and consciousness of humanity. Now we understand that in this manner alone a new light could have been kindled; and for the most active and intelligent part of the whole human race a new element was prepared through Christian civilization. Our century has explained this enigma; a century which, inheriting the sufferings, the mental efforts and labors and the rays glimmering through the preceding ones, begins to transform into a social fact, what by the past was scarcely conceived as a vision.

The eternal aim towards which mankind gravitate becomes more distinct and perceptible, and therefore the destinies of special nations, peoples and states show more visibly. If for the ancient notion of individualism, egotism and exclusiveness, Christianity substituted at first theoretically the conception of humanity, we enter the era when this conception, from a theological abstraction, will become the source and the spirit of a new law, of a new order. Association will no longer be only a practice in religious worship and prayers; no more will it be confined within the walls of a church, considered at best but an abstract spiritual bond: it will become the corner-stone of every future social edifice. It will go forth into the world and rule it. Further, the two great human and progressive phenomena marking the setting of the last century; the French social revolution, and the political emancipation of America, are the first great and positive results of the application of what must be called the Christian doctrine. Its essence is love, fraternity or fraternal accord, equality as was thought once in abstract, or before God. But love, fraternal accord, can only exist and flourish in the atmosphere of liberty, which thus becomes the soul of Christian civilization. Equality before God includes logically equality among men in their mutual relations, and before their laws. However, how dim a light did all these primordial rays of Christianity, forming its only and exclusive revelation, throw on the first vacillating path of nations, collecting under its sign. For centuries and centuries the pure Christian conception was misunderstood, misrepresented, defiled, and distorted, often faithlessly, by doctors, philosophers, moralists, religious and ethical teachers and preachers; most generally applied by them, *ad usum Delphini*, or in behalf of the strongest, the oppressor, the enslaver, against the feeble, the oppressed, the enslaved. The real human, Christian essence, even now is scarcely beginning to be considered as the source of a positive social order and organization. The past cannot be eliminated at once; its influence is perceptible, and in many ways it asserts its right, usurping on the present. For all this, however, the past is undermined; the new light penetrates, its rays begin to warm the mind, and soon nations and people, will grow and develop under their generous and reinvigorating action. Those who for the present lead the march of the whole human race, the European races, true representatives of humanity, will before long act in harmony with its purer and loftier tendencies. Selfishness and hostility will begin to melt and disappear from their hearts, as well as from their actions, before the dawn of fraternal concord. If this concord is not active, if it does not regulate human affairs in general, still its time approaches, in proportion as the comprehension of destinies brightens and becomes more manifest. The impediments, the counteracting forces of darkness, are the so-called governments, the keepers and bearers of power; the kings, and in an absolute meaning the superior social classes, be they called divines, experienced councillors, aristocracies of various kinds and distinctions, rising above the generality by some kind of privilege, are here and there eager to carve out or get a new privilege. It is principally these who rend asunder nations and peoples, otherwise destined to move harmoniously and in peace in the orbit of modern civilization. By their ministry and interference, past falsehoods are made the plea for new ones. The natural tendency of men is to associate, to exchange peaceably intellectual as well as material products. For this reason, all high discoveries, the results of any labor of the mind, the world-illuminating lightnings of genius, become at once the property not of the creator or inventor, not of the community or nation amidst which the inventor dwells, but of the whole human family, who hail in him a common benefactor, a general light. He is for all as the sun rising, giving life to the whole creation. Not envy, jealousy, and eternal conflict, are the final destinies of our race; the time is at hand when fraternity will be no more an evanescent phenomenon. Soon people and nations will conceive and understand, that they form a general brotherhood, where each has a task more or less difficult to accomplish, a more or less heavy burden to carry; thus all will contribute to raise the great enlightning pile, to co-operate to the general welfare of the human family.

Moreover the positions either usurped or formed by historical events and accidents, still prevail and fetter the people—but their hours are counted. Their existence is solely that of a barren fact, like a corpse without a soul, like a centenary oak, rotten and decayed, in the primitive forest—no more shooting out fresh leaves and buds—standing there until a tornado finally overthrows it. It no longer draws new invigorating juices through the withered roots. In the same manner, the rulers, and the artificial superiorities of the European world, have no roots in the feelings or in the voluntary and spontaneous adhesion of the masses. Their existence has no moral basis in national sentiments, nor does it derive any vitality therefrom. And through the whole of history; what has become extinct as an idea inspiring a nation or a people, has disappeared after a longer or shorter time, and disappeared finally from the world. The manifest destiny of all such excrescences is to perish.

The great, harmonious combination of aims and tendencies in which consists the future, can alone be realized in liberty, based on equality; in one word, in a real, genuine democracy. Thus it is a manifest destiny, that democracies are to spread and form an electric chain over all regions where European, Christian civilization is already implanted. Then only will brutal force begin successively to disappear, and peace and order, right and justice to prevail. Whatever may be said to the contrary, there has been more uprightness, honesty and patriotism among the imperfect democracies hitherto known in history, than under any other form of government. Not the democracy of Athens, but the Spartan aristocracy was accessible to the gold of the great king at Susa, and conspired against Greek autonomy and independence. That democracy fought against the Spartans, introduced into the heart of the city by the oligarchs and aristocrats; it backed Demosthenes against Philip, and fought with Philopœmen. The aristocratic and elegant Xenophon, sees with indifference, if not with applause, the ruin of his native Athens, and extols Sparta and the royal Agesilaus, scarcely mentioning the patriotic Pelopidas, the great, immortal, democratic Epaminondas. Not the plebs but the patricians of Rome were accessible to the gold of the Numidian kings. The Guelfs, or the popular party of the Italian republics, combated all foreign interference, and the supremacy of the German emperors, invoked and introduced into the country by the Ghibellins the pure aristocrats of Italy. Savanarola corrupted not the Florentine republic, but the Medici, the Pitti, the

Guicciardini. Phidias, and Michael Angelo belonged to the Demos, and are democratic produces. Not the democracy or the French people saluted cheeringly the invaders of 1814, or in 1815 speechified redundantly when great actions were needed. Not the Demos of Paris raised the price of stocks on the exchange, after the national disaster at Waterloo. The people mourned; noblesse, priesthood and bourgeoisie radiated with joy, in their servility to the foreign masters and invaders. Every where the people, the Demos fought for the country, the upper classes submitted or betrayed it. History teems with the like evidences, and to close them: Christ belonged to the Demos; his words swayed the multitude. The rude, poor, unlettered fishermen of Genesareth, heard his words with their hearts; the common people listened gladly and followed him.

As a lamp when going out throws its strongest light, so old, withered notions, destined to disappear, seem to act more strongly, and as at the present moment to win the upper hand over the bright hopes and generous expectations spreading through and penetrating the masses. Ancient prejudices of race are not to last for ever; hatred, jealousy of nation against nation, fostered by the personal interests of the few, will give way. All these recurrences of absolutism, oppression, and the temporarily apparent submission to them of the European world, are so many forebodings of the new era—are the last flashings of the dying lamp. The oppressors, the privileged, the drivers or masters of society, have no faith in themselves, in their own vitality: they fear and doubt the necessity of their social existence, already doubted and contested by the reason of the masses; and the fear, the doubt, in itself helps to impair their strength. Every where the continual and widening deflection from these solitary pillars of the past is clearly visible. Fraternity and solidarity are ideas already sinking deeper and deeper into the consciousness of the people, and the time must come when they will be established social facts; their advent is the manifest destiny of humanity.

The destinies of the European world are not limited to that part of the globe, but have already received a signal manifestation in America, the historical offspring of Europe, and the loftiest social application of the European—the Christian idea. Thus what is here already a life, what inspires, and morally and socially elevates millions and millions, must react on the old world, and reinvigorate it sooner or later. Europe must have, for her corner-stone, the same absolute social principle, whatever may be the form by which it will be asserted or shaped out. Again, the destinies of Europe cannot take a higher flight, if a part, a preponderating branch, shall stand apart in gloomy and hostile isolation; the whole must ascend together. The Russian people are now in this isolated position; if therefore a purer light is to beam over the West, and evoke there a new and fresh life, the Russians and Slavi must likewise be penetrated and warmed by its rays.

It has become very common of late to compare the growth of America with that of Russia; to look for a similitude in their development and progress; and finally, to divide the future of the two hemispheres between these two ascending states. As far as it concerns the rude, material, geographical extension over unpeopled regions or decayed countries, or the power which compactness of population must necessarily exercise over less peopled and weaker neighbors; and further, regarding and comparing the growth of internal, material resources in extensive regions, scarcely yet touched or opened by the share of cultivating labor or industry; the comparison may have some plausibility on its face, but there ends the similitude.

At the first and superficial look, both of them seem to be new-comers among the community of states. But Russia is old as well as new; she represents an old historical element, which for uncounted centuries, has prevailed and generally established the great phenomena of the old world, that is, the element of race. America is new, not only as an historical appearance, but likewise as the realization of a higher, nay, the highest conception, that of humanity, blended and melted together without distinction of descent, creed, and origin. Thus America represents the concrete of the human family, Russia only one of its members; and thus what Russia represents in history is inferior to what is revealed by America. No further analogy can be found existing between the two except in the thoroughly opposite characteristics of two extremes. America is the light, and Russia the darkness; the one is life, the other inertia, depending on the will of one. Russia is saddled by despotism, that old inheritance of the East and of heathenism; America initiates history and humanity into a new era—which a century ago was looked on as an Utopia—constructing a social order on the foundations of equality and liberty, realizing in a broad manner the sole principle of social truth. The one raises the broken-down, the degraded by oppression and misery, restoring to him the enjoyment of right and the dignity of man; the other, if she does not introduce slavery and serfdom in her conquests, subjects them to an all-crushing, all-levelling despotism; both being accursed twin brothers. In America real progress rules; in Russia there prevails a sham-imitation of progress. In America every object, social, material, or from the realm of mind, already receives, or will receive in due time, a more correct and enlarged exposition. The study of man will be better and more fully developed. His nature, the real play of his faculties, passions, and feelings will be better observed, examined, understood, and explained than has yet been done by psychologists, metaphysicians, and anthropologists. Henceforth man can be a subject of observation in his true element, in his exclusively congenial atmosphere, in that of full, real, daily enjoyed liberty and equality. Hitherto, for all such studies and observations, a kind of abstract being has been constructed, set out with speculative attributes; this abstract very generally differing from the man of common daily life, from the mass, from humanity. Higher moral science must use a criterion realizable in imagination, never in actual life; liberty became transformed into a mental and spiritual faculty, instead of being laid down as the exclusive life-giving source for the human race. Rational, positive equality was wholly overlooked or banished in theory and practice from all human relations. Thus one misrepresentation generated another, and from it sprang the scientific division of society in three principal classes or strata: the toilers, workers, or supporters of the others; the central, the scientific, teaching class, or priestcraft; and the fighters, the defenders, or rulers. Science, by elaborate argument, consecrated the work of violence and oppression. And if the human reason and conscience sometimes raised their voice against the like falsehoods, not only theology, but unfortunately philosophy recognized these divisions as forming the true basis of social relations. Thus a mystical expounder of history, like the fiery Goerres, as well as Hegel the greatest logical metaphysician, both of our epoch, concurred in adopting the above view, not to speak of many other writers of all nations. They forgot that if the discoveries and rules of physiological anatomy apply to the whole race, psychology and anthropology, to be of any real worth, ought not to deal with ideal types, but with concrete, large, every-day realities.

All these absurd incumbrances disappear successfully in America, where man stands in his real nature.*

Two opposite axioms, equally truthful, cannot be deduced from one and the same principle; there is only one right line among millions of deflections; in the same manner, there can exist only one way and one law for real grandeur and progress; and a nation deprived of self-consciousness and of the intellectual manifestation of individuality, cannot move on the real and right track. Civilization has there neither deep roots in the people, nor does its light radiate freely in all directions; it is rather like a will-o'-the-wisp, erring unsteadily on the surface. In America the individuality of every one is raised to the dignity of social truth; in Russia individuality is a fault, sometimes a crime. Every thing is implanted artificially, or as the result of brute force. In Russia, a sickly unreality, resulting from convulsive efforts of despotism, compresses the inward national vitality; in America, reason shoots off freely in all practicable radii, every thing rises, grows, and unfolds itself, germinating from an inborn, vital force. In Russia, as yet, one absorbs in himself the life, the activity of the whole nation; in America, every one and all act and live according to their own will, propensities, and impulses. In Russia, the government is the soul and the life, it is the exclusive medium for the respiration of millions; in America, there exists nowhere a government according to the ancient meaning of this word. It is an association of freemen, cemented by the principle of equality. Every individual is a type of humanity, his rights are equal to those of every other, and thus the rights of men form the corner-stone of the association, the govern-

* Any philosophical appreciation whatever of America, can only be applied to the free States.

ment being only a delegation to attend to its various business. The holders of the reins of government in Russia, nay, in the whole of Europe, look down on nations as on creatures existing for their pleasure, on which they prey with more or less ferocity. Here the government is only partly invested with a power, whose completeness and source resides with every member of the association. In Russia, the sword of Damocles is suspended over the Czar, as well as over the whole social order; every new day of the existence of America is brighter than the past one, is marked by a material as well as by a social and moral improvement and ascension. There we see a master or driver of millions; here millions of independent, intellectual, freely-moving beings. Here the legislator is the people; there the law is the result of the will of one, often of his whim. In the self-consciousness, in the self-reliance of each individual, is founded the greatness of America; in Russia an order from the government is the only life-inspiring agency. The government in Russia, as in the whole of the old world, is obliged to take a minute care of the prosperity of its subjects, as of a hot-house plant; here it grows freely and prospers in the air—in an atmosphere loaded with liberty, in the social soil of equality. Therefrom intelligence, energy, elasticity, self-consciousness, and self-reliance, pour into the individual, and to them exclusively is due the prosperity so envied by the governments of the older hemisphere. Not in physical conditions, not in geographical position is the arcanum of this wonder—the like conditions, and some others even more fully acting and developed, exist in other countries and regions; but the all-powerful source thereof is equality and liberty limited by reason or its laws. Those believing in the interference with human affairs, or in their benediction from above, can find a palpable manifestation thereof in the prosperity of America, because she alone is true to the eternal laws and conditions of the existence of human nature. Nothing is checked and depressed here by artificial barriers; free will and free action have full play. But every thing is hampered, circumscribed, restricted in Russia, as every where else; and these restrictions are a curse continued through centuries. Thus while other countries move rapidly towards a dreadful cataclysm, America has before her an immense and bright horizon; and if some clouds may be visible on it, they never can extend to a war of elements, to social tornadoes like those hovering over Europe. America is thickly thronged with humanity; Russia is as yet peopled by docile tools. Russia has some tint of superficial varnish and polish; America bears in its womb a true human civilization. Of this no superficial refinement forms the criterion; no fastidious culture prevailing among some few privileged ones; not even the high literary and artistical creations of a few men of genius constitute the primordial aims of civilization, or are its real fruits, but the rights of all asserted, recognized, respected. When this is obtained, refinement, culture, delicacy of taste, arts, will follow and flourish, completing and adorning the healthful society. In saloons or palaces, in sumptuous dwellings, the European, and above all the Russian civilization is confined; the American blossoms in district schools spread over the country, in townships, villages, and hamlets, accessible to every body, even the poorest, and where many a European, besotted by kings, nobles, and priestcraft, is aroused, and feels the amaurosis dissolve from his mind's eyes. These are some among the agencies at work for the manifest destiny of America, but nowhere existing in Russia. The accidental conformity in some material, and secondary respects, cannot and ought not to be taken as a revelation of equal and corresponding destinies.

America's manifest destiny, as felt and proclaimed by her people, is to extend around her the reinvigorating institutions of which she is the focus; to teach and implant farther and farther the principle of self-government with the free and alone supreme action of law; in one word to continue the work of the emancipation of man, restoring him every where to his inborn rights and dignity. Therefore her future extension ought to harmonize with the broad and luminous principle in which she initiates history. America should attract by the power of example, —and, daily extending the gulf which separates her from the past, she should no more recur to, or use, violence and invasion as means of propaganda. If unprovoked, America ought for ever to renounce brutal force. No doubt that in the past, war and the sword have been awful and fierce agencies, turning sometimes beneficially, and forwarding the aims of civilization. How much soever one might wish to have seen American history purified from this obsolete and barbarous stigma—still the war of Mexico served to illustrate the vitality of the American constructive principle. California conquered, raised in a twinkling from the most chaotic and complicated turmoil of passions and interests—to the dignity of a well-organized State, organized by the common sense and understanding of the in-pouring Americans—those social Pelasgi of modern times—without any effort, without special leaders, legislators, men of learning (savants) and deep statesmen. At the same time, what a sorrowful spectacle was shown in the old world. Two of her most civilized nations—where learning and instruction, if not general, still teem and flow over in certain classes—called together *all* their individualities, of any social, political, or scientific celebrity. The representatives of all new social ideas and theories, as well of historical schools and doctrines, were chosen by the people to meet together. No interference from without, no foreign power meddled with them, or prevented their action; masses of people, full of cheerful expectation, were ready to receive their biddings, to follow their word. They had the sublime mission of devising the means for the renovation of society, now crumbling to pieces. Their long-protracted deliberations ended by opening more widely the doors to domestic despotism in France and Germany.

Russia represents an ancient historical and social element, still prevailing in the territorial divisions, in the formation of states, in one word in the whole national economy of the old world; that is, as before stated, the element of race. Russia moves on the old track, and her destinies—whatever they may be—must run and be partly, at least, fulfilled under the pressure of the imperious laws of warlike force. Slavic and Russian destinies point towards Asia,* to the East. For their realization Russia will be obliged to appeal to the old law of force; but in her future relations with the West, Russia, emancipated from despotism, must contribute to fix the emancipation of Europe on a firm and civilized basis. Thus between Russia and Europe there ought not to exist in the future any reasons of hostile feud.

If until now and for a short time to come, Russia represents in history darkness and the most stringent absolutism, this cannot last for ever. There is enough of latent

* Some eighteen years ago, in one of my writings published at Paris, I was the first foretelling that the activity, the destinies of Russia, would turn in that direction. Russian reviews and periodicals, written by statesmen, or under their direction, called me, "the man who first laid his hand on the curtain veiling the future of Russia." I mention this as a proof that I touched a chord in the national feelings.

life in her people to prove that the present passiveness is not a result of debility, and prostration. For some reason or other thickly veiled to the human understanding, history is directed by various seemingly illogical, cruel laws and even principles. Why must nations and humanity, through bloody toils, carve out their way towards the higher regions of light? why is progress thus laborious, difficult, and often interrupted? Why has the consecration of blood hitherto been the only initiation to life? Why does the initiator perish by the initiated? The slow and successive transition from one social state to another, and better one, is among the great laws of historical movement. The Slavi and the Russians are now in darkness, and under the freezing action of despotism and caste: but the nations of western Europe were for centuries troddon down by kings, priests and nobles, and how far even now are they emancipated? Where is a real people in Europe?

Often, very often there prevails in history a law in direct opposition to the ethical principles of daily life. Thus, what in itself is a crime, has often historically beneficial results. Why it is so, very likely will remain for ever unanswered. But the fact rises, terrible, above humanity—as a granite rock above the surface of the ocean.

Without the injustice of the British Ministry and Parliament, the independence of America would not have been so soon evoked; humanity and history would have been deprived for a longer time of this realization of their most sublime aspirations, and yearnings. And ascending higher; without the cruel atrocious persecutions of the primitive Christians, Christianity would not have shown its value; would not have moved the masses, and would not have spread and scattered in all directions the sparks of a new civilization. When all the world bowed to the Imperial idol—the Christians alone maintained and asserted the freedom of conscience, of conviction.

In Russia despotism is preparing, nay, facilitating the ways for a new era. The stronger the compression, the more vigorous will be the reaction, as in fountains the height of the jet is regulated by the volume and the pressure of the water. The people, submerged now in darkness, will in due time awake to the higher influences of truth. One can already hear the eternal waves of human rights splashing and beating on the artificial rocks of despotism and privilege. They will be broken, washed away, and ingulfed. Liberty alone is an enduring substance, and a principle; all other social forms are transient manifestations, and—notwithstanding their existence—still doomed to destruction.

The Slavi, as well as the Russian people, must put on the robe of manhood, because democracy is as absolute and irresistible as the laws of the physical world. Chronologically, the Slavi and the Russians appear the last to act prominently on the scene of history, therefore they have suffered the longest time. Their emancipation will sum up the emancipation of the European world. To contest and doubt the emancipation of Russia, is to doubt final justice and wisdom.

Having re-established the true balance in Europe, the Slavic and Russian current will undoubtedly turn towards Asia. There, in those vast spaces, is the immense field opening for their action. And no other nation or race can fulfil this mission. If mankind is to form in the future a harmonious whole, the solitudes of Asia must be stirred up, vivified, and the deathlike quiet prevailing there must be broken. Culture and civilization must dispel the atrophy, north as well as south of the Himalaya.

To electrify these regions, an uninterrupted contact and friction, exchange and excitation are absolutely necessary. The chain must be as mighty and gigantic as is the region to be awakened and remodelled. Those intrusted by nature's law with this mission ought to be conterminous, ought to stand shoulder to shoulder with the East. This is the case with the Slavi, and principally the Russians. The people to whom this task is assigned, must be in possession of powerful material resources, and enjoy in full their rights and faculties. An active mass is to press against an inert one. Such a labor can in nowise be accomplished by scattered commercial factories, nor even by religious or political missionaries: but only by the concentrated activity of a mighty people. Whoever observes history with an unprejudiced eye, will discover this almost incontestable fact, that maritime intercourse—unless combined with colonization—never brings about an assimilation or permanent exchange of ideas between nations. Ideas are propagated by land; contiguous races, even if differing in civilization, have a certain similarity of habits and notions, which, fostered by the facility of contact in peace or war, and by other physical circumstances, such, for instance, as navigable rivers and open plains, act as so many connecting links between the adjoining races. And so are the Russians with all the Asiatics. Tartary, Thibet, Mongolia, the snowy northern regions of Asia deserve as much a human, European, civilizing solicitude as Asia Minor, India, parts of America, or any other spot whatever on the globe. In justice these northern regions, less favored by nature, ought to be compensated by civilization. The members of the human family scattered there ought to be protected against the inclemency of the elements, and wrapped in the folds of sheltering, preserving culture. Whatever may be at present the black stains on Russia, neither its government nor its people are laboring under the inhuman and heinous prejudice against any difference of race, against any variety of shape or color in the human family. Descendants of Calmucks and Tartars count among the Russian *Knaïzïa* or Princes; Pouschkine, the greatest Russian poet, had African blood in his veins from the maternal side, and spoke of it with pride. Already in contact with various Asiatic tribes, the Russian does not dispossess them—either by law or by violence; the Baschkir of Orenboug along the Ural, is protected by law in the property of gold-yielding sands as well as would be any genuine Russian, who, enslaved himself, treats kindly those whom he subdues, conceding to them even more rights than he enjoys himself. The Russian neither exterminates nor transforms into bondsmen, serfs or slaves, any conquered people. The change of form, the transition from despotism to liberty, can neither alter nor endanger the real destinies of Russia and the Slavi. On the contrary it will widen and clear up the horizon, inspire with a fresh vigor, give a mighty impulse. Some of the works undertaken by despotism, for its own glorification or interest, will be continued in a new and humane manner.

Various are the agencies, various the ways and means through which the genius of humanity reaches her transitory or her final ends. Various are the mental and physical instrumentalities; the one as ideas, the other as races and nations, through which great historical events are prepared and executed. The history of people and nations, of their formation as states and empires, is a continual reciprocal action of just and unjust influences, of atrocity, cunning and cruelty, if to the events of the world is to be applied the criterion of common morality. And tragical complications still leave in history indestructible and often beneficial traces. No century and no nation can go by, without illustrating this phenomenon. Through how many bloody, and apparently unjust and exterminatory wars, was attained and established the unity of the Roman Empire. But this unity cleared up the way for Christianity, facilitating the labors of the apostles, and of the fathers. It can be said historically, that Augustus surrendered to Christ the world as an unit. The Franks, or rather France carried on her shoulders for nearly ten centuries, the destinies of the continent. Charlemagne put an end to the chaotic rovings of tribes, began to construct a new social edifice; the battle-axe of Martel crushing the scimitar of the Moslem, preserved the west from the temporary domination of the Koran; Franks and France emancipated the Bishop of Rome, and were thus the instruments of consolidating the Papal unity for good and evil. In the 16th century France alone raised a barrier against the attempts of Charles V. to establish an universal western monarchy. She prevented the absolute fusion of the Pope with the Emperor, and thus preserved Protestantism from being strangled in the cradle. To accomplish these various tasks, strength and unity were the first conditions, and to frame it out several centuries were laboriously devoted. Nearly eleven various nationalities, differing in descent, race, language, domestic and forensic customs and feudal investitures,—were to be melted into one powerful nation. How many murders, crimes, forgeries, broken treaties and various other offences were resorted to before the unity was obtained. The great revolution of the last century, initiatory of a new era, which is working still and will work uninterruptedly until the past is destroyed; one among the greatest events in the world's history, would never have attained its providential signification, if attempted or even carried out by a small state or nationality. But the cry of emancipation shouted simultaneously by twenty-six millions, shook the world, and unhinged the past for ever. When the head of Charles I. fell under the axe of the Independents, no one of the sovereigns of Europe felt himself less secure on his throne: how differently were they all affected by the act of popular justice executed at Paris on the Place of the Revolution. France elaborates and scatters abroad ideas with unsparing profusion, because she is the focus of a powerful unit, of a mighty people.

In the history of Russia, and above all during the last hundred years, there are many events, which, if only partly understood now, will, however, be justly appreciated by the coming generation. Some of these mournful historical dramas are well known, and have been mentioned here; we seem to approach the winding up of an event, startling, menacing, cruel, in the opinion of some, but nevertheless unavoidable, and very likely to occur before the end of the present century.

The empire of the Ottomans, at least in Europe, is rapidly approaching its end; no human aid can preserve it, and the real question is, what banner shall, finally, be implanted on the walls of Constantinople? It is Russia, and Russia alone, which, for more than a hundred years, has uninterruptedly drawn nearer and nearer, with a bold, aggressive, and steady pace. It is an old struggle, often renewed. It began nearly ten centuries ago, not between Turks and Russians, not between Christians and Moslems, but between Byzantium and its emperors and Kïeff and its grand dukes. At that time, the heathen Ros more than once appeared in view of the imperial city, and his savage warwhoop often startled its purple-born masters. We have already mentioned that old chroniclers and geographers of the East, Armenians and Greeks, ten centuries ago, called the Euxine, *Mare Russicum* (Russian Sea). For the last hundred years the Russian, cross and bayonet in hand, has marched, surrounded by a cloud of fire, towards *Carigrad*, the imperial city, to replant the holy sign on the cupola of St. Sophia.

Very likely Czarism may fulfil this work. But Czar and Czarism are tools used by the genius of history, who will break and shatter them after their task shall have been done. In the foregoing drama the Czar, wrapped in his toga of despotism, is after all an agent of the national tendencies.* He hews out the path for the future, loading on his shoulders the malediction of the moment, and is thus the sin-offering of the nation. In the present imminent crisis, as in several past ones, history, which is seldom anomalous or commits errors, stands opposite to the sympathies and to the excited feelings of the moment. Generous, and to a certain extent seemingly well-deserved wishes, surround the fate of the Turks. But inexorable history marches onward, unfolding events from its womb, and unmindful of the clamors or sufferings of the day. There are some features in the character of the Turks commanding respect; but still they cannot avert the doom overtaking them. As Lamartine said, years ago, they are "encamped in Europe." They have put forth no roots during nearly five centuries of their occupation, but have continually formed an insurmountable barrier to the onward spirit and energy of Western Europe. It seems that all the branches and tribes of Scythic or Ouralian, Finnic, Hunnic, or Turkoman descent—all connected together—that these tribes were never predestined to grow and prosper on the European soil. Some of them even encir-

* See Appendix C, The Testament of Peter.

cled by Christian civilization, as, for example, the Magyars, have remained for a thousand years without increasing in any way, by any idea or notion, the bulk of European culture. All of them appeared, or entered Europe, on horseback, ravaging and pillaging, and producing hussars or spahis; and on horseback, they successively disappear from the European arena.

The Turks laid waste the most beautiful regions of the ancient world, where culture and civilization flourished more or less from the dawn of history until overthrown by the Turkomans, as Egypt, Asia Minor, Syria, Greece, and Constantinople. Among all the contumely so unsparingly poured over the last Byzantine epoch, it ought not to be forgotten that in Byzantium was light when all the West was in darkness; that there the remains of the ancient classical civilization were preserved and kept alive, and therefrom they were transported to Italy and to the rest of Europe. The old, fierce, religious fanaticism of the Turks is dying out, and with it the only spring of their political existence is destroyed. No momentary reforms, sparingly spread over the surface, can inculcate a new life, not springing from within a nation. The Moors, who were the benefactors of Spain, adorning her with arts, culture, refinement, poetry; who even in many points taught Europe; who spread larger and deeper roots in the Peninsula than the Turks in any soil occupied by them; the Moors, who resided in Spain nearly twice as long as the Turks this side of the Hellespont, finally gave way and disappeared from the part of the globe not fated for the growth of the crescent.

The Turks, as individuals, as a state, or a nation, seem unfit to become imbedded or intwined in the development of the principles admitted as fundamental in modern civilization, which cannot justly be named otherwise than Christian. Its true focus, its life-giving idea, is the substitution of humanity for the ancient selfishness, heathen or Jewish, looking with contempt from Saïs, Olympus, or Sion, on all other members of the human family. The Koran inherited in full this ancient, hostile, isolating creed. In love, in humanity, and fraternity is contained the moral, philosophical essence of the Christian idea. They alone throw the light of promise, and from their source pours all that is elevated and pure in modern Christian development. Whatever be the muddy alteration of this spring, however slow and obstructed its current, still the essence remains unabated and unstained by the mire spread around it. Thus the darkest clouds change not the beneficial glare of the sun. With the above triad alone is progress possible, and the real mental and social emancipation of men to be attained. What, therefore, is encircled in the Christian idea, what breathes life from it, even in the remotest manner,—all this is progressive, and possesses the seeds and possibility of a higher development. The influence of the Christian idea seems to decide the question that the human race is to be for ever progressive. In the whole ancient world history points only to one people, to the Greeks, and even among them almost exclusively to Athens, where existed a spring of unborrowed progress within the people itself. The light now kindled can never more be extinguished, and each people belonging to the Christian world contributes to nurse this sacred flame. All that is out of the Christian orbit remains fatal and stationary, deprived of spirit and elasticity. It opposes and counteracts all civilizing, cultivating activity, and as a barren fact, void of an inspiring idea, it is destined finally to perish. That is the destiny of the Koran, whose historical existence has been in unabated opposition to the Christian or European world.

At present the Turks rather submit to, than admit some, modifications pressed on them by the current of events: but they never can undergo a thorough reform in the spirit of their cardinal institutions, without ceasing to be what they are now. To them may be applied the celebrated saying of the General of the Jesuits, when the Pope Ganganelli proposed to him a reform of the order, "*Sint ut sunt aut non sint*" (they must remain as they are or not be at all). Whatever may be said to the contrary, Russia is in the Christian orbit, however distorted, and even in some respects pushed aside, may be the real application of its higher principles. The pure spark is deposited in the people, and will finally prevail against the unchristian Czarism. In the same manner the destiny of the Russian people will, in the end, prevail over the fate of the wandering Turks.

No one can tell precisely when the last hour will strike and Constantinople change its masters; neither the Czar nor his antagonists. But the world is prepared to witness it. The general fears of its consummation are so many proofs of its unavoidability. Without discussing how far other states will submit or participate in an offensive or defensive manner in this great historical drama, some forethoughts may be expressed as to the influence on the future of Russia when in possession of this key of the ancient hemisphere.

The conquest of Constantinople will be the satisfaction of an old—and in the feelings not only of the Russians but of all the southern Slavi, of a pious—covetousness. On the way thither difficulties greater than crossing the Danube or passing the Balkan will be met and overcome, by sacrifices and bloodshed unequalled perhaps in history. Whatever is now the alleged, or, partly even, real humanity of the Turks, it ought not to be forgotten that in the European regions occupied by them there exists not one single Christian and aboriginal family—and nearly three quarters of the Christians are of Slavic race—which, from generation to generation, has not some fresh and bloody tale clouding over the domestic hearth, some tale of its members murdered by the Turkish yatagan. How long is it since the Giaour has come to be considered as a human being by the Mahometan? What was sown by centuries in oppression, extermination, and blood, a few years or even decennia cannot so easily heal or blot out. Further, for more perhaps than thirty centuries, the Slavic race, posted on the eastern limits of Europe, received the first shock of all the Asiatic invaders, of Finnic, Ouralian, or Mongolian origin. In those struggles the Slavi were always alone against fearful odds. During the duel fought between the cross and the crescent, and above all in the last six centuries, the Slavi shed more of their blood against the Moslems and the Turkomans than did all the other nations of Europe taken together. Neither England nor France ever assisted the Slavi, and the Emperors of Germany, as well as the Republic of Venice, resisted the Osmanlis by battalions formed mostly out of Slavic soldiers. When, therefore, the moment for the expulsion of the Turks shall come, the utmost exertions will be required to prevent a cruel and merciless retaliation, the long-concentrated wrath increasing by the probably desperate resistance of the retiring foe.

For Russia, for the present or any future Czar, the complication will really begin with the possession of Constantinople and its Turkish dependencies. The destinies of the nation, of Czarism, and of Europe, will then enter a new phasis. From whatever point of view we may consider this eventuality, sure it is, that the political past of Russia will approach its last stage with an accelerated velocity. For any one acquainted with the Russian history and character, it is clear that in the event of the Czar becoming master of Constantinople and of European Turkey, there will be nothing like an immediate erection of the conquered country into an independent state with a Russian prince at its head. It is true that such a project is cherished by a certain class of politicians, who, at different times within these last twenty years, entertained similar schemes with regard to Poland, Greece, and even Hungary, but any thing like this was never thought of in Russia and in St. Petersburg. If the Turks are subjugated or driven out of Europe by Russian power and policy, their territories, and all that belongs thereto, will at once form a national possession, as inalienable as the most ancient provinces of Russia proper. Gained by the nation, to the nation it must belong. Desired and sought for centuries, the object of prophecy, of aspiration, and of faith, to separate it from the whole would be like dismembering the empire itself. Peaceably it could not be done. No sovereign would dare to undertake it. The step could never be understood, never accepted by the people. It would be regarded as high treason against the national unity and the national existence, and would prove sufficient to shake any Czar from his throne. No one could resist the flood of unpopularity which such a measure would arouse. Even the courtiers would repudiate it, and reject all measures of political expediency which might be urged in its favor. The Russian people would look on the act as a mutilation of their glory and their inheritance, and as the avowal of national weakness and individual imbecility. Or it would bear the equally repulsive aspect of submission to foreign powers, and would thus raise the national spirit in rebellion. The lowest peasant in Russia regards Poland, Finland, and Georgia as national acquisitions, and parts of one united, indivisible domain. Much more will this be the case with Turkey, whose appropriation lies through gigantic difficulties. To erect a distinct sovereignty and government at Constantinople would be an insult to manifest destiny, an outrage on the universal convictions and feelings; it would be something unheard of in Russian history, and no Czar would venture to erect it into a separate kingdom even for one of his sons. Nor would the most ambitious among them accept a sovereignty which would either be a delusion, or must else bring him into hostility with his kindred and his native land. In this new domicil he would be surrounded and obliged to get accustomed to new faces, to new associations, a dear sacrifice, if not, at least partly, compensated by realities of power and sovereignty. A grand duke at St. Petersburg, as long as it lasts, must occupy a position much superior to that of a sham monarch at Athens or Constantinople. And to become a real, independent monarch there, he must fight for it against Russia.

The conquered country will then remain Russian. The precise nature of the administrative divisions and organization is a problem which time and circumstances alone can solve. It will be easy to proceed there as in any other conquered province, distributing the whole into counties and governments, according to the Russian home system. Nor will any hinderance be found in replacing the decrepit Turkish administration by a new one, or introducing and adapting there the Russian civil and criminal laws. The beginning is simple and easy, but it is the end which we are endeavoring to foreshadow. No doubt it must be something such as the greedy autocrat and his counsellors do not imagine.

The traditional appellation of Constantinople among

the Russians is Czarigrad—the city of the Czar. One day the imperial court will be transported thither in fulfilment of the destinies of the city. Constantinople will exercise its everlasting spell, and attract the Czars. Its irresistible and various fascinations will tempt them. This is not aimed at, but it cannot be avoided. The monarch and his grandees will yield to the temptation. They will abandon the cold, misty, frozen, marshy, mouldy and gloomy region of St. Petersburg, with its monuments of murder and of parricide, for the unrivalled beauty of the Bosphorus, where in their ambitious intoxication they will believe themselves the masters of the world. But history attests that to conquer and occupy Byzantium, is to sink into effeminacy. The families transplanted to the south in the cortège of the throne will soon disappear one by one. Roman families settled with Constantine and after him in Byzantium; still they disappeared after a short time from the court and from public life, and scarcely a family of Roman descent appears prominent during the Eastern Empire. The Greeks, the Fanariote, the Slavic Rajah of the South will soon prevail in the palace —it may be in the modern seraglio—against the genuine Russian. By and by they will surround the master, creep into his councils, and crowd out therefrom the man of the north. Even the cunning and servile German, so influential now in the northern capital, will be pushed aside. Teutonic prilgrimages of fortune hunters from the Baltic provinces, as well as from Germany, will be not so easily performed to Constantinople, as they are now to St. Petersburg. In one word, the court in Byzantium or Czarigrad will soon cease to be Russian; it will become estranged to the nation, and autocracy will soon become disabled. It will lose its control over the people, its old indigenous flavor will disappear, the historic ties between the Czar and his subjects will be rent asunder; the man of the North will cease to recognize his hereditary master in the despot revelling on the Hellespont. We may expect to see there a varied reproduction of the worst Byzantine epoch—and that the throne of Peter may disappear in the ashes of some modern Sardanapalus. The Muscovite despotism has muscles of iron, and nerves of steel; let these relax and it dies. Let it become Byzantine or Sultanesque, and the nation will rise for its overthrow. Nobility, clergy, the men of Moscow, of the Don, the Wolga, and of the Baltic, all united in the common cause, will execute its doom and close its history, more easily and surely than would be possible in the Kremlin or on the Neva.

Thus the possession of Constantinople seems necessarily fatal to the power of the Czars. There remains the alternative of the conversion of the city into a mere satrapy, and the appointment of some noble or general to govern it. But this is hardly possible. What subordinate could safely be intrusted with the power and influence inherent to such a position? Among the actual or possible possessions of the Empire, there is none whose control would so stimulate ambition or furnish such resources to gratify it. Mehemed Ali in Egypt was far more dependent on the Sultan, and had less the means of gaining power for himself, than a Russian governor would possess in Constantinople, where contact and communications with Europe and with the world are more easy and immediate than from St. Petersburg. No police will prove sufficient to watch there over the lieutenant of the Czar. Besides, no Russian will become a Pole at Warsaw, a Georgian or Armenian at Tiflis, and identify himself with the conquered and espouse their cause; how easily the sternness of his national feelings would be dissolved amid the recollections of Greece and of Byzantium, surrounded by an unwonted life, and breathing an atmosphere teeming with new and irresistible aspirations. There is not a man in all Russia that an Emperor would long trust there. Fatality will oblige him to govern himself with such consequences as are shown above.

The annexation of Turkey, and the possession of Constantinople, will influence the destinies of the Russian people in a manner directly opposed to that in which it must affect the autocracy. Constantinople will become a mighty opening valve for Russia, a channel connecting and uniting her, really for the first time, with the European nations. A great mart will be opened, not only for the exchange of goods but likewise for that of ideas. Through Constantinople the Russian people will mix freely, not only with the few foreign merchants and speculators visiting or established in St. Petersburg, but with the world at large. This broad opening for commerce will, like a pioneer, carve the way for other and more bright results. Nowhere will commerce prove to such an extent a mediator of civilization, as when Constantinople shall initiate the Russian people to the trade of the world. All the forces and resources of the country will turn naturally towards the south, following the lordly currents of the Dnieper, the Don, the Wolga, and its affluents. Now, during six months of the year the Baltic is frozen, but the communication through Constantinople will know no interruption. The Russian products for export must laboriously ascend towards the north, where empty only the Neva, the Dwina, the Niemen, secondary natural channels, and running through less fertile regions. The Mediterranean is still, and will be for a long time, if not for ever, the rendezvous of the world, while the Baltic, and above all its Finnic bay, is frequented only by few nations. The Russian people are no more to be excluded from the general communion. and the safety of other nations requires their admission. When Russia shall become a maritime power, then only will her movement keep time with the other nations; her development will become regulated and orderly, and no longer spasmodic and discordant with itself. St. Petersburg is now the principal outlet, affecting the nation as a powerful vesicatory applied on the surface of a body to stimulate the activity of its various parts, attracting it artificially to a given point. The impulse towards Constantinople will be natural, like sliding on a gentle slope. " St. Petersburg," says Kukolnik, a Russian poet, " is a window cut out into Europe by the axe of Peter the Great." Constantinople will prove an immense gate, not only opening to Europe, but to all the world. In St. Petersburg despotism, with its vast civil and military mechanism, stands day and night a watchful and menacing sentinel to intercept every breath of air which may impart a moral contagion. No such quarantine can possibly be established on the Hellespont, and no police can maintain there its impervious nets. Western ideas and culture will make their way, and irresistibly stimulate the whole empire. What is now benumbed will be raised to elasticity and to cosmopolite intercourse. Odessa is already one of the most liberal and facile spots in Russia, where despotism is felt less painfully. Intercourse on a large scale with other nations will result, and the Russian, the man of the people, will no more be kept, as now, isolated from his brethren. His suspicion against every thing foreign—a sentiment carefully nourished and fostered by the government—his sulky coyness will successively melt away and disappear; the inborn sociality of his character will prevail, rendering him generously friendly with the foreigners. The genius of history in her multifarious workings is directed by higher aspirations, her views are loftier and more keen than those of every-day politicians She prepares the future; they scarcely discern the seconds of the present. Thus she leads the Russian people to the sacrament of initiation into the community of nations, through the future possession of Constantinople. Once there, the man of the people, burgher, merchant, or peasant, will feel more keenly the necessity of education, of culture of mind and intellect, whereof he is now deprived by the cruel care of the government. No preventive measures can then prove stringent enough to check and bar the inborn human impulse to see the outer world, to travel, to observe, to learn. Then not only noblemen, officials, or the favored few, but the man of the people will mix with Europe and become acquainted with her condition. The people will begin to appreciate events by personal observation, to ponder good and evil by themselves, and not through the medium of Czarian proclamations. The national character will unfold its more generous side, be better known and appreciated by others. The extension of trade, of commercial affairs, will clear and widen the mental horizon; the Russian will be enabled to make a large choice of mental goods, to introduce and raise them carefully at home. He will adopt goods as well as ideas by his own judgment, and no longer scantily receive every object at second-hand, through the minute and narrow interference of the ruling master. The nation will thus rise to the level, feel the impulses, claim the advancing rights of civilized humanity, and share in the ebb and flow of the European social tide. Through this Hellespontic gateway the people shall enter the scene of the world, and no longer be represented there by the autocracy and its hirelings.

The expulsion of the Turks and the future possession

of Constantinople have been considered for years as the highest problem for European politics. On its solution depends not only the future political configuration of Russia, but her supremacy over the old hemisphere. Prophecies are at hand that the oscillating waves of the shock which is to ingulf the empire of the Ottomans will be deeply felt through the whole globe. Sinister and terrible consequences are associated with that eventuality. Without in the least contesting its grandeur, it may be contended that what is now represented as ominous of evil, will, for reasons mentioned above, prove in the end an harmonious incident in the great drama of human affairs. It will become a galvanic spark, applied to the combustible and explosive elements, accumulated in Russia for centuries. Whatever may be the ambitious purpose of the Czars, and their hostility to the triumph of the principles of liberty and democracy, the enterprise set on foot against the world's welfare will turn against them. Emancipation and the destruction of autocracy will rise from the dreaded conflagration.

In the pages of this book an attempt has been made to show that in the nature, and in the feelings of the Russian people, as well as in its institutions, and in its present or eventual geographical extension, are contained seeds of better destinies for the whole Slavic race, and promises of a civilized and peaceful onward march for the European world. The time, the hour, for the unfolding and growth of these germs—thickly veiled now—will be revealed and sounded by the ever-watchful genius of humanity.

APPENDIX.

A.

THE AMAZONS.

THE appearance and the disappearance of the Amazons in the most remote history, is one of the enigmas, left and transmitted to posterity, almost from the mythical times of the infancy of mankind. At the dawn of history, the Amazons were considered as being already an echo of bygone times, belonging to the most distant heroic epoch.

The investigations into the origin of races and people, trace back to the primitive migration that divided the great human family. It is supposed that the grandsons of Noah parted from each other, and formed families, groups, and tribes. Thus originated the races, which spread over, and populated the whole globe, assigned as the habitation and patrimony of men. The origin of the Amazons ought to belong to, and to be connected, at any rate, with one of the races which issued from the great trunk. The Amazons cannot be considered as belonging to the Shemites, for antiquity does not place them among the peoples of Shemitic descent. The question is, to lift the veil of time, and determine to which branch according to the Biblical genealogy the Amazons belonged.

Whoever is willing to listen attentively to the murmur of the earliest traditions, of the infancy of mankind, and especially to the traditions of those families and races which took possession of Europe, from the shores of the Euxine and the Hellenic Archipelago to the Atlantic, and from the columns of Hercules to the frozen seats of the Laponians—traditions transmitted by the belief of those peoples, and gathered by historians and chroniclers; such an one entertains no doubt, that, from the time of the primitive settlements, the vivid recollections of those first pioneers, and the pious reminiscences preserved by following generations—all run back to a primitive and common cradle. All of these traditions point to the East, to heights which the ethnography of nations demonstrates to be situated in Asia, around Mount Ararat and in the Caucasian chain.

Thus what Moses teaches in his books, seems, to a certain degree, to be confirmed by the traditions of the earliest people, and by the science of our times. The masterly publications of Ritter, that irrefutable geographer, and those of the immortal Goerres, admit the fact of the concentration of the primitive families in the Caucasian Mountains, before their distribution over the globe. From these heights they descended, one after the other, spreading in every direction, as torrents falling from mountains overspread and fructify the plains. As well to-day, as in the historical yesterday, the names of the forefathers of almost all Japhetic families, both European and Asiatic, are still to be found in Caucasus and Armenia.

Setting out in the search of the distant regions, designed for every family and race as their special and definitive fatherland, these families left the Caucasus by the descents of the north, south, east and west. Part of the last emigrants undoubtedly remained near the shores of the Black Sea.

Among these first pilgrims, are also to be found the people of the Eniochi—Enetes—Venetes, to whom classical writers assign a most remote antiquity. These Enetes or Venetes moved forward towards Europe slowly, for ages, remaining in different spots which they peopled, and whence they sent out colonies in different directions.

Paphlagonia seems to have been one of the more protracted stopping places of the Enetes, during their transmigration towards Europe. Ancient testimonies are very explicit as to this fact. The father of history, whose authority, denied for a moment by the skepticism of the last century, daily regains ground with all who know to what voices a lively attention must be given, in order to understand the old traditions of different nations: Herodotus, speaking of the Italian Enetes,—Venetes, tells us, that they arrived there from Asia. In his book Terpsichore, he says: "Enetos qui sunt in Adria—se colonos Medorum dicere—qui quo pacto coloni Medorum fuerint ejusdem non quo cogitare, sed fiat quod libet in longo tempore." Flavius Josephus, in his Antiquities, mentions the Enetes as the oldest inhabitants of Paphlagonia; positively asserting that, in remote times, these Enetes were also named Riphatos, or descendants of Riphat, according to scripture, the son of Gomer. The testimony of Homer is not wanting, that the Enetes inhabited Paphlagonia.

> "Paphlagonorum hanc ibant, ductore Pylomene, turmae
> Ex Henetis mulas quæ terra enutrit agrestas."

Relying upon this testimony of the poet, Strabo asserts, that it was the Enetes who preserved and conveyed to posterity the art of breeding the best horses, and that of procreating mules. "Etiam apud Græcos pullorum Venetorum fama innotuerit, idque genus longo tempore in prætio fuerint." In another place: "Veneti—imitatione priscorum qui procreandis mulis equos alebant." Strabo collects almost all the traditions upon the sojourn of the Enetes in Paphlagonia, of whom however, in his time, there were no remains in that country. He attempts to explain their disappearance. "Primarum Paphlagoniam gentem fuisse Enetos, e qua fuerit Pylomenes, quem et plurimi ad bellum fuerunt secuti, qui eversa Troja, amisso duce in Thraciam, abierint vagantique deinde in Venetiam parvenerint, sunt qui Antenorum et filios ejus socios ejus profectionis fuisse perhibent, et ad intimum Adriæ sinus recessum consedisse." In another place: "Alii Venetorum Paphlagonum quosdam e bello Trojano cum Antenore eo locorum evasisse tradunt"—Probabile est, ergo hac de causa Enetos defecisse ut in Paphlagonia nulli reparientur."

As already stated, these Enetes were a horse-breeding race, and apparently a race of horsemen. In their neighborhood.

on the south of the Black sea, tradition and ancient fable point out to us the Amazons.

The customs of the Amazons, their warlike life, their horsemanship, their hatred of men, their customs, as for instance, that of mutilating one of their breasts, to enable them the better to manage the bow, are all generally known; as well as what is called their history. The aim of the present article being to assertain, if possible, their orign, and to discover with what race they were connected, I shall not delay upon what has become quite proverbial through the world.

The Amazons did not remain strangers to the great duel fought by the nations of these countries, which, in the following period, have been surnamed and divided into European and Asiatic. I will observe here, that the appellation of Asia is wrongly bestowed upon these countries, at the time of the siege of Troy. Strabo, whose authority on those matters is the most decided among the writers of the classical world, speaks thereof in the following manner. "Neque Europam neque Asiam nominabant Homero vivente, nec dum divisus erat in tres continentes orbis terrarum, continentibus reliquis non dum divisis, ne Tanaidis quidem opus habuit mentione."

The Amazons hastened to the defence of Troy. Homer enumerates them, with other nations gathered together in the city of one hundred gates. Their queen, Penthesilea, fought there, and probably she followed Pylomenes and his Paphlagonians. The verse,

"Divi in locis monumentum nempe Myrinæ,"

alludes to the Amazons. This Myrina was also one of their queens, and founded a town in Eolia, named from her.

The Amazonian region, situated on the south of the Pontus Euxinus, was contiguous, on the west, to Paphlagonia, and the very ancient country of Polymenia, where, in a later period Pompey founded the town of Pompejopolis, which outlived the founder but a short time. On this side, also, they bordered the settlements of the Eniochi, Enetes—Venetes, being separated from them by the river Halys. This Amazonian region was included from old Phanaroea, between the rivers Lycus on the south, along the Yris, and both sides of the Thermodon and the plains of the Themiscyra, having on the east, the Chaldeans and the Amazonian mountains.

The scholiast of the Argonautica of Apollonius narrates, that, in the vicinity of the fields of Doias, which together with the Ackmonian thicket, were situated on the banks of the Thermodon, three cities were built and inhabited by the Amazons. One of these cities was Lycastia on the banks of the Lycastos or Lycos, Lych, (the original root of the name of Lech ;) the second was Themiscyra, near the mouth of the river Thermodon; the third was Chalybia, near Mount Henetos, afterwards the residence of the Alybes, called sometimes Chalybians, who instead of silver possessed iron. This town, Chalybia, is the same as Alobe, Alopa or Aloa, in ancient fable, the silver city, afterwards transformed to the iron town, or castle. According to this commentator, the Amazons of those regions, were also divided into three branches: the centre on the Thermodon, the east near the Chaldeans of the country still named Kuldir. These Chaldeans had a periodical intercourse for procreation with these women. Finally, the third branch extended west, along the banks of Lychus, and bordered on Paphlagonia.

This was one of the regions inhabited by the Amazons, in antiquity so remote that the light of history is scarcely able to disperse its darkness. The fame of the labors of Heracles, by whom their queen Antiope was killed, preserved also to posterity the remembrance of this warlike woman, as it does the lay of the great poet of the mythological world, and as does also the popular fable.

But this fable of the existence of the Amazons in the night of time, was not confined to that region only. Antiquity has traditions of them in other countries also, both on the Tanais and in the burning Libya. It is difficult, almost impossible to specify the period and the causes which led to this irruption of the Amazons. They shook Asia Minor and extended their inroads to Greece. The Libyan Amazons, Diodorus Siculus believed to be only a colony of those of Themiscyra, whom according to his description they resemble in every respect.

In the first feeble twilight of the middle ages, Orosius of Hispano-Goth extraction, the pupil and friend of St. Augustine, one of the fathers of the church, and after him the first originator of the philosophy of history as founded on the intervention of Providence in human affairs, and in this manner the precursor and intellectual sponsor of Bossuet—Orosius tried to draw together all the different traditions concerning the Amazons. He attempted to establish between them a link of filiation, and even a dynastical succession. But he mingled together the different traditions and legends, and confused the places. Casting them all in one and the same mould, he exerted himself to prove the Amazonian descent to be originally from a Scythic family, which, expelled from the North, reached the Thermodon guided by Plyros and Scolopytos.

Antiquity in conveying to us the recollection of times which can be called ante-historical, pretends not to give with any precision their chronologic epoch, a thing impossible in itself. The epoch in which the Amazons shook Asia, confounded by Orosius and his followers with the exclusive existence of the Amazons of Themiscyra, might belong to that period, the memory of which reached Herodotus as an echo of long bygone times, in which the Cimmerians of the Pontus, expelled from their seats by the Scythians, and fleeing before them, arrived in Media and Asia Minor—Melpomenec: "Scythas Arraxe transmisso in Cimmeriam abiisse." *Clio*: "Cimmerii a Scythis nomadibus ejecti."

The Amazons, connections of that race to which the Cimmerians belonged, probably followed them. Both the Cimmerians and Amazons met, it seems, south of the Black Sea with other tribes belonging originally to the same race; and in this manner both were strengthened. The Cimmerians mixed with the Eniochis-Riphatides—the Northern Amazons with those of Themiscyra. The names of different towns, as well as the names of different rivers, fountains, etc., show the course of this irruption. Generally over the whole globe, and in all times the mountains, rivers, valleys, wells, and springs tell the history and form the nucleus for the oldest legends of nations. The Amazons seem to have formed the staples of this irruption, judging from the cities whose foundation is ascribed to them. Such were Maza, Mazec, in Bythinia; Cyme, called also

Amazonium in Eolide opposite Lesbos, Myrina also in Eolia, Myralea, Pygelle, and others scattered in different directions, of which Ephesus—burnt and ransacked by Cimmerians, and the Amazons—seems to have formed the centre.

Finally the Amazons called Scythian, mentioned by Herodotus, and said most improbably to have fought and overcome Cyrus, are known history by the fables concerning their existence. These lived north of the Caucasus, in a portion of the country between the ancient Tanais and the Rha, Araxes, called now the Volga. In the south of this Amazonian region ran the river Imytyus, and it reached north, where Appianus and Ptolemeus placed the *Mithridatica regio.* In the west it was bounded by a chain of very elevated hills, called by the ancients, Hyppian (horse) afterwards Gordian, also Riphean mountains. These Amazons descended from the same stock as those of Themiscyra.

The Pentateuch gives to Noah three sons, and the ethnography of some races seemingly coincides with the tradition. Very likely already in the Caucasian cradle, the descendants of Riphat, son of Gomer and grandson of Japhet, separated and spread themselves by three primordial branches. As was mentioned, the Enetes, one of these branches, issued by the mountain passes of the South; and another branch made choice of the northern declivities for their pilgrimage. To the last belonged the old Cimmerians of the Pontus. The Amazons of the Tanais belong to the northern branch of the children of Riphat.

On the authority of Herodotus, many writers looked upon these Amazons as the mothers of the Sarmates. Tradition or fable tells us that a young son of some Scythian king seized by surprise some Amazons, made acquaintance with their queen, and was rejoined by some of his youthful companions—and that this was the origin of the Sarmates. Although the existence of the Sarmates is averred in the first centuries of the Christian era, nevertheless, without going back to a remote antiquity, their origin wants historical evidence. They appeared in Europe without ascertained ancestors, and they disappeared in the fifth or sixth century, leaving no undeniably established historical posterity.

History mentions first the Sarmates on the west of the Hyppian hills bordering the country of the Amazons. The appearance of the Sarmates, although greatly posterior to the disappearance of the Amazons, took place in the neighborhood of the country occupied by the latter. These two circumstances taken together formed the source from which the fabulous origin of the Sarmates started. Indeed, when the writers of the time of the Roman empire, in speaking of the Sarmates give a description of their usages and manners, and especially of those of their women, there is to be found a striking resemblance to the Amazonian modes of life.

Nicolaus Damascenus, friend of King Herodus, writes in the following manner upon the Sarmates: "Uxoribus in omnibus obtemperant tanquam dominabus (δεσποιναις) regina dominante.———Virginæ non prius nuptias concedunt quam hostem aliquum interfecerit."

The testimony of Strabo, relating to the disappearance of the Enetes from Asia Minor after the Trojan war, will be recollected. Goerres, one of the most erudite men of our century (who died about eight years ago) supposes that the disappearance of the Asiatic Amazons coincided with that of the Enetes. These latter abandoned Asia for definitive settlements, as no portions of that part of the world seem to have been intended to be finally peopled by the race to which the Enetes belonged. Their sojourn there seems to have been only a protracted stay in the course of this primitive pilgrimage.

And as the migratory bird does not construct its nest before it has reached that region to which nature directs it,—so the first pioneers of mankind proceeded in their pilgrimages until they reached those lands, which by the decree of Providence were to be their final home. For then, as now, nothing was abandoned to chance in life and in the movements of mankind.

Disappearing from Asia, the Enetes appear again in Europe—in Italy according to classical writers. We have seen the testimony of Strabo—but he is not the only one who relates it. In the fragments of Cato is to be found,—" Venetis cunctis origo Phaetontea est." Polybius says, "Loca vero mari Adriatico vicina—antiquum ex Paphlagonia genus colit. Hi Veneti appellati." Pliny as well as Ptolemeus, enumerating the ancient nations and those of their time, prove the Paphlagonian origin of the Enetes—Venetes. T. Livy begins his books thus speaking of the nations preceding the Romans in the land of Ytalos: "Antenorum cum multitudine Henetum—qui seditione a Paphlagonia pulisi—venisse in intimum maris Adriatici sinum."

Before this colonization in the Italiotian* country, this branch of the Enetes continued its migration through Thrace, and the Hyemus, toward a final home. This was in the south-east of Europe, on the banks of the Danube, and among the Krapak mountains. From thence they extended along the Elbe to the Baltic, and toward the west probably to Vindelicia. In the last centuries of the Roman Empire, the Enetes or Venetes, then united with other branches of the same trunk, make their entrance into history, bearing the general name of the whole race. Pliny, Ptolemeus, Amm. Marcellinus, and others, assign to the different tribes of the Enetian branch, the lands from Illyricum to the Baltic. All these tribes take, at least finally, the name of Slavic. After the fall of the Roman Empire, and the extinction of the classical world and its writers, the chroniclers belonging to the first centuries of the Middle ages, the Byzantine historiographers, and finally the erudite of the fifteenth and sixteenth centuries, acknowledge the Enetes or Venetes to be Slavi.

Bishop Jornandes, a Gothic chronicler, speaking of the inhabitants of the north-east of Europe, calls them Vinidi—Veneti. "Ab una stirpe exorti tria nunc nomina reddidere; id est: Veneti—Antes—Slavi." Procopius, Constantinus Porphyrogenos, and others, say the same.

All these testimonies establish the fact that the inhabitants of the banks of the Elbe are descended from the ancient Enetes, or Venetes—and that they belong to the Slavic race. It is undeniable to every historian that the Enetes and other tribes of

* The predecessors of the Romans are called Italiots, from Italos, and their successors are Italians.

the same branch, spoken of by Pliny and Ptolemy, are the Slavi of the fifth and sixth centuries. As such they are acknowledged by subsequent writers, among others by Roger Bacon, the intellectual giant of the middle ages, by the chronicler Helmodius, and finally by Philip Melancthon, who says: "Nam Heneti gens Asiatica, lingua, moribus, et vitæ institutis different a Sarmatis id est a Tartaris. Ergo Germanos Heneti proximi viverunt, quanquam nunc Heneti utramque ripam Vistulæ tenent, sed passim in ultimis finibus Germanis fuisse admixtos Henetos apparet appellationibus."

When these different Enetian families extricate their denominations from classical qualifications and terminatious, reviving their unchangeable radicals, the Slavic names are heard on the same spots where the nations of Pliny and Ptolomeus sojourned. Thus arises the name Tschechia (or Bohemia). As soon as the Tschechs took strong root, the Amazons plainly reappear among them with the same characteristics according to the new Tschechian legends, as distinguished them in the ancient classical traditions. They emerge on the banks of the Elbe in new places under Slavic names, but showing all the outlines of the violent passions with which they have been endowed by antiquity.

Among the whole descent of Japhet, among all the nations who went forth from Caucasus and Armenia, and especially among these who peopled Europe from the Hellespont to Gades and to the countries of the Celtic Britons, it is only by these Tschechs in the West of Europe, that the mythical existence of the Amazons is revived.

The Tschechian legends gleaned verbally from the people by the national chroniclers relate that Wlasta, according to some a daughter of the prince Crac, Cracus, by others said to be pupil to the queen Libussa, who married a ploughman named Premysl (intelligence) and was a mother and benefactress of the country—put herself at the head of women and founded an Amazonian state. Wlasta, wlast, signifies power; she erected a town or perhaps a castle whose name was Devium, Devia, Devicograd. (*Deva*, *Devica*, maiden, *grad* town—castle.) These women waged a most destructive war against men, killing the male children and carrying off the female, from whom they cut off one breast. They were generally on horseback, etc:—and every one will recognize in these descriptions the mythical Amazons of antiquity.

The fables of the infancy of Poland also show an instance of a woman ruling the country. So the national reminiscence of Wanda, daughter of one Cracus, founder of the town Cracovia, to whom she succeeded. This legend was brought most probably to Poland from Tschechia with the dominator Cracus.

In the quick and fiery spirit which fills the veins of a certain class of Polish women of the present time, can be seen the traces of Amazonian blood and filiation.

It has been mentioned, that one of the branches of the descendants of Riphat, son of Gomer, issued from Caucasus by its northern declivities. In search of its predestinated patrimony, it wandered along the banks of rivers and near mountains on a course towards the north. In this manner this branch seems to have followed the course of the old river Nardanus or Hypanis, now Kuban; crossing afterwards the Meotis, it extended itself between the Borysthenes or Dnieper, and beyond the Tanais or Don, leaving every where colonies and tribes. Ascending the basin of the Borysthenes, it entered that of the Dwina, in the vicinity of lake Ylmen and the sources of the Rha or Volga. The mountains called Woldai, generally classed by antiquity among the Riphean mountains, seem to have been the terminus of the wanderings of this branch. It took possession of these countries as its final fatherland. There were its holy hearth and holy forest, and there its traditional and religious mysteries were revived. In these countries antiquity situates the mythical Hyperboreans so highly esteemed by Herodotus and all the classical world, of Pliny, Pausanias, Apollonius, Pomponius and others. Ammianus Marcellinus calls them Arymphæos, so also do all subsequent writers and chroniclers. So also are they named by Roger Bacon and the anonymous old geographer of Ravenna, in his ethnographic hours, as well as afterwards by Martinus Zellerius, and other geographers of the XVth and XVIth centuries.

The traditions of the Amazons emerge in these new settlements of the Riphatides, and again animate the legends. On the heights of Woldai, and around lake Ylmen, the women war against men, and found and govern cities. There was situated the *terra fœminarum or land of women* of the Northern chroniclers of the Xth and XIth centuries. According to one of these legends, the ancient city of Novgorod (New town, (near lake Ylmen, which, in the earliest Christian centuries—probably in the IVth or Vth—may be looked upon as the New-York of the North, being then ruled by republican institutions, was built by women on their return from some warlike excursion on the banks of the Danube.

The chronicler Adamus Bremensis relates as follows what reached him in relation to this *terra fœminarum* (Women-land): "Circa littora maris Balthiei ferunt esse Amazones quod nunc terra fœminarum dicitur. . . . . Sunt etiam qui referrunt impregnari a preteruentibus negotiatoribus vel ab eis quos inter se habent captivos . . . generant Cynocephalos qui caput in pectore habentes in Russia saepe videantur captivos." In another place: "Filius regis (Dane or Norman) nomine Amund a patre missus ut dilaterat imperium quum in patriam fœminarum venisset quos nos Amazones vocamus, veneno quod ille fontibus immiscerunt tum ipse quam ejus exercitus perire."

Here finishes the Amazonian fable in European legends and recollections. Many centuries afterwards, one of the Spanish leaders in South America, in going up one of the rivers, in this then newly discovered world, asserts that he met a whole population of armed women, who resisted his troops most desperately. He believed himself to have encountered Amazons, and named after them the river. But I think no one of his adventurous successors mentions such a striking event, and this in a time so near our own, and of which we possess most minute relations. This single and unsupported mention of so remarkable an appearance, justifies a doubt in the reality of these newly discovered Amazons. Probably they were armed women, who, with their husbands, or in their absence, defended their homes against these invaders. In a land where every thing appeared unusual and surprising, the exalted Spanish fancy, seeking for the marvellous, created instantly an analogy with, and believed itself to have realized the long lost fable of the Amazons. That the leader gave to these warlike women this name can be explained; for probably in that time, as now, every woman whose taste and occupations were rather masculine, was called an Amazon. In this manner every country, city and village had and has its Amazons. Thus the Carthaginian women, those of Saguntum, the mountaineers of the primitive cantons of Switzerland, fighting on the shores of Lake Lucerne against the French invasion commanded by Brune; and those of Saragossa, as well as those of the Greek war of independence, should be all classed as Amazons. But those armed women, struggling and defying death in the defence of the holiest interests, are not Amazons in the historical meaning of the word.

In thus recapitulating the various relations transmitted to us by antiquity, as well as tracing out the ethnography of spots which were inhabited by the Amazons, I think I have proved that they made their appearance generally and almost exclusively by the side of branches issued from, and belonging to, a distinct race, and this during all the phases of the wanderings and different denominations to which these branches have been subjected. It has some probability that these branches are descents of Riphat, through Gomer, grandson of Japhet, and if the historical evidence of the Genesis be admitted, ancestors of the Slavic race. Thus, also, the Amazons most undoubtedly must be acknowledged as belonging to it by blood. Especially is this proved by their reappearance in the legends of the Slavic inhabitants of the Elbe and the eastern shores of the Baltic alone.

B.

THE FOURTEEN CLASSES OF THE RUSSIAN PUBLIC SERVICE; OR, THE TSCHINS.

CLASS.	MILITARY.	CIVIL.
I.	Field Marshal.	Chancellor.
II.	General in Chief.	Real Privy Councillor.
III.	Lieutenant General.	Privy Councillor.
IV.	General of Brigade.	Real Councillor of State.
V.	Brigadier (no longer existing).	Councillor of State.
VI.	Colonel.	Councillor of Court.
VII.	Lieutenant Colonel.	Councillor of College.
VIII.	Major.	Assessor of College.
IX.	Captain.	Titulary Councillor.
X.	Captain of the Staff.	Secretary of College.
XI.	Lieutenant.	Secretary of Government, or County.
XII.	Second Lieutenant.	Clerk of Chancellery.
XIII.	Cornet.	No special denomination beyond that of Tschinownik (keeper of office).
XIV.		The same. Both these lowest classes have the privilege of being exempted from corporal punishment, and wear a small sword with the uniform.

C.

THE POLITICAL TESTAMENT OF PETER THE GREAT.

Throwing a glance on the continual expanse of Russia, on all points of her extensive frontiers, witnessing the arrogant manner with which she comes forth in her recent attack on Turkey, considering the haughty attitude assumed by the Czar in the affairs of the world, one easily is inclined to perceive or to try to detect in this mounting tide of Russian ascendency, deeply laid schemes for enslaving at least the ancient hemisphere. It is not only supposed, but positively asserted that this world-embracing activity is the fulfilment of a hereditary legacy inspiring and directing the wide-spread actions of one Czar after another. Thus at present Russian horses quench their thirst in the Danube, Russia incites, as it is said, her nominal vassal the Khan of Persia, to attack Herat, and form a Russian vanguard towards Affghanistan, and in due time towards the British possessions. Russian steamers disturb the waters of the Lake Aral, navigate the Oxus and Jaxartes, and it is rumored that armed corps are ready to land towards Khiva, Bokhara, Khokand; Russian Engineers survey the table-land between Altai and Thibet, and raise forts along the skirts of the salt lakes of the grand steppe of Tartary; Russian armed battalions and Cossacks gather along the frontier of China, menacing on the west the little Bucharia, and Mantchouria on the northeast; Russian fleets begin to appear in the Pacific, and the flag with the two-headed eagle will soon make its appearance among the diplomatists in the Sandwich Islands; Russian colonists and merchants navigate from Ochotsk, Kamtschatka or Sitka down to the shores of Japan, founding cities on the Ainos on the edge of the Mantchou-land. From the Euxine to the Pacific opposite to Yesso, extends an uninterrupted chain of armed vanguards, forerunners of a storm ready to hurl on the more conspicuous points of this immeasurable line.

By these facts is sustained the assertion that the lineage of the Czars advances with unabated pertinacity to fulfil the destiny traced by the prophetic spirit of its great protoplast. Politicians and other writers have settled it almost beyond contestation, that with Peter the Great originated the idea of this universal dominion, and moreover, that he foretraced to his successors the ways of its execution. It is almost a general belief that Peter wrote a will whose decisions are religiously carried out by his successors. In this mysterious document the dismemberment of Poland is said to be specially recommended and enjoined, as well as the final destruction of Turkey and the conquest of Asia. The route to the British provinces could not have been traced there, as at that time England did not hold the East Indies. All this would be superhuman, and prophetic, if true. Had Peter done any thing like this, it would raise him above all statesmen known in history—nay, he ought to be considered as gifted with more than human powers. We are sorry for the sake of the vagaries constructed upon this will of Peter, to oppose a flat denial to its existence. There is no where such a Czarian relic. At any rate, it does not exist in the state or family archives of the Romanoffs or Gottorps. Besides, history explains by herself most clearly the source, the reasons and the agencies at work in the ambitious encroachments of Russia, without being obliged to have recourse to any such striking fallacy. If there exist such a legatee, it is the whole nation. This we shall show. The Czars are only carrying out that which, rising upwards from the bottomless depth of national aspirations, becomes a fact by itself. The encroachments of Russia cannot be contested. But the movements of affairs around, play rather her game, clearing up the way to her ascendency. If finally the nature of the source is to be ascertained, it is not an apocryphal and imaginary command, but deeper, larger, and inexhaustible, and thus more dangerous for the moment than any individual hereditary ambition. It runs powerfully through all strata of the nation. Men rising from nothingness have in the last 150 years embodied these ambitious incitements, and the sovereigns have acted under the national impulse. Peter the Great, to be sure, started Russia on a new orbit. He opened communications by sea, and brought her nearer to the busy European world. After him, other elements, new and unforeseen events, made her roll onwards to the present day. The principal aim of Peter was to bring his country to the Baltic, to navigate the Black and Caspian seas, and to unite the northern and southern navigation by internal water communications. Thus he opened a channel between the Volga, the lakes and Neva, and attempted unsuccessfully to cut one from the Don to the Volga, by which the Euxine and Caspian would have been married. As to dreams of universal monarchy for himself or his successors, his ambition did not go beyond the wish to become a member or the Roman or German empire, by the purchase or conquest of the small dukedoms of Holstein or Oldenburg. He respected so far the power of the German Emperors, as to ask from them the grant of titles of princes and counts for his own subjects, as was the case for Menchikoff, Sheremeteff and others. In this his successors followed his example, Paul being the first who created new titles in Russia. Peter was likewise far from thinking of partitioning Poland, and still less would he have recommended it to his successors. During his wars with Charles XII., Russian troops occupied for years various parts of Poland, whose political existence was for a moment nearly annihilated. One part of the nobility submitted to the orders of Charles XII., and followed the treacherous Leshtshynsky, a king of his creation; others remained faithful to the freely elected, but by Swedish troops expelled, Augustus of Saxony. Lithuania was divided in deadly feud between the powerful houses of Patz and Sapieha. At that time Peter could have easily cut off as much from Poland as he might have found useful or necessary. He could have done it even with some appearance of diplomatic justice, as half of the nation or nobility fought with the Swedes against him, and his ally Augustus, overpowered by Charles, was obliged to conclude a separate treaty to save his Saxon possessions, renouncing the crown of Poland and the Russian alliance. Peter's victories restored him to the throne, and put an end to the Swedish dominion in Poland. He never abandoned the interests of his faithless ally, or attempted to jeopardize the independence of Poland. In his correspondence with his commanders, Menchikoff and Sheremeteff, he speaks always with great commiseration and indulgence of the various sufferings of the nation. He explains to them and even justifies the treachery of Augustus and the continual tergiversations of the Polish nobility; joining now the Russians, now the Swedes; recommending to the generals not to be revengeful against the poor people or the individuals. It is a notorious fact for any one half-way acquainted with the history of the 18th century, that the partition of Poland originated with Frederic of Prussia or his brother Prince Henry, and was decided and concocted at first between the cabinet of Berlin and Kaunitz, or rather the virtuous Maria Theresa; who, piously hypocritical, after having received at the confessional the absolution of her Capuchin monk, cheerfully signed the partition treaty, urging the accession of the immoral but reluctant Catharine. True it is, that, this political slaughter once decided, Catharine then and afterwards took care to have of the victim as large a slice as possible. The idea of the destruction of Poland was strange to the cabinet of Petersburg, to such an extent, that Potemkin—the great favorite of Catherine, who for more than forty years directed all-powerfully the foreign diplomacy of the empire—seeing in the last years of life his influence and power decline, formed the project of dethroning Poniatowski and of declaring himself king of Poland. It may be said of Potemkin, who owed his rise to an accident, that he was the first who gave a new positive shape and direction to the national aspirations concerning Turkey, the expulsion of the Moslems from Europe, and the possession of Constantinople. Peter never extended his projects so far, and under his successors it was never thought of. The lascivious Elizabeth, his daughter, and the fourth after him on the throne, detestin gany trouble, avoided war if there was any possibility to do it; and even Bestucheff her chancellor, or Worontzoff her favorite, never nourished any ambitious project against Turkey or any other country. Potemkin evoked it from the recesses of the national feelings, and inscribed it for ever in the governmental policy. The expulsion of the Turks was for him as the "delenda est Carthago" for the old Roman. The wars under Catharine were mostly incited by him. During the famous journey of Catharine to southern Russia, where cities, villages, and populations emerged in theatrical scenery created by the almighty favorite, several finger-posts were erected with the inscription, *The way to Constantinople.* Potemkin consolidated the Russian power in the Black Sea. He conquered and annexed the Taurian peninsula, or Crimea; he is the founder of Cherson, Nikolaeff, Sebastopol, the restorer of Kertsh and of many other cities there. The peninsula began to be cultivated under his impulse, and among others he introduced the culture of fruit-trees, which now give a large income, and are exported to the whole empire, even to the market of Petersburg. With Potemkin originated the idea of giving to the second son of Paul the name of Constantine, as a foreboding of the restoration of the ancient Byzantine empire.

Thus, not even then did the Russian policy or cabinet think of eventually annexing their conquest. But, as the French proverb says, "*L'appetit vient en mangeant;*" and the idea of universal dominion, if there is any, was evoked by various successive events. All that in this direction is undertaken or accomplished by Russia, all that startles and fills other governments with awe, is the work of accident rather than the result of a far-reaching, preconceived plan in the head of an individual or of a dynasty. The individual ambition of rising favorites did the whole, independent of any incentive from the reigning sovereigns. Thus here, as often happens in history, small causes produced gigantic effects. The Orloffs, likewise of obscure descent, rivals of Potemkin in the favor of Catharine, as ambitious, but his inferiors in large conceptions, shared with him his enmity to the Turks. Gregory Orloff, having under his command the Englishman Elphinstone, won against the Turks the naval battle of Tchesme and received for it the name of Tschesmynsky. Alexander's ambition was principally attracted towards the west; and it is Napoleon, if any body, who contributed to introduce the Russians into the centre of Europe, who cleared the way for their preponderating influence in the affairs of the world. Without his overthrow of the Prussian monarchy after the battles of Jena and Auerstadt, the Russians would not have been called in, and the kingdom of Prussia, then in possession nearly of the whole present mock kingdom of Poland, and backed by Germany, would have formed a bulwark to Russian interference. Napoleon, flattering Alexander, holding out to him the mirage of a division of the world between them, thus did every thing to rouse ambitious projects. It is a well-averred fact, that at the interview at Erfurt, and afterwards during his matrimonial views for one of the sisters of Alexander, and until the beginning of hostile relations in 1811, Napoleon offered several times to give up the new-formed dukedom of Warsaw or Poland for an alliance with Russia against England and the world. All this was more than sufficient to give the Russians a consciousness of their power, and it may be said that the lures proffered by Napoleon acted more efficaciously on the Russian statesmen and noblemen surrounding Alexander than on the Czar himself. The heroic resistance offered by the Russian people to the invasion of 1812, was not inspired in the nation by the Czar, but, on the contrary, Alexander was tempered by the national, characteristic, and unyielding stubbornness. Public opinion prevented any conciliatory settlement after the soil was invaded; several battles were lost the enemy in the heart of Russia and in possession of Moscow. When the French army retired to Poland, Alexander wished to end there the pursuit of the enemy; but his Russian *entourage*, as Wolkonsky, Balashoff, Kutuzoff, and many others, full of revenge, urged him on to continue the war to the final overthrow of the foe. Thus events put the Russians at the head of Europe in this struggle against the French Titan. How little Alexander acted under the impulse of any preconceived plans may be judged from his answer to the celebrated Madame de Staël, that "he was only a lucky accident." The acclamations of the whole of Europe might have been sufficient to turn his head, and make him believe himself "the man of destiny," as Napoleon was called, or to strengthen his faith in hereditary ambitious transmissions, if in reality any had existed. The Czars head a national machinery, powerful in itself—but not one of them can be considered as inspiring a powerful soul into it, as creating and preordinating all the multifarious and extensive manifestations of its activity in the various points of the empire. Thus Richelieu, a Frenchman, favored byAlexander, created the port of Odessa in spite of the court of Petersburg, and thus contributed mightily to strengthen the Russian influence on the Black Sea.

The Greeks, the Moldavians, the Ypsylantis, the Cantakuzenos, the Comnens, and many others in the service of Russia, continued for more than half a century the work commenced by Potemkin, alimenting and throwing fuel into the animosity of the Russians against the Turks. Now, as three hundred years ago—when the enterprise of the Strogonoffs, merchants of Moscow, and the daring spirit of Yermack, the Cossack, a pirate on the Volga, conquered Siberia—it is the ambition of individuals shooting from the mass of the nation, and not even the descendants of ancient powerful families; it is the craving for influence and name that does the work, extending the Russian frontiers, and penetrating deeply and more deeply onward, on the whole line, from the Danube over Thibet and China to the Pacific.

During the last years of the reign of Alexander, among the general apathy prevailing in all branches of the government, the national pride, personified in a Yermoloff, stirred up the regions over the Caucasus and extended the awe of the Russian name and power among the mountaineers, the tribes on the Caspian, and the Schaihs of Persia. The attempts to get hold of Khiva and Bokhara, to conquer these regions, frustrated some fifteen years ago but now renewed again, originated exclusively with General Peroffsky, a man without an ancestry, by birth the bastard of a grandee, once a youthful playfellow of Nicholas, and now his favorite. His projects, opposed by all the influential statesmen and courtiers, were accepted by the Czar as procuring an occasion for the general to distinguish himself, and not at all as a scheme deeply pondered or forming part of a general preconceived plan. The Emperor wished principally to be able to bestow on his courtier the grand cross of the decoration of St. George, which can be worn only by the conqueror of a province. Peroffsky, haughty, ambitious, enterprising, became governor of the territory of Orenburg, and sent therefrom, on his own hook, agents to explore Khiva, mark the military route across the steppes, and even to stir up Persia, and the Affghans, and penetrate to India. One of his agents, Witkewitch, a Pole, was met by the English officers in the Persian army at the siege of Herat, and at that time terrified the English agents and politicians. Peroffsky failed then, for various reasons, but now he is again in Orenburg, about to renew the old enterprise. The start thus once given by an individual, the government continues the work. When Peroffsky was recalled, steamers were sent to the Lake Aral, to Oxus, Jaxartes, and thus the way prepared for a new and more successful attempt.

The frontier of China, Mantchou-land, Japan, and the Pacific, are now alarmed by Russia. This is the work of Mourawioff, for two or three years the governor-general in Eastern Siberia, as active, ambitious, and enterprising as any man in Russia. Until his time all was quiet there. Such individuals put the government on the track, inspire the Czar, instead of receiving their inspiration from him. They receive the power to act, and the utmost that is recommended *sometimes* to them is, to see what can be done. All this reminds one of the extension of the power of Spain in America, accomplished by Columbus, Cortez, Pizarro, mostly in spite of the sovereigns and their councils.

Such are the agents at work in the all-grasping progress of Russia. Men issuing from the mass of the nation, giving utterance to the national ambition, rather than instruments of any far-reaching scheme of the Czars. Which of these two ways is more dangerous or beneficial for the world, or at least for Europe, only the future will prove.

D.

It may be interesting to see how the appearance of Russia was considered in her relations to Europe some three hundred years ago, in the middle of the 16th century. The orthography, punctuation, and even the bad Latin of the chronicler, are faithfully copied.

Extract from an old chronicle, "*Historiae quae advenerunt in gubernationem Ferdinandi I. Imperatori Augusti: Simone Schardio collecta.*"

* * * "Moschi antea artium nostrarum rudes, successu temporis solertissimi effecti sunt, et tormenta ex metallis fabri-

cata quam plurima in aciem nunc secum adducunt. * * * Ac constat belli smalcaldici tempore, praefectum quendam equitum ex Moschia oriundum, Divo Carolo V. quatuor millia equitum pollicitum fuisse; caeterum quod tardius advenerat bello jam confecto; eam tamen gratiam ab optimo principe pro beneficio oblito retulisse, et quosdam artifices ex Germania permissu Caesaris conducere licerat, quos secum in Moschia advectaret. * * * Itaque inter alios Architecti, Typographi poetae, Fabri ferrarii, et quod plurimum internat, tormentorum libratores ac magistri conducti sunt."

The members of this expedition were arrested by the magistrate of the city of Lübeck, but released by the express orders of the German Kaiser. The chronicler thus continues:—

"Non solum autem in bellicis munitionibus prohibendis, insigni solertia usi sunt lubecensiis ac magistratus septentrionis, verum etiam omnium navalium rerum scientiam Moschis praeripere satagerunt; ne si aliquando classe instructus hostis barbarus quid in inculta ac silvestri regione materia non deesset nemoris excidendi, omnem non solum Germaniam sed universam Europam posset debellare; qui ter centana millia voluntariorum equitum in aciem cum vellet educeret, et militantes arctissima in disciplina non secus, atque conditione servos contineret. Occasionem itaque omnem resecare decreverant, quod ea sublata eventum quoque lugubrem sane futurum impediri posse, animadverterent. Itaque Legati maritorum civitatum quos Ansas nominant communi decreto, Lubecae quondam habito conventu, Narbensem profectionem omnem ita sustulerant ut pro infamibus omnes eos haberi pronunciarent qui et merces suas advectarent, jure denique omni mercaturae exercendae interdicarent, et bona insuper eo advehenda, aut inibi comparata, actionibus factis publicari fiscoque attribui conserunt. Videbant enim id quod res erat: Fureas Hellespontum Ligurium avaritia transgressos ad invantibus, Graecis transfugis et piratis quum classae pollere occiperent, non solum ipsam Constantinopolim Imperii dominam, sed universam pene Graeciam, Macedoniam, et Illyricum et alia loca vicina Imperio suo subjecisse; ita Moschos quoque omni Septentrione terra marique invaso et predomito, ubi classis potestas fieret,

Narbae et Iwangrodi emporio condito, et peritia rei navalis accederet, quod quidem in emporiis facile contingit: in interiora Germaniae innumerabili effuso exercitu facile posse penetrare. Hoc itaque metu deterriti, negotiatores a navigatione interdicta, usque ad hoc tempora abstinuerant, adeo quidem ut neque paulo honestior civis ibi domicilium haberet." * * *

THE END.

APPLETON'S EDITION OF THE BRITISH POETS.

PROSPECTUS

OF A

New and Splendid Library Edition

OF THE

POPULAR POETS AND POETRY OF BRITAIN

EDITED, WITH BIOGRAPHICAL AND CRITICAL NOTICES,

BY THE REV. GEORGE GILFILLAN,

AUTHOR OF "GALLERY OF LITERARY PORTRAITS," "BARDS OF THE BIBLE," ETC.

In demy-octavo size, printed from a new pica type, on superfine paper, and neatly bound.

Price, only $1 a volume in cloth, or $2 50 in calf extra.

"Strangely enough, we have never had as yet any thing at all approaching a satisfactory edition of the English poets. We have had Johnson's, and Bell's, and Cooke's, and Sharpe's small sized editions—we have had the one hundred volume edition from the Chiswick press—we have had the double-columned editions of Chalmers and Anderson—and we have the, as yet, imperfect Aldine edition; but no series has hitherto given evidence that a man of cultivated taste and research directed the whole."—*Athen.*

The splendid series of books now offered to the public at such an unusually low rate of charge, will be got up with all the care and elegance which the present advanced state of the publishing art can command.

The well-known literary character and ability of the editor is sufficient guaranty for the accuracy and general elucidation of the text, while the paper, printing, and binding of the volumes will be of the highest class, forming, in these respects, a striking contrast to all existing cheap editions, in which so few efforts have been made to combine superiority in production with low prices.

Under the impression that a chronological issue of the Poets would not be so acceptable as one more diversified, it has been deemed advisable to intermix the earlier and the later Poets. Care, however, will be taken that either the author or the volumes are in themselves complete, as published; so that no purchaser discontinuing the series at any time, will be possessed of imperfect books.

The absence in the book market of any handsome uniform series of the Popular British Poets, at a moderate price, has induced the publishers to project the present edition, under the impression that, produced in superior style, deserving a place on the shelves of the best libraries, and offered at less than one half the usual selling price, it will meet that amount of patronage which an enterprise, based on such liberal terms, requires.

The series will conclude with a few volumes of fugitive pieces, and a History of British Poetry, in which selections will be given from the writings of those authors whose works do not possess sufficient interest to warrant their publication as a whole.

It is believed that this will render the present edition of the British Poets the most complete which has ever been issued, and secure for it extensive support. The series is intended to include the following authors:—

ADDISON.	COWPER.	GRAHAME.	OPIE.	SPENSER.
AKENSIDE.	CRABBE.	GRAY.	PARNELL.	SUCKLING.
ARMSTRONG.	CRASHAW.	GREEN.	PENROSE.	SURREY.
BARBAULD.	CUNNINGHAM.	HAMILTON, W.	PERCY.	SWIFT.
BEATTIE.	DAVIES.	HARRINGTON.	POPE.	TANNAHILL.
BLAIR.	DENHAM.	HERBERT.	PRIOR.	THOMSON.
BLOOMFIELD.	DONNE.	HERRICK.	QUARLES.	TICKELL.
BRUCE.	DRAYTON.	HOGG.	RAMSAY.	VAUGHAN, H.
BURNS.	DRUMMOND.	JAMES I.	ROGERS.	WALLER.
BUTLER.	DRYDEN.	JONES.	ROSCOMMON.	WARTON, J.
BYRON.	DUNBAR.	JOHNSON.	ROSS.	WARTON, T.
CAMPBELL.	DYER.	JONSON.	SACKVILLE.	WATTS.
CAREW.	FALCONER.	LEYDEN.	SCOTT, J.	WHITE, H. K.
CHATTERTON.	FERGUSSON.	LLOYD.	SCOTT, SIR W.	WITHER.
CHAUCER.	FLETCHER, G.	LOGAN.	SHAKSPEARE.	WILKIE.
CHURCHILL.	GAY.	MACPHERSON.	SHELLEY.	WOLCOTT.
CLARE.	GIFFORD.	MALLETT.	SHENSTONE.	WOLFE.
COLERIDGE.	GLOVER.	MARVEL.	SMART.	WYATT.
COLLINS.	GOLDSMITH.	MILTON.	SMOLLETT.	YOUNG.
COWLEY.	GOWER.	MOORE.	SOMERVILLE.	

The following Authors are now ready:

JOHN MILTON, 2 vols.; JAMES THOMSON, 1 vol.; GEORGE HERBERT, 1 vol. JAMES YOUNG, 1 vol.

www.ingramcontent.com/pod-product-compliance
Lightning Source LLC
LaVergne TN
LVHW020222110826
845151LV00003B/799

* 9 7 8 1 4 2 5 5 3 2 6 1 1 *